Living Spirit

LITERATURE

AND RESURGENCE

IN OKINAWA

Living Spirit

FRANK STEWART

EDITOR

KATSUNORI YAMAZATO

GUEST EDITOR

Featuring photography by Higa Yasuo

Editor   Frank Stewart

Managing Editor   Pat Matsueda

Designer and Art Editor   Barbara Pope

Associate Editor   Sonia Cabrera

Abernethy Fellow   Eleanor Svaton

Staff   Moriah Amey, Kathleen Matsueda

Corresponding Editors for North America
Barry Lopez, W. S. Merwin, Carol Moldaw, Michael Nye, Naomi Shihab Nye, Arthur Sze

Corresponding Editors for Asia and the Pacific
CAMBODIA   Sharon May
CHINA   Howard Goldblatt, Ding Zuxin
HONG KONG   Shirley Geok-lin Lim
INDONESIA   John H. McGlynn
JAPAN   Leza Lowitz
KOREA   Bruce Fulton
NEW ZEALAND AND SOUTH PACIFIC   Vilsoni Hereniko
PACIFIC LATIN AMERICA   H. E. Francis, James Hoggard
PHILIPPINES   Alfred A. Yuson
SOUTH ASIA   Sukrita Paul Kumar
WESTERN CANADA   Charlene Gilmore

Advisory Group   William H. Hamilton, Robert Shapard, Robert Bley-Vroman

Founded in 1988 by Robert Shapard and Frank Stewart

Mānoa is published twice a year. Subscriptions: U.S.A. and international—individuals $30 one
year, $54 two years; institutions $50 one year, $90 two years; international airmail add $24 per
year. Single copies: U.S.A. and international—individuals $20; institutions $30; international
airmail add $12 per copy. Call toll free 1-888-UHPRESS. We accept checks, money orders, Visa,
or MasterCard, payable to University of Hawai'i Press, 2840 Kolowalu Street, Honolulu, HI
96822, U.S.A. Claims for issues not received will be honored until 180 days past the date of
publication; thereafter, the single-copy rate will be charged.

Mānoa gratefully acknowledges the continuing support of the University of Hawai'i
Administration and the University of Hawai'i College of Languages, Linguistics, and Literature;
and the grant support of the National Endowment for the Arts, the Hawai'i Council for the
Humanities, the Witter Bynner Foundation for Poetry, and the Hawai'i State Foundation on
Culture and the Arts. Special thanks to the University of Hawai'i Center for Okinawan Studies,
the Mānoa Foundation, and Dexter and Valerie Teruya for their generous support.

http://manoajournal.hawaii.edu/
http://www.uhpress.hawaii.edu/journals/manoa/

CONTENTS

Editor's Note   *vii*

ESSAY

Maternal Deities and the Ancestry of Humanity   60
   Takara Ben

Possessed by Love, Thwarted by the Bell: An Overview   83
   Kathy Foley and Nobuko Miyama Ochner

A Living Legacy   135
   Ōshiro Sadatoshi

Images of the Sacred   147
   Frank Stewart and Katsunori Yamazato

FICTION

Round-trip over the Ocean   1
   Sakiyama Tami

The Dog Snatcher   27
   Nakawaka Naoko

Mabuigumi   112
   Medoruma Shun

Riding a Bus in a Castle Town   151
   Ōshiro Tatsuhiro

The Wild Boar That George Gunned Down   188
   Matayoshi Eiki

The Paper Plane at the Empire State Building   254
   Nagadō Eikichi

POETRY

Three Poems 21
Yamanoguchi Baku

Hawks 23
Kawamitsu Shinichi

Okinawan Shaman Songs 50
Christopher Drake

Nothing Can Compare: Okinawan Folk Songs 65
Wesley Iwao Ueunten

Ryūka: Okinawan Lyric Poetry 71
Traditional

The Love of the Red Soil 141
Yonaha Mikio

Three Poems 178
Makiminato Tokuzō

Two Poems 184
Takara Ben

DRAMA

Gods Beyond the Sea 74
Ōshiro Tatsuhiro

Possessed by Love, Thwarted by the Bell 98
Tamagusuku Chōkun

The Cocktail Party 213
Ōshiro Tatsuhiro

About the Contributors 280

Editor's Note

Living Spirit: Literature and Resurgence in Okinawa is a collection of extraordinary literary works from the Ryūkyūs, most of which have never been translated into English, or are newly translated for this volume. The selections range from the oldest poetry born in the islands to contemporary prose and poetry.

The publication of *Living Spirit* is another important step in the resurgence of Okinawan literature that began in the 1960s. Together with the book's 2009 sister volume, *Voices from Okinawa*—a collection of plays and essays by Okinawan Americans—*Living Spirit* displays the richness and beauty of a literature that has been relatively unnoticed for far too long. For example, despite the fact that Okinawan authors have been awarded Japan's highest literary award, the Akutagawa Prize, Okinawan writing has been largely marginalized or subsumed in the larger category of Japanese literature. Okinawan literature, however, is not a subordinate category but a literature with its own history, traditions, and sensibilities. It stands on an equal basis with Japanese and other world literatures. *Living Spirit* is an invitation for English-speaking readers to experience the many strengths and surprises of Okinawan writing in several genres.

In addition to Okinawan prose and poetry, *Living Spirit* offers another treasure from the Ryūkyūs: a series of remarkable photographs by Higa Yasuo. For over three decades, Higa studied the ancient and sacred religious festivals of Okinawa and was able to record cultural practices that, unfortunately, are rapidly disappearing. These foundational rituals preserve the essence of Okinawan culture, temperament, and ways of being in the world, and Higa's images are therefore a vital complement to the work of Okinawan authors.

The importance of the resurgence of Okinawan literature and culture today can be best appreciated by knowing something of Okinawa's history. By the twelfth century, an independent, centralized kingdom had emerged in the islands of the Ryūkyūan Archipelago. The Ryūkyū Kingdom flourished until 1609, when the Satsuma (Shimazu) clan of southern Kyūshū invaded the kingdom and took control. According to the "father of Okinawan studies," Iha Fuyū, the invasion transformed the kingdom into "an ingenious

Higa Yasuo: Maternal Deities

Inviting and Greeting the Gods (Kami-nkē)
Aguni Island, Yagan Utaki
1990

organ" of exploitation, and for the next 270 years Satsuma plundered the resources of the Ryūkyūs and used the kingdom for organized smuggling while other parts of Japan were closed to foreign countries. An exception was the Dutch trading depot on the island of Dejima, in Nagasaki harbor, which the Tokugwa shogunate in Edo used for trade and for gathering information on foreign countries. The clan also imposed a heavy tribute-tax on the people. Under the severe and uncompromising control of Satsuma, the Okinawan people became, to use Iha's word, "slaves."

It is not surprising, then, that during the Satsuma era, Okinawan culture lost its vigor and liveliness, and the arts declined rapidly. The invasion and domination by Satsuma, Iha wrote, were the greatest tragedies in Okinawan history, and he believed that even in the twentieth century, the people were still suffering from the trauma of three centuries of Satsuma "enslavement." The 1879 annexation of the Ryūkyūs by Japan—though another act of colonization—ended the islands' economic ruin; Iha called it an "emancipation" of the people from a bitter period of "slavery." In using such terms, Iha was of course aware of the parallel he was drawing with the history of slavery in America. But he was equally aware, of course, that annexation by Japan further suppressed Okinawan culture and language.

Iha made these observations in his 1947 essay, *"Okinawa rekishi monogatari"* (A Story of Okinawan History). At the time, Okinawa was occupied by the American military, as it had been since the end of World War II. Iha concluded his essay with these words:

> I will not ask under what political system Okinawans should live to become happy because this question is outside Okinawan history. But I will add that when imperialism comes to an end on this earth, Okinawans will then be liberated from the "bitter world" [*nigayo*] and enjoy the "sweet world" [*amayo*].

Iha died one month after finishing *"Okinawa rekishi monogatari,"* and did not see his hopes realized.

Nigayo and *amayo* are from the vocabulary of ancient Ryūkyūan sacred poetry. According to Iha, they mean, respectively, "a year of bad harvest" and "a year of abundance." *Nigayo*, in Iha's modern interpretation, seems to refer to the many afflictions that Okinawans endured—not only the Satsuma invasion and Japanese annexation, but also the fierce battle that took place in 1945, primarily on Okinawa Island. The Battle of Okinawa is regarded as one of the cruelest conflicts ever fought: after eighty-two days of horrendous fighting, nearly one hundred thousand civilians perished, the great majority of them trapped between the armies of Japan and the United States. The battle had a traumatic and lasting effect on the Okinawan imagination—and we see this reflected in the literature.

Iha's use of the word *imperialism* in his essay is controversial. Did he choose the word hastily? What did he really mean by it? It seems to me that he was referring to all political and social systems that violate human rights and that use political and military might to enforce policies of discrimination, oppression, or aggression. Seiyei Wakukawa—an influential leader of the Okinawan diaspora in Hawai'i, who became a disciple of Iha's in the 1920s—wrote that "Okinawa is unblessed with history." Iha meditated on this "unblessed history" in his last essay, and how such a history has shaped Okinawan identity.

The last sentence in Iha's essay refers to two forces in the Okinawan psyche: the struggle to be free of "imperialism," and the yearning to reach the ideal state he called *amayo*. Today, sixty-six years after the Battle of Okinawa, Okinawans continue to be caught between Japan and the United States. But readers of *Living Spirit* will notice a growing resistance to the political situation in Okinawa, and the determination to realize Iha's ideals.

Despite Satsuma's severe control of social and economic systems, Okinawa experienced its first "renaissance" in the eighteenth century, according to Iha. Adversity could not prevent a flowering of genius during this period. Among the notable figures was Tamagusuku Chōkun (1684–1734), who created *kumi odori,* a new performing art integrating music, dance, and poetry. Iha compared Tamagusuku to Zeami, the Japanese originator of Nō plays, and to Frédéric Mistral, the French poet who revived the language and literature of Provénce. Other figures in the renaissance included the outstanding painter In-Genryō (1718–1767); the legendary poet Unna Nabī (born about 1660), whose *ryūka* are still sung throughout Okinawa; and the skilled politician Sai On (1682–1761). Sai On was regent, instructor, and advisor to King Shō Kei. Under his influence, the king introduced land reforms, conservation projects, and various initiatives that encouraged official government recognition of Okinawan craftsmen, artists, and performers. It was because of Sai On's wisdom that the "Golden Age" of Ryūkyūan arts flourished.

The second major renaissance of Okinawan culture began in the latter half of the twentieth century, and we are in its midst today. One of its early manifestations was the 1967 selection of Ōshiro Tatsuhiro as the first Okinawan to win the Akutagawa Prize, the most prestigious literary award in Japan. Until then, people had believed that it would be extremely difficult or almost impossible for Okinawan literature to cross the Shichitō Nada (The Sea of Seven Islands)—the rough waters between Amami and Yaku Islands—and receive due recognition in the north.

But the sea was crossed, and after Ōshiro won the prize, three other Okinawan authors—Higashi Mineo, Matayoshi Eiki, and Medoruma Shun—won it. In the 1990s, Sakiyama Tami was nominated for the award twice. In Tokyo, Okinawan writers were winning other literary awards as well.

Much contemporary Okinawan fiction experiments with the languages of two cultures. For example, the authors mix Okinawan language with standard Japanese in ways never before tried. Their works also courageously tackle controversial issues, and this has had a great impact on contemporary

Japanese literature. Okinawan literature has become the focus of enthusiastic scholarly studies, especially among the younger generation of academics in Japan. It is as if Okinawa's culture, history, myths, and folklore—which once seemed so distant and exotic—are finally understandable to Japanese readers and scholars.

The popularity of Okinawan literature has not been limited to fiction. Yamanoguchi Baku, who left Okinawa as a young man and spent most of his life writing poetry in Tokyo, has been increasingly acknowledged. While many Okinawan writers went to Tokyo before 1945 to seek recognition for their work, Baku is unique in that he became one of the most popular poets in Japan even though his "mother tongue" was Okinawan. Like Anglo-Irish poets and writers who created modern English literature, Baku invented a simple but deep vocabulary accessible to all readers. Using standard Japanese, he democratized Japanese poetry. But before he became popular, he endured the fate of many Okinawans in the cities of the northern Japanese islands—itinerant, poor, socially isolated, and almost homeless.

In the 1950s and the 1960s, a group of young writers established the radical journal *Ryūdai bungaku* (Ryūdai Literature), through the University of the Ryukyus Literary Club. These young poets and writers wrote critically of their society's political situation and managed to alarm the American military authorities who governed Okinawa. As a result, in 1956 *Ryūdai bungaku* was suppressed, and six students were expelled from the university under heavy pressure from the Americans. The students were censored and punished merely because they spoke out against the unfair and undemocratic treatment of Okinawa by the United States military. The incident is still remembered as a scandal of the Cold War milieu in the 1950s, when Okinawa Island was a U.S. outpost, bristling with weapons, in the Western Pacific. The freedoms that the United States was supposed to be protecting were hardly present in the Okinawan Islands, which America governed.

And so, just as Okinawa's first renaissance took place in the midst of Satsuma's colonization, the second resurgence of culture and arts took place during the repressive American rule of Okinawa. Many great literatures, in many places, have been born in reaction to injustice and adversity, and in this way Okinawa shares similarities with other world literatures, bearing witness to an "unblessed history." Today, Okinawan literature has clearly achieved the qualities of—and deserves to be regarded as—an international literature. Imperialism has not disappeared from the earth, as Iha Fuyū hoped it would. But Okinawans surely have learned from their history, and have broken out of their "years of bad harvest." Resistance and the resurgence continue, and a new literature is being written in Okinawa that is planting the seeds for Okinawa's "years of abundance." I wonder what Iha would have said if he had lived long enough to see the new flowering of literature and culture in the second half of the twentieth century. The "years of good harvest" show every sign of continuing.

Acknowledgements

I vividly remember meeting Professor Taira Buntarō when I was a young instructor of American literature at the University of the Ryukyus in 1977. He was an esteemed pioneer in translating Okinawan literature into English and had retired by then. I told Professor Taira that I was grateful for his translations of *ryūka*, and that as a student I had used them in a term paper, for which I had received an A. Without the slightest smile, Professor Taira looked straight into my eyes and said, "Young man, why didn't you translate the poems for yourself?" Stunned and ashamed, I was speechless. I told myself that someday I would translate Okinawan literature and leave that speechless young man behind.

More than thirty years have passed, but I always feel indebted to Professor Taira for his words, and for his small bilingual book *My Fifty Favorite Okinawan Poems*, published in 1955. His goading of me set me off on this adventure of translating Okinawan literature into English. Thus, for more than one reason, *Living Spirit* is a dream come true for me.

I'm grateful for the hard work of *Mānoa: A Pacific Journal of International Writing* in shaping this dream into the carefully made book you are now holding. Without the unstinting efforts of Frank Stewart, my friend and coeditor, *Living Spirit* would not have been possible in this form. We were ably assisted by managing editor Pat Matsueda, staff members Sonia Cabrera, Eleanor Svaton, and Moriah Amey, and book designer and art editor Barbara Pope.

Of course, such a project cannot be done by just a few people, and there are many others to thank.

For their kind and generous support of this effort to bring Okinawan literature to readers everywhere, I want to extend special thanks to Dexter and Valerie Teruya.

Professor Joyce Chinen, director of the Center for Okinawan Studies at the University of Hawai'i–Mānoa, enthusiastically helped with this effort, and her center contributed funding. "Compatriotic" collaborations with her and her sister, Karleen, editor of the *Hawai'i Herald*, have always inspired me and resulted in valuable discoveries.

My fellow translators should be thanked. Colleagues at the University of the Ryukyus and friends accepted challenging work when Frank and I approached them and shared our plans for this book. Shinjō Tomoko and Hamagawa Hitoshi were especially helpful with reading galleys and suggesting improvements.

I wish to thank Mrs. Higa Nobuko for generously giving us permission to publish Higa Yasuo's timeless photography. Ōshiro Hitomi, curator at the Okinawa Prefectural Art Museum, graciously assisted with transmitting the digital data for the images. Ōshiro Sadatoshi and Yonaha Mikio, poets and critics, not only allowed Frank and me to publish their works, but also advised us on the selection of other writing. Takara Ben, whose essay and poems are included here, introduced me to Mrs. Higa Nobuko and facilitated the editorial process in innumerable ways.

Last but not least, I would like to thank my family—Marie, Akiko, Ken, Kinuko, and Kohei—for their support and encouragement.

Katsunori Yamazato
University of the Ryukyus

Round-trip over the Ocean

A commotion of light stirred at their backs, as if someone were creeping across the water toward them. She spun around in alarm. Suspended over the misty cape of T. Island, the setting sun glowed like a red ball of fire. Fragments of broken light flew at her eyes and scattered in all directions. As she blinked rapidly, a blanket of vermillion unfurled toward them and converged with the color of the sea.

From a distance, the surface of the ocean appeared to be a gently undulating blue carpet; viewed up close from the boat, it was a heaving expanse of high crests. Crashing through towering waves one after another, the boat struggled through the heavy seas.

It was 6:20 in the afternoon. The small fishing boat, midway between two islands—one receding behind them, one drawing closer—continued to plunge ahead across the ocean. An hour and ten minutes had passed since the roofless boat, under the gaze of the heavens, had departed from the northern port of T. Island with its three passengers: Akiko; Kinzō, who was ill; and Old Man Kāre, the helmsman. They had timed their departure so they wouldn't be seen leaving T. Island and so they could avoid the intense glare of the sun. More important, they wanted to arrive at O. Island under the cover of falling darkness.

The stench of fuel oil and leftover fish turned Akiko's stomach, and the spray of seawater made her feel clammy. The vibration of the boat and the endless drone of the motor made her nauseated. Just then, Kinzō began shaking violently. Since departing, he had stared at the bottom of the boat and sat rigidly, as if nailed to his seat. But with every jolt or shimmy of the boat, he glanced over at Akiko with inflamed eyes. His contorted face was splotched black and blue. Akiko unzipped her bag, pulled out a bath towel, and draped it over his shoulders.

"Are you in pain, Dad?" Fighting back the nausea that brought tears to her eyes, Akiko reached out to rub Kinzō's back. But he brushed her hand away and resumed staring at the bottom of the boat. She took a deep breath and turned her gaze to where he was looking. Sitting diagonally from each other, they awkwardly avoided eye contact.

"Kinzō, hang in there a bit longer," said Old Man Kāre, gripping the helm at the rear of the boat. "Look! There's Nishino Beach!"

Higa Yasuo: People of Compassion

Old woman showing hajichi marks

The place the old man motioned towards with his chin looked like a crushed, cream-colored jug lying on its side. It was the sandy beach on O. Island's northern coast. That was where the boat was headed.

Ten days earlier, Kinzō had proposed that, as the last remaining child of his family, he himself would retrieve his deceased mother's mortuary tablet, which had been left behind in the abandoned house, cared for by a stranger. It had remained there without any grieving family member for seventeen years. His words had sounded like a pronouncement rather than a proposal.

His wife had glared at him at first. "In your condition? You're being unreasonable." But in the end, she was no match for the headstrong invalid who ignored all objections to his plan for a twenty-four-hour round-trip between the islands.

"Once you get an idea, you're pigheaded to the end. You've got your mother's stubbornness." Akiko's mother frowned and heaved a sigh. Then she turned to Akiko as if pleading for help and said, "Well, perhaps if you'd go with him…"

It had been two and a half years since Akiko had quit the part-time job at the post office she'd taken to keep busy and earn some spending money. Now, confined to a daily schedule consisting entirely of taking care of Kinzō and doing a few odd chores, Akiko couldn't think of any reason for refusing her mother's request. Kinzō's taciturn nature had gotten worse over the past several years, and his stubbornness—which could not be blamed simply on his invalid condition—was oppressive to everyone around him.

Long ago, after the family's affairs had been settled, Kinzō had resolved never to set eyes on anyone from O. Island again. That was why he had come up with the idea of going to Old Man Kāre—who had relocated from O. Island to T. Island and now fished occasionally—to charter his boat for a quick trip to the island and back. Kinzō wanted at all costs to avoid the regular boat service and the risk of encountering someone from O. Island. The plan—conceived by an ailing man who had been cut off from society for over ten years—seemed ridiculous. What had persuaded Akiko to go was her growing suspicion that her father harbored a secret obsession that somehow concerned her, though she was doing nothing more than spending her days in idleness.

Kinzō had hardly said a word since they had cast off—as if he feared that opening his mouth even a crack would allow his intense pent-up pain to spew out.

The ocean spray blew higher as the wind rose and turned against them.

"Old Man Kāre, you said we were almost there. How much farther until we get to Nishino Beach? We've been able to see it for a while now."

Akiko glanced back at Old Man Kāre. He was gaunt, but also tanned and sturdy. Perhaps out of habit, the old man never sat down. He stood hunched over the helm.

"Oh, I don't know. We should be there in twenty, thirty minutes."

He again motioned with his chin towards Nishino Beach. His face was tinged red from the reflection of the sun. For some time now, he had been gazing at a single point on O. Island, which seemed to be neither getting closer nor receding into the distance. It occurred to Akiko that his blank face had remained emotionless and unchanging all this time. With this thought, a nostalgic image swelled up in her breast like the sea foam surging around the boat.

She was suddenly overcome with emotion. In her mind, the distance they were now crossing between O. Island and T. Island was like the distance across the U. River, which flowed in a northeasterly direction down the center of O. Island, separating the old village from the new one.

Many years ago, Old Man Kāre had ferried villagers across the U. River. Even then, he had stood hunched over the helm. Though short, he had long legs and a shriveled upper body, giving him the appearance of a hunchback. He had lived in a hut on the bank of the river and had avoided intimate contact with people on both sides, preferring to spend his days simply watching the current. No one knows how it began, but the islanders fell into the habit of calling him Old Man Kāre, playing on the local word for river, *kāra*.

Each year, when the scorching subtropical heat began to abate, the old village on one side of the river held a festival to mark the change of the season. Austere on the first day and lively on the second, the festival featured all sorts of events. As a child from the new village, where traditional festivals were rarely held, Akiko would cross the river with her friends to see the boat races that marked the festival's climax. Every year during the celebrations, the cheerful sounds of the old village would drift across the river into the silent monotony of the newer community of migrants.

"Old Man Kāre! Get the ferry moving!" the children would call out in front of his hut. Silently, a sluggish, hunchbacked man would appear. It shouldn't have taken ten minutes to cross to the opposite bank, but the boat meandered with the river's current and seemed to drift about for ages. Each time the old man raised his long bamboo pole from the riverbed, it traced a semi-circle through the air, raining beads of spray on his passengers' heads. When the bottom of the boat scraped against the shallows upon arrival, Old Man Kāre gave no signal that they had reached the opposite shore. Holding the bamboo pole, he waited patiently until the clamorous children disembarked, their skirts and trousers pulled up and their shoes tucked under their arms.

"Old Man Kāre, see you on the way home!"

Akiko and her companions were always the first to arrive. Without waiting for the later groups, they dashed off along the road that led to the old village. Old Man Kāre would slowly maneuver the boat around and then head back. Glancing behind her as she ran, Akiko could make out the figure of a hunchbacked man, his shadow trailing on the river's surface behind the swaying boat.

According to rumors, Old Man Kāre's hunchback was not congenital; it was due to his having worked for such a long time in the coal mines, starting when he was very young.

The boat suddenly made a wide turn. While Akiko's gaze had been directed inward, the ocean had grown dark. Nishino Beach now loomed before them. The helmsman steered away from the beach and anchored in the shadow of a towering rock that jutted out towards the offing.

"Can you go ashore first to make sure there's no one near the beach?" asked Kinzō. His voice sounded as tense as ever. He was still determined to avoid being seen by any of the islanders. Old Man Kāre nodded, turned off the motor, and secured the anchor line. Then he climbed out of the boat. Chest deep in the water, he waded along the rock face to the beach, then plunged into the thick shrubbery. The retreating silhouette of the old man's short, crooked body was sucked into the gloom.

The boat bobbed up and down beneath the rock. The dazzling sun had vanished. The sunset had faded, and the island seemed as insubstantial as a blurry black-and-white movie. Their view blocked by the rock, the only thing Akiko and Kinzō could be sure of was the cramped space inside the boat, where they sat facing each other. Even that space swayed insecurely. The expanse of surrounding water, immersed in the falling darkness, had gathered into a black mass.

Akiko slowly looked up and peered into the dark. She leaned forward, trying to get a glimpse of the old village—so close and yet out of reach.

Just beyond the thicket into which Old Man Kāre had disappeared, several hundred meters down the meandering road through the bush, stood the house where Akiko's family had once lived. Akiko's grandmother had reluctantly agreed to abandon the house and move with her family to town on the main island. But after leaving O. Island she had said, "I just can't survive in this place," and had returned to the house after only a month. She lived by herself and, less than two years later, died of complications resulting from a common cold.

The family had hastened back to the island and, in a daze, had gathered around the grandmother's discolored corpse. By then, nearly all of the postmortem arrangements, apart from the burial, had been taken care of by the villagers. This was partly done out of spite: those who had remained on the island wanted to show their disapproval of the family that had left. Reluctant to interfere with the burial rituals, the family could only stand aside. The death of the grandmother, who had boasted of her excellent health at age sixty-six, had taken everyone completely by surprise. At the funeral service, the grandmother seemed to be merely pretending to be dead in order to chastise her children and grandchildren for abandoning the island and her. The family members had hung their heads in embarrassment. Shortly after the first anniversary of her death, Kinzō had been stricken by a strange collagen disease with no known cure.

The growing darkness made Akiko and Kinzō increasingly anxious. Akiko felt that if she didn't speak to her father, or do something, they would both vanish into the blackness. She reached out to adjust the towel on his shoulders. The boat lurched to one side and Akiko feared they might capsize. She grabbed the side of the boat to steady herself, and bracing her feet on the bottom of the boat, she clutched Kinzō's arm. Pitched towards Kinzō, she lost her balance, then fell back against the opposite railing. The boat lurched back to its original position.

"Akiko!" On his hands and knees, Kinzō called out, moaning in pain.

Akiko tightened her grip. "What? What should I do?" she asked.

Instead of answering, Kinzō pried her hand from his arm. The weak, insubstantial feel of the soft flesh of Kinzō's hand, like that of a woman's, lingered in Akiko's mind. Kinzō gave her a look of stern rejection, as if to say he had never intended to call out to her.

"Old Man Kāre's taking a long time," he said, biting down on his frowning lip. "Maybe he ran into someone."

Her father was so stubborn! There was no approaching him. Realizing she was reacting to him the same way her mother always had, Akiko heaved a sigh. But a moment later, she recognized that she had inherited part of her father's nature, and she smiled to herself at the irony.

Akiko was in her late twenties and had no particular accomplishments to speak of. Whenever she tried to act decisively in a group, she always felt uneasy and out of place. As she struggled to avoid conflict with other people, she became obsessed by a secret desire to be alone and to avoid all contact. Akiko's behavior was viewed by her parents as somehow entangled with the dark circumstances of the family's relocation and the last wishes of her grandmother.

Akiko raised her head and turned in the dark toward Kinzō, who was muttering.

"Listen, Dad," Akiko ventured, knowing full well that her words would be repulsed. "When we get to the village, shouldn't we at least tell old Hatsu Nakamori that we've come? No matter how hard we try to keep it a secret, word will eventually get out that we were on the island."

As Akiko had expected, Kinzō gave her a menacing look.

Paying no heed, Akiko continued. "She cared for Grandma to the end. Since we're removing Grandma's mortuary tablet, I don't think it's very polite to not even say hello. Especially since this is our first visit in over fifteen years."

Infuriated, Kinzō flung away the towel draped over his shoulders. Akiko stammered, then fell silent. At wits' end, she silently retrieved the towel from where it had snagged on the boat's railing.

Before they had started out, Akiko's mother had in fact contacted Hatsu Nakamori. Akiko's mother had been on friendly terms with her since the time the family had lived on the island. Hatsu had agreed to look after Akiko's grandmother after the stubborn woman abruptly returned to the island and began living on her own. To somehow bring Kinzō in contact with Hatsu during the journey was one of the duties Akiko's mother had entrusted to Akiko. Kinzō had not been to the island since the first anniversary of his mother's death; neither had anyone else in the family, including Akiko's two married, older sisters. Ever since Kinzō had fallen ill, the family had had little choice but to honor the strictures he had imposed on himself in an apparent attempt to deal with his feelings of guilt.

Also standing in the way of this journey's mission was Akiko's grandmother's dying wish: that her remains, or mortuary tablet, never be removed from the island. Out of a desire to protect the death-bed wish that had been entrusted to her, Hatsu had pledged that "promises made to the dead must be kept no matter what, or the living can never rest easy." For seventeen years, Hatsu had overseen the annual memorial services for Akiko's grandmother. Now, she must be well over seventy years old.

The grandmother's dying wish made living in town on the main island extremely uncomfortable for them. As long as they avoided returning to the old island, there seemed to be no escaping their situation and shame. Moving back, however, was out of the question, as they had no way to make a living there. Since they had no choice but to continue living where they were, they badly needed to come up with some kind of solution— even after all the time that had passed.

"If I say I'm not seeing anyone from the island, I'm not seeing anyone from the island!" spit out Kinzō, as if to emphasize the determination he continued to express from his sickbed. The words seemed to be a spell he cast on himself to help him persevere.

Old Man Kāre still had not returned, and Akiko began to worry. It wasn't just her shaky emotional state that made his delay so distressing: it was already past eight o'clock, and there was not a glimmer of light in the cloudy September sky. The place where they were anchored was now in complete darkness.

Though they had left town just that morning, Akiko, unaccustomed to being away from home, felt that several days had passed and that she and Kinzō had been bobbing up and down on the water for ages. Would they ever be able to set foot on the island? Or would they just drift out to sea? As long as Kinzō insisted on avoiding the villagers, and as long as Old Man Kāre remained gone, the young woman and the invalid—both ignorant of how to operate a boat—could do nothing but stay put, swaying side to side on the pitch-dark sea. Akiko began to feel disgusted at herself for having so imprudently and casually agreed to Kinzō's plan. Nevertheless, since she was already here and O. Island lay before them, there was no turning back.

The boat was shaking. She looked over at Kinzō and noticed that he was shuddering; a hissing came from his clenched teeth.

"Dad, are you cold?"

Kinzō shook his head. But suddenly his trembling grew worse and he fell down, writhing. He began striking the bottom of the boat with his fists. A chill ran down Akiko's spine. As she had feared, he was having a seizure.

Kinzō had undertaken the voyage without permission from his doctor. He brought with him an entire week's supply of pills, a dose of which he'd been instructed to take every eight hours. Out of stubbornness, Kinzō took the pills every six hours. What's more, he took with each dose one more pill than was prescribed. His seizures were a withdrawal symptom that occurred when the effect of the steroid medication—taken to suppress the pain and retard the progression of the incurable disease—wore off. He had taken a dose three hours earlier, in the harbor village of T. Island just as they were casting off, so the medication should not yet have worn off. However, for Kinzō—who had spent the last ten years coping with his illness at home or staying at the hospital—the stress of an airplane flight, a taxi ride, and then a voyage on a small fishing boat to the island must have been an intense strain. Although it was early for another dose, Akiko took out Kinzō's medicine. She pressed three Prednisone pills into his trembling hand, and he gulped them down without water. As he continued to writhe in agony from the convulsions, the boat tilted so far over that the sides nearly slipped below the surface of the water.

Weeks and months had passed when Kinzō had been assailed day and night with nearly every known symptom: splotches and swelling all over his body that, like burns, appeared suddenly but healed gradually; headaches and shivers that made him writhe on the floor; vomiting; ringing in the ears; fever; and numbness. Over the past year, the symptoms had abated to the extent that he was able to consider making this trip to the island.

Once a seizure had begun, Kinzō had no choice but to endure it until the medicine started to take effect. Worried about the tilting of the boat, Akiko occasionally remembered to rub Kinzō's back.

Just then she heard something swooshing in the water. Startled, she sat up and saw the black shadow of Old Man Kāre, his arms flapping like wings as he waded towards them through the dark shallows.

"Oh! Old Man Kāre's back!" Overcome with relief, Akiko impulsively reached down and pulled Kinzō up from his prone position.

When at last she stepped onto the beach, Akiko was delighted by the feeling of sand between her toes. She, Kinzō, and Old Man Kāre walked until they reached a group of small boats that had been pulled up to the shrubbery at the high-water line. She scanned the area with the flashlight that Old Man Kāre had given her. Barely visible through the darkness, the narrow trunks of a cluster of *mokumaō* trees towered before her, their branches swaying in the ocean breeze. The scenery seemed to have remained unchanged for the past twenty years. Her heart was stirred with emotion.

Akiko could now appreciate the meticulous schedule of Kinzō's seemingly ludicrous plan. If they had arrived at midday, with the sun shining overhead, the island probably wouldn't have looked this way. Had the landscape been blazing white under the merciless sun, she would have had to avert her eyes and would have felt disoriented and confused.

They followed a gently meandering road that led towards the center of the village. At a point where the white sand began to change to soil, they came upon a plot of land about two hundred meters square enclosed by a hedge of Ryūkyū hibiscus. Inside the hedge stood a traditional home shoddily constructed of rough-hewn boards. Through the open doorway, they could see a Buddhist altar. To the right of the entryway was the guestroom, which had an alcove; to the left were the living room and the kitchen; and at the back were the sleeping quarters. The interior walls did not reach all the way to the ceiling's soot-covered beams, so it was possible to hear what was going on throughout the home. Always dark and shadowy, even when the sun was high, the dwelling crowded the family into a small space, as all the village houses did.

O. Island was relatively large compared to the surrounding islands. The broad U. River divided the island in two. On the west side was the old village, which had been protected by the river from the spread of an infectious malaria that had decimated the village on the east side. When the malaria had subsided, newcomers had resettled the site of the village that had been ravaged.

Over the past dozen years, the island had grown increasingly poorer and more desolate. The principal cause was an earlier boom in real estate. Tourist companies had speculated in the island's most scenic property, driving up land prices. Islanders who owned land jumped at the opportunity to sell, using the cash to begin new lives on other islands. However, after a temporary spurt in new construction, land values had dropped and the island had again become poor. Kinzō had been among the first to sell his land and move away. Shaking off the censorious looks of the old villagers who stayed behind in poverty, Kinzō forced Akiko's bitterly objecting grandmother to accompany the family to town on the main island. That had been twenty years ago.

Kinzō's slow pace forced Old Man Kāre and Akiko to stop many times. Kinzō would catch his breath, then lean on Old Man Kāre, take another dozen steps or so, and stop again. Carrying the bags and lighting the way ahead of them, Akiko had to turn around each time and put down the bags.

"Old Man Kāre, can I sit down for a while?" Kinzō freed himself from the old man's arms and, exhausted, sunk to the weedy ground. His legs, withered as tree branches, were splayed, and he hung his head. Old Man Kāre squatted close behind him.

"Listen, Kinzō," he said, sounding like an innocent schoolboy. "It's only my opinion, but about your plan to return to T. Island today: I wish you'd reconsider."

Kinzō's body quivered. His head spun around, and his face stopped inches from Old Man Kāre's.

"What do I need to reconsider? If it's my health that concerns you, you've got nothing to worry about. It's not a big deal."

"Your health's a big deal, I'd say."

"You promised me," Kinzō said in a half-supplicating tone. "You said we could get back in a day. Isn't that why I hired you?"

Old Man Kāre nodded slowly, then spoke in a low voice. "I've been crossing rivers and the ocean for years, so for me, it'd be easy to head back to T. Island right now. I know how determined you are. But listen, Kinzō. If you want to take Grandma Makato's mortuary tablet from that house, that's up to you. But to just carry it off without having a memorial service or anything? I don't know about that."

Kinzō's eyes seemed to gaze inward, as if Old Man Kāre's words were sinking deep into his heart.

Holding a memorial service to move someone's mortuary tablet, even a makeshift ceremony, required following certain procedures. If Kinzō absolutely refused to spend the night in the village, then it was necessary to dispense with the time-consuming formal procedures and make an informal ceremony as brief as possible. Akiko's mother had already asked Hatsu Nakamori to make arrangements for a ceremony—though it was not clear how elaborate it should be. Hatsu had agreed to meet them at the deserted house around eight o'clock. Along the way, Akiko was supposed to persuade Kinzō of the necessity of a ceremony.

"After all this time, I know it's unfair to bring up the feelings of the dead, especially when the living have got things they have to do. But I hope that you, as the remaining child, would consider Grandma Makato's feelings."

At this point, Old Man Kāre turned his shriveled face towards Akiko, then looked back at Kinzō.

"Think about what you're doing from Akiko's perspective as a grandchild," he said. "I'm sure she wants to do what she can."

As far as Akiko was concerned, this strong speech from the normally reticent Old Man Kāre was a miracle. It was a relief to her to realize that she might count on the old man to do the persuading.

"We didn't prepare for any memorial service. We can take care of that sort of thing when we get back to town." Kinzō spit out the words in disgust. But his confidence was obviously shaken, and his voice trembled.

"Of course you could. But Grandma Makato's spirit wants to be here on the island. Surely, you know that more than anyone. Just because you carry off the mortuary tablet doesn't mean her spirit will follow. You should observe the proper rites, and also pray for her forgiveness."

Old Man Kāre's words stung Kinzō's heart. In response, his body began to tremble again. He pressed his fists into the ground and stiffened his shoulders.

"What the hell do you expect an invalid like me to do? I don't want people to see me like this. All I want is to get back to town without being seen. That's my only wish. If we have the memorial service here, we'll have to call a *yuta* shaman. And there's no way one of them would want to help me after all this time."

"There's old Hatsu Nakamori," said Old Man Kāre. "She can't do anything large scale, but if it's a simple ceremony, she can recite the basic prayers. At least, that's what she said."

Kinzō's hardened face turned from Old Man Kāre to Akiko and then back again. His suspicious, exhausted eyes turned downward, and he lapsed into silence. There was a long pause. Kinzō showed no sign of responding, so Old Man Kāre draped Kinzō's arm over his shoulder and pulled him to his feet.

"Well, Kinzō. Your house is just ahead."

In pain and without the energy to resist, Kinzō allowed himself to be dragged along. He didn't have the strength to even keep his head steady, so it bobbed up and down with each step.

In a gap in the darkness, Akiko recognized the shape of her old home. She quickened her pace. She passed through the opening in the hedge of Ryūkyū hibiscus and saw light coming through the open front door, like a sweet odor. In the faint light, she placed her hand on the door jamb and lingered in the entryway. Just then, she noticed someone moving inside. She recoiled in surprise when a plump old woman appeared before her.

"Aki-*chan!*" The round-faced old woman, squinting through moist eyes, was Hatsu Nakamori. When she glanced over Akiko's shoulder and spotted Kinzō being dragged along by Old Man Kāre, her expression suddenly clouded over, and she covered her cheeks with her wrinkled hands.

Inside, the abandoned house was covered in cobwebs and strewn with trash. Even so, the frame showed no signs of warping. Visible in the ceiling, the roof tiles were so solid as to appear new. Except for the rubbish and missing sections of wallboard, the house had more or less retained its original appearance. The altar room near the entrance was the only room to have been kept clean. Hatsu appeared to have taken special care of the mortuary tablet, which stood in the middle of the Buddhist altar. The only light in the house came from the candles placed on the altar and throughout the small room. On a low table were a traditional multitiered box and a lacquer tray decorated with offerings of fruit and various cakes, all of which created a strangely cheerful atmosphere.

Hatsu pulled Kinzō in front of the altar and had Akiko sit beside him. Old Man Kāre knelt down on the floor behind them.

Smoke from the incense, blown by the draft seeping through the tattered wallboards, drifted over the group and flowed outside. Hatsu sat on her haunches, her old body curled into a ball. She lowered her folded hands onto her knees and bowed deeply, her body trembling. Slowly, she straightened up and began speaking in a solemn voice to the mortuary tablet.

> *O most precious!*
> *Most honorable gods and ancestral spirits, we summon thee!*
> *On this blessed and holy day, we summon thee!*
>
> *O most precious!*
> *Your child and granddaughter entreat you!*
> *With offerings of food and fragrant incense!*
> *And offerings of sacred* sake…

She repeated her chant several times, and it seemed that it would probably go on for a long time. When she began the third repetition, her face was sweaty. Intoxicated by her chanting, she glanced over at Kinzō.

"Kinzō," she said, "relax and don't be so tense. Grandma forgives you." Hatsu was apparently already communing with his mother's spirit, and Kinzō did as he was told.

Hatsu's chanting had been mumbled at first, but gradually became more confident and clear, filling the room. Soon her upper body began to sway excitedly, and her hair came untied.

Akiko could hear the rhythm of the ocean outside: the roar of breaking waves, the hushed pause as they receded, followed by another roar. The sound, in company with Hatsu's chanting, stirred a memory in her. A yearning began to overwhelm her and gradually intensified. With her eyes lowered, she surrendered to the sounds and sensations. When she closed her eyes, she heard a swooshing that sounded less like crashing waves than like trees falling in a forest. The prolonged sounds faded away into the distance, then drew closer, and finally crashed loudly. When she listened more intently, the sounds seemed to be calling to her from outside.

Her legs were numb from sitting in a formal *seiza* posture. Nevertheless, before she realized it, Akiko was standing outside the house. The white smoke of the incense had been wafting over her, and now she was saturated with its smell.

She crossed the yard and found a path leading from the house to the beach. Once, there had been four or five other houses scattered along this path, far from the village. Now, there were no signs of them. By the dim light of the moon, Akiko plunged into the heavy undergrowth of shrubs and small trees.

Suddenly, she could see nothing but a huge shadow in her path. When she looked up, she saw a tangle of black trees, their twisted branches spiraling high above her, the entire mass blocking her way. She was in a thicket of *yama-bashō* banana trees; their layers of broad leaves were pressed together in an impassable mass.

Akiko realized that she was in a zone of profound silence. Immediately she knew she was experiencing something that had lain dormant and now had risen to the surface as a result of the unexpectedly strong spiritual power of Hatsu, an amateur *yuta*. A bluish-white space opened up before the thicket, and in it was an apparition of a young-looking Grandmother Makato sitting on the ground next to a girl. Makato was peeling bark from cut sections of *bashō* trees. At her side, a four-or five-year-old girl with a disconcertingly small face followed the movements of Makato's hands. Whenever Makato glanced over at the girl, the woman's stern expression broke into a smile and her eyes twinkled.

Aki, don't make fun of me like your parents and others do. You need to listen carefully to what I say.

Speaking in rhythm with the movement of her hands, Makato chose each word carefully. The girl nodded at everything she was told. Did she understand the implication of Makato's words? Akiko drew closer to the apparitions in order to speak to the girl, but their forms faded into the brush and disappeared.

Every year in early summer, Makato would plunge into this thicket of *yama-bashō* trees to cut down saplings just before they bore fruit. The sounds that Akiko had heard, she realized, were the trees falling one by one. After the trunks were peeled, they could be split into fine strands, boiled in a wood-ash solution, then washed and dried to produce dark, yellowish fibers for weaving. Makato would cut down these *yama-bashō* saplings in a deter-mined attempt to make a living with her weaving in the deserted village.

Her biggest obstacle was that the fibers used to make high-quality *bashō-fu* cloth didn't come from plants like these, growing in the wild. Only the fiber of a cultivated variety, the *ito-bashō,* yielded soft fibers and fine thread. The stiff fibers of *yama-bashō* plants tended to break, no mat-ter how carefully they were handled. Such fibers were completely unsuited for weaving. This fact notwithstanding, Makato continued for many years to weave with thread made from *yama-bashō*, since it was all she had. Eventually, however, her efforts came to an end. A pile of unspun fiber probably sat on the dirt floor in a corner of the shed.

Akiko wandered farther into the thicket. Although this time of year was usually hot and humid, she felt wrapped in coolness. The thicket seemed both to welcome her and to expand, making a rustling sound.

Originally, the *bashō* trees were not dense enough to form a thicket. In the wild, *yama-bashō* spring up across the plain in clumps of two or three plants. Akiko's grandmother had created a thicket in the belief that she needed many trees to produce enough thread to weave cloth. Sometimes Akiko had helped her strip off the lower leaves on the *bashō* plants when they had grown to a height of about five feet. It was only many years later that Akiko found out her grandmother's fruitless efforts had dumbfounded her parents and older sisters and had made the old woman the laughing-stock of the village. Akiko's memory of her grandmother—who was ignored by everyone except the uncomprehending young grandchild—came back to her.

Akiko stood near the thicket for some time. When she looked up, she saw the dense thicket rustling even more. Frightened, she wanted to fall back on her haunches right there. But she had the feeling that if she did so, she'd never be able to escape. So she turned to leave.

Reentering the old house, Akiko was struck by the strong smell of incense. Piles of salt and incense sticks had been placed in two corners of the doorway as guideposts for her grandmother's spirit. Inside, Kinzō had gotten up from the altar, and he and Old Man Kāre were eating while Hatsu chatted with them. Hatsu smiled at Akiko when she entered. Her genial round face looked possessed and fatigued.

Akiko sat down opposite Kinzō. Old Man Kāre sat to the left and Hatsu to the right. The candles behind them cast their faces in shadow. The configuration suggested a scene of solemn ceremony, and made the disrepair of the house seem oddly appropriate.

Hatsu had finished the first stage of her ministrations. She stood up and took the mortuary tablet down from the altar as the others turned to watch her. She carefully spread out a somber purple *furoshiki* wrapping cloth, picked up the mortuary tablet, and placed it on the cloth as if she were handling a newborn baby. Just as she was about to wrap the tablet in the *furoshiki,* Akiko reached out and took it in her hand. Seeing that it was just a thirty-centimeter-long piece of dark-colored wood, she turned it over and read what was written on the other side:

SECULAR NAME: MAKATO NAKAMA
DIED: OCTOBER 2, 1965
AGE: 67

Reading the date on the tablet, Akiko reflected on the passing of time. Suddenly, the quiet was broken by Kinzō, who rose and began folding up the sheet he had been sitting on. The tension in his face had returned, spreading apprehension throughout the room.

"Oh my! Wait, Kinzō, wait! If you leave at this hour in such a small boat, the waves are going to be rough," Hatsu said. She tried everything to cajole him into staying, but he was done listening to her and the others. Akiko reluctantly stood up to accompany him.

"Kinzō, if this is really what you want to do, that's your choice," Old Man Kāre said calmly. "But as long as we leave before the villagers wake up, it won't matter if we wait a little longer."

Kinzō stopped his faltering preparations to leave.

"If you rest here for a while, and we leave while it's still dark, you'll be able to avoid meeting any villagers, just as you wished. And that will give Grandma Makato more time to lament her departure from the island."

Trapped between the old man admonishing him and Hatsu nodding her support, Kinzō stood in confused isolation. Pain and exhaustion seemed to have weakened his resolve.

"Well, if I can avoid meeting any of the islanders," he said in a resigned tone of voice.

It was resolved that Kinzō and Akiko would spend the rest of the night in the abandoned home, consoling the spirit of Akiko's grandmother. With relief, Hatsu carried in the bedding that she had prepared in advance. She checked the items one by one; still, she had misgivings about leaving the invalid Kinzō and his daughter alone in the old house. She dawdled and stood for a time in the doorway. Realizing she couldn't stay forever, she squeezed Akiko's hand and then plunged into the darkness and headed back to the village. Old Man Kāre returned to the boat, promising to pick them up at the appointed time.

Akiko lay down next to Kinzō and gave herself over to the sound of near and distant winds outside. Meanwhile, Kinzō had fallen asleep from his medication. Akiko's nerves had caused cramping in her arms, legs, and back, but she gradually began to relax and her eyelids grew heavy with drowsiness. Her mind, however, remained alert. She turned onto her back and stared up at the rough-hewn ceiling, sensing the heavy darkness enveloping the silent house. Abruptly, she was jolted by a bottomless darkness that seemed to crawl across the ground and threaten to assault her. She glanced over at Kinzō. Seeing that he was asleep, she quietly slipped out from under the bedding and stepped outside.

She walked noiselessly past the vague, indistinct shapes of trees and brush and headed to Nishino Beach. The sounds and smells on the wind led her to the shoreline. The surface of the ocean at low tide dully reflected the light of the nearly invisible moon, and the dim glow faded from the inlet's beach as if in retreat. Old Man Kāre's boat, anchored beneath the rock face, sat motionless and small, like a child's toy floating in a puddle. In this desolate and somehow oppressive environment, Akiko had the feeling that something inside her was boiling to the surface. Unstoppable, it suddenly tore through her.

"Old Man Kāre!" Alarmed by the sound of her own cry, she called again even louder. The old man's silhouette appeared on the boat. She waded into the sea. She struggled through the swirling water, her feet slipping on the slime of sand, pebbles, and rocks. When she reached the boat, the old man pulled her up. Her soaked jeans and undergarments clung to her skin. The old man blinked at Akiko in astonishment and smiled self-consciously.

"How thoughtless of me. How could I expect a young woman like you to have a good night's sleep in a place like that?"

In his own way, the old man tried to rationalize the strangeness of the situation. He shook out the khaki blanket that smelled of fish and that he had used to cover himself. Awkwardly, he draped it over Akiko, who was wet through and through.

As if something had just occurred to him, the old man hauled in the anchor and started the boat's engine.

"Akiko, it'd be too bad if you left without seeing any other part of the island. If we circle around the three capes on the east side, we'll reach the U. River. How about we make a run?"

Akiko nodded in agreement, and the old man cautiously steered the boat away from the rock face and into the deeper water. The boat cut through the waves, disturbing the stillness and solitude. The wind stirred up the strong smells of the ocean. Akiko reached over the gunwale and touched the surface of the water. She felt against her palm the heavy resistance and flow. The water's sharp chill reawakened her exhausted nerves.

The boat followed a course as close to the coast as the ebbing tide would allow. By the time they had rounded the first cape, Akiko's eyes had grown accustomed to the darkness, her field of vision had begun to expand, and she could see farther inland.

Three villages were spread out along the coast between Nishino Beach and the U. River. Started by people who had come after the war, when the economy in the area had been most unstable, the villages had been built on the sites of previously abandoned ones and were barely managing to sustain themselves. The inhabitants were mostly people who had fled during the fighting and had found their way back. Some had migrated from elsewhere.

A cleft in the blackened landscape revealed a glimmer of light that looked especially desolate to Akiko. She thought it must be from the village built by workers in the coal mines.

"Is that S. Village over there?"

Old Man Kāre looked to where Akiko was pointing and slowly nodded. He had lived there long ago, before moving to a hut next to the river.

"There are people living there even now, aren't there?" Akiko murmured, not expecting an answer from the old man.

"The faces have changed, but they're still scraping by."

Akiko nodded—not so much to the old man's words as to the moisture in his eyes. The old man's gaze was riveted on the village. Suddenly he shook his head, as if freeing his thoughts from an old memory. He sucked in his cheeks and moved his wrinkled lips as if trying to find the right words. "I used to work in the mines with a guy from that village," he finally said. "He's dead now."

Old Man Kāre looked gloomily at Akiko. "Besides him, I had one old friend who died like a real fool just before I left the island. So he's gone, too."

Surprised at the intensity and bitterness of the old man's words, Akiko stared at him for some time. Then the old man licked his lips and began telling his story.

"There was a young guy named Matsuo. He was a couple dozen years younger than me. Unlike me, he had a family—five kids in all. He didn't have any skills other than working in the coal mines. During all his years on the island, I never saw him plowing fields or going out to sea. And yet he was always talking big…"

Vague memories of the Matsuo family began coming back to Akiko.

Each village had had what was called a cooperative shop, a nonprofit co-op that sold everyday necessities on credit. The Matsuo family also had a shop, but unlike the co-ops it was privately owned and they were attempting to make a profit. The shop sold goods that the Matsuos had bought wholesale. This was many years after the collapse of the coal-mining industry, which had been started by investors from mainland Japan. Most of the miners had been day laborers, and when the mines failed, they left the island. Newcomers to the village mingled with the few mine workers who had remained. Akiko vaguely recalled that the newcomers started to gain power by sticking together. They shunned the stragglers from the mines. In the midst of the complex relationships among the villagers, Matsuo had to find work outside the network of businesses and farms controlled by the newcomers. But Akiko couldn't remember anything that connected Matsuo to Old Man Kāre.

"He stayed on the island because the girl he married was from here. Apparently, at first he wanted to leave, but then the kids were born one after another, and he had no choice but to stay. Of course, his wife was the one who struggled bringing up the five kids. And then, when his oldest kid left the island, right about this time of year, he hanged himself."

The old man's mouth clamped shut as if to sever all connection with Matsuo. He looked down at the surface of the water. Moved by his story, Akiko too gazed at the ocean. Suddenly, she pictured Kinzō's contorted face during the rough journey to the island. She tried to block out the image that rose up in her mind.

At that moment, there was a dull thump from under the boat. The next moment, the boat lurched up and came crashing back down into the water. The old man lost control, and the boat took off in a zigzag pattern, with no signs of steadying. Akiko noticed that the tide had ebbed considerably and that patterns of ripples stretched in all directions. A coral reef had emerged as the sea near the coastline had become more shallow. The boat had apparently scraped against a reef. Embarrassed by his carelessness, the old man quickly steered the boat into deeper waters. Soon, a second cape came into view, and the dim light of S. Village faded into the darkness.

Akiko looked out to sea and stared wide-eyed at what she saw. The reef surrounding the island rose above the surface like a marine creature. Before her eyes, the ocean appeared to be drying up, revealing a vast expanse of reef that seemed connected to the land. In the past she had watched from the shore as the tide ebbed, but viewing it in reverse—while on the water—made her acutely aware that the island was connected to the bowels of the earth, far below the sea.

"Oh! So this is how quickly the tides can move in and out!" Akiko exclaimed with a sigh.

"At times like this, you can't relax when you're steering. You carelessly take the wrong route, and you end up running aground."

Gripping the rudder more firmly, the old man concentrated on their course. Akiko looked again into the outward flow of the tide. She could see only the reef pushing its way through the dark surface.

When the tide was out, the shallows covered an extensive area and could have been mistaken for land. The boat took a course just outside the large reef. Before long, they passed a small, uninhabited island and then the second cape. There had once been a small village of newcomers near the mountains. But because she couldn't see even a faint light, she wasn't sure it still existed.

Akiko could see a beach, white and forlorn against the black contours of the island, rising in the narrow stretch of land between the inlet and the forest. She couldn't tell whether or not any villages were there.

From her new perspective, looking towards the island from out at sea, Akiko realized that its shape was the opposite of what she had imagined. While she had been living in town, she had believed that if she returned to O. Island, it would be the same as it had always been. Now, however, the island's shape—so stable in her memory—had been altered, and she was thrown into a state of uncertainty. She felt as if she were seeing a shadow of the island instead of the place she had been so sure of. She thought of having been at Nishino Beach several hours ago, when powerful emotions had arisen in her by touching the trees, hearing Hatsu's chanted prayers, and seeing Makato and the little girl in the banana grove—and she wondered whether these were only illusions inside the night shadows.

Akiko continued watching the hazy image of the island as it flowed by. She then focused on the spot where land and sea blended together, but felt only the movement of the boat. Though she stared, the island's shape seemed to become even more unclear.

When the sea began to lighten in the approaching dawn, she saw a wave at the bow rise up—a dull flash of blackish green. The fathomless depths had given her a glimpse of the abyss that at any time could swallow the tiny boat. The boat passed close to the border between the shallows of the reef and the ocean's immense depths. Large whirlpools were forming in this zone, where the outgoing tide sucked at the reef, spouting and gushing. She was suddenly seized with the desire to locate the precise place where the reef and the deep water created a fissure. Without realizing it, she was leaning far over the gunwale.

"That's dangerous, Akiko! Could you sit up, please? There's nothing around here to look at. Nothing but water—as far as the eye can see." The old man's warning pulled Akiko back from the seductions of the deep.

Old Man Kāre stared at the ocean directly ahead of them. The tide continued to ebb, and Akiko understood that if he were careless for even a minute, they'd run aground on the reef and be immobilized on the ocean until the tide turned.

Rounding the third cape, the old man cut the engine and the boat slowed. The cold wind slackened. Akiko's drenched pants had begun to dry.

The boat headed up the river. Trees grew along the banks so that the winds subsided even more. The seductive odor of rainwater drifted in the air. The trees and undergrowth grew denser on both banks as they continued into the depths. The river narrowed and the shadows of leaves floated on the dark surface of the water that carried the boat along. Akiko wondered, as if searching through the wreckage of a dream upon waking, if she had ever passed through trees lining a river like this one. The idea of having once before been lured from the ocean into a waterway that cut through a narrowing and deepening conduit—and of drifting without end—began to dominate her thinking. It was as if she were recalling an experience from long ago, or as if the image had descended upon her from a distant source and was coming to life within her.

Akiko was suddenly overwhelmed by a desire to get at the truth of Kinzō's obsessive behavior. She needed to see what he—with his unwavering self-discipline and with his obligations to Makato's last words—was trying now to excise from the island.

Before she realized it, the boat had drifted to a standstill. The calm, glimmering surface of her thoughts was disturbed, and the riddle of her father's behavior disappeared beneath it. Fish jumped out of the river, and ripples spread along the water and towards the thicket of trees. The old man, who had been fixated on the scene in front of them, suddenly spoke.

"He hanged himself in this forest," he muttered, "right over there. He was hanging from the branch of a tall *akagi* tree."

Though the old man had spoken in a whisper, the black clump of towering trees seemed to stop swaying in response to his words.

"I was the one who found him. I was also the one who brought him here."

Stunned, Akiko was quiet.

"Matsuo was in an unusually good mood that day, and he asked me to ferry him up the river. He was friendly, like when we used to work in the coal mines together. So I didn't doubt him when, on the spur of the moment, he said he wanted to set boar traps. When I came back to pick him up at the appointed time, I waited. But he never showed up. He couldn't have. By then he was already hanging from the *akagi* tree."

The old man looked steadily into the forest as he spoke. He was no doubt looking at the very tree from which Matsuo had been hanging. Akiko had the feeling that the old man's story held the key to the riddle with which she had been struggling.

"If we don't head back soon, we won't be able to keep our promise to Kinzō to leave before dawn." The old man's tone of voice had changed, and his words rang out and echoed off the water.

The broad reef that had been exposed was now hidden below the waves. Early morning light drifted over the surface. Dawn had not yet broken, but the deep purple sky could lighten in an instant. Akiko began to regret having left Kinzō alone in the abandoned house.

The return course began to swell with the rising tide. Waves surged on the horizon, but the winds were less forceful than on the ride out. The boat picked up speed and headed west.

As soon as they reached Nishino Beach, Akiko dashed across the sand and hurried to the abandoned house. She flew into the yard, breathing hard, then threw open the front door. Kinzō was prepared to leave and was waiting for them with a surprisingly calm expression. Oh! It must've all been an illusion! An upwelling of relief nearly brought Akiko to her knees. Kinzō looked as if he had been sitting in the same position since the evening: cross-legged, his hands on his lap, clutching Makato's mortuary tablet. Without demanding any explanation from Akiko as to where she had been, he stood up as if to leave at once.

"It'll be light soon," he said, then walked out of the door ahead of her. Akiko hurried after him, carrying their bags. Kinzō strolled through the darkness with his head held high. He was as unsteady and feeble as always, but composure and confidence seemed to have returned to his step. Akiko watched him with a puzzled expression.

It was 5:40 in the morning. The boat moved out of the shadow of the rock and headed into the offing. The densely confined darkness that hung over the island began to dissolve between the water and air and then to fade into the distance. When the boat picked up speed, a thin wall of water rose up on each side. As if passing through a transparent veil, the boat ferried its passengers away from the island.

Kinzō, holding Makato's mortuary tablet, sat with half-closed eyes. He looked as if he were still clutching something that could never be relinquished, as if his emotions had been truly conveyed to Makato in Hatsu's ceremony. Akiko, however, couldn't determine his exact thoughts from his quiet, somber demeanor. Whatever he was thinking, the strange composure that had returned to his expression made her deeply uneasy.

Even if Kinzō managed to carry Makato's mortuary tablet back to their home in town, he still faced a moribund, overmedicated life, plagued by pain and illness. He was returning to town only to be thrown back into an existence somewhere between living and dying—the same state he had been in for the past dozen years. Akiko tossed her head as if to shake off the dawning awareness of why Kinzō had made this voyage. It didn't matter anymore. If they arrived on T. Island in time to board a flight to the mainland, they would be at home in the early afternoon. Her depressing obligation would then be over. More than anything, she wanted to regain her sense of tranquility as soon as possible.

Then something rose up in Akiko that she did not expect and that could not be shrugged off, swirling around her like a whirlpool. She stared straight at Kinzō. The image of him with his eyes closed peacefully, sitting with Makato's mortuary tablet in his hands, caused her to see through her father's scheming determination. She stared at Makato's mortuary tablet, clenched in his hands as though to prove he had been granted permission to carry out his mission.

Looking towards the horizon, Akiko could see no sign of the sunrise, though the ocean was a faint, bluish white. The boat had crossed the border between the coral reef and the deep sea. The ocean ahead was turning gray, indicating the boat was entering the deeper waters. Akiko stood up and twisted around towards the stern. Swaying there in the gathering signs of dawn, she comprehended the abyss of water surrounding the island and saw that the island was a black mass stretching from the surface of the sea into the bowels of the earth.

The next moment, she reached out and seized Makato's mortuary tablet from Kinzō's hands and, just as quickly, hurled it through the air over the abyss. The wooden tablet traced a high arc, alighted on the quiet surface of the sea, and then vanished amidst the waves.

Unable to rise and powerless at first to grasp what had happened, Kinzō merely stared in the direction that the tablet had been thrown. Reaching out to him, Akiko spoke in a tense voice that was compelled by a will not her own.

"This is how Grandma feels," she said. "More than any memorial service, this is what she wanted."

Coming to himself, Kinzō clutched the side of the boat. The mortuary tablet had completely vanished, but again and again he beckoned for it to return. Akiko wrapped her arms around him from behind, for fear he might jump into the sea.

The boat tilted violently. Listing far to its side, the gunwales nearly touching the water, it headed to T. Island.

Translation by Sminkey Takuma

Three Poems

A CONVERSATION

"Where are you from?" asked the woman.

Where am I from? Well, I light a cigarette and think about
a place where the clothes are dyed with images of tattoos
and songs are played on snakeskin-covered *shamisen!*
                                                            Way over there…

"What do you mean by way over there?" asked the woman.

It's just way over there… actually the southernmost point
of the Japanese islands. Does she want to hear that the custom
in my homeland is for women to carry pigs on their heads
and everyone goes barefoot?
                                                            Down south…

"What do you mean by down south?" asked the woman.

Down south; just down south… place of unending summer,
islands rising from indigo seas, century plants, deigo, screw pines,
and papayas huddled in the glaring white season. Where stereotyping
says the people are not Japanese and don't understand the language!
                                                            The subtropics…

"The subtropics?!" exclaimed the woman.

Yes, the subtropics, my woman… but can't you see the subtropics
are right in front of you?! Like me, the people there understand
your Japanese well, though the world associates us only with tribal
chieftains, natives, karate, and *awamori* liquor.
                                                            Close to the equator…

A LETTER TO MY SISTER

She asked a friend to tell me:

> *Brother, I am certain you will be a big success.*
> *Brother, where in Tokyo are you living now?*

I feel you watching over me in your message,
and though for six or seven years I have tried
I cannot write you of my struggles to survive,
of poverty that keeps me from marrying,
I cannot write that your brother's appearance in Tokyo

is like that of a hungry dog. How can I write such things?
Nor can I write that your brother lives hand to mouth,
with no fixed address. Unable to tell you the truth,
yet finally cornered by your stinging questions,
it takes all my strength to write these few words:

> *Dear sister, I hope you are all doing well.*

INTRODUCING MYSELF

Gentlemen gathered here today,
I have been thinking of your status for some time,
And now I have noticed myself thinking of you.

Well, I don't wish to sound arrogant.
But me? I am proudly one of the poor.

Translation by Katsunori Yamazato and Frank Stewart

Hawks

When the first cold winds of October shiver
Through the pandanus groves on the far hills
Daylight darkens, the valleys are smeared shadows
     —And spirits of land and sea begin appearing.

The weary boy tending his family's poor
Farmland hears voices in the wind's
Shadows, chanting to him
     "Time to go home, child, time to go."

Though his eyes are watery,
He does not weep yet. He begins softly to sing
Above the murmuring voices
     To blur the grieving in their calls:

     Cold winds of October, bring the young hawks,
     Cold winds, seasonal winds, invite them
     To find the fields, where they will be fed.

Migrating hawks from the far reefs
Hear the boy singing, chanting their names,
And hurry to the pandanus hills
     From the low-lying Panari Island in the east.

Hawks are the spirits of ancestors, restlessly flying
Out to sea and back again as the seasons turn.
But why the eternal pilgrimage, and why return?
     Even the elders of the village don't know.

When the first cold winds of October blow
The spirits of the hawks cry out, weeping,

And the people weep with them
    Wishing to share in their grieving.

Hawks, spirits of our ancestors, restlessly arriving
On our poor island as October winds begin blowing,
What can we do but capture these hawks to feed ourselves,
    As our ancestors did when they were living?
    Alive because of each other, now and always.

Translation by Katsunori Yamazato and Frank Stewart

Higa Yasuo: Maternal Deities

Inviting and Greeting the Gods (Kami-nkē)
Miyako Island, Karimata, Ryūgu-nigai
1975

Higa Yasuo: Maternal Deities

Inviting and Greeting the Gods (Kami-nkē)
Amami Oshima Island, Akina, Hirase-mankai
1990

The Dog Snatcher

The stone tombs stood side by side in a row against the cliff, behind a concrete barrier. Hibiscus and banyans drove their roots tightly into the cliff's jagged face, their foliage softening its rocky surface and partially concealing many of the tombs. Just knowing they were there, however, behind the trees and bushes, sent a sharp pain through my body. I felt my body becoming tense whenever I looked toward the cliff.

The wailing of a speeding ambulance approached, then rushed by. The sound shrieked through the room and made the glass door shake. I suddenly thought of the man who had recently been reported on the news as lost at sea. Had he been found yet?

According to the article in the morning newspaper, the man had gone fishing and had not returned. Late the following afternoon, his family had called the police and a search had begun. Apparently he was an experienced weekend fisherman. He had set out to sea as usual, by himself. The article speculated that his boat's engine must have broken down, or some other emergency had arisen. For some reason the details in the article were still fresh in my mind—he was a forty-one-year-old electrical engineer, with a wife and two daughters.

As I lay in the darkness with all the aluminum windows shut, I could not hear the rain, but the smell of its moisture hung in the air.

Without getting out of bed, I slid open a window and parted the curtains. By the dim outdoor lights I could see rain striking the walls of the veranda and the glistening foliage. The drizzle fell as silently as fog, like white threads blowing in the darkness. It was the first rain since I had moved in.

The house was located in the countryside, a little north of the closest town, on a street with a few other houses. The street sloped gently upward before ending near the tree-covered cliff. Below the cliff was a broad plain, crowded with trees. The house was the only dwelling standing close to the numerous large tombs set among the thickets at the base of the cliff. A few houses were scattered in the distance, but the surrounding area was mostly farmland. A mountain range was visible in the distance.

I had looked at a number of other properties before finding this vacant, two-story house set amid the surrounding graves. A new, two-lane road ran past the graveyard, but the house was down a side road on its own. I had the impression the old house had been built on reclaimed land, since the house site was slightly elevated and the ground around it looked unnaturally flat. When I had seen a FOR RENT sign on the door, faded by the sun, I had entered the walled yard and walked around to the back. The weedy, over-grown kitchen garden looked like it had once been well tended. But it was the red hibiscus in the corner of the yard that caught my eye. The flowers were in full bloom, the curved petals so abundant that they weighed down the gangly branches.

As soon as I saw this house, I knew it was exactly what I had been looking for. I imagined the door suddenly opening wide, and a dear old voice wel-coming me—*you're back!* I tried to hold on to this cheerful image. It was my grandfather's voice that called out to me in my fantasy. Perhaps it was the red flowers in the long-neglected backyard that made me think of him.

It had been twenty years since I left home, at age seventeen. Years later, when I heard that my grandfather was dying, I wasn't able to return in time to be with him the day he died, and was also too late for his funeral, even though I rushed to be there. He outlived his wife, and died peacefully of old age. I felt remorse over not having visited him even once since leav-ing home. At that moment, the bond between my family and myself seemed to me completely broken. To say goodbye to Grandfather, I vis-ited his tomb on my own. It had been built when my grandmother had passed away. Grandmother had continually pestered my mother for a son to carry on the family name and tend to the family grave—*A boy, first of all!*—but she died before her wish could be fulfilled.

The traditional turtle-shaped stone tomb, bounded by a garden and hibiscus trees, was large; the size clearly expressed my grandparents' fervent hope for a long line of successors, all of whom would be buried there. Because Grandfather was a second son, he was expected to establish his own branch of the family, to be continued by his eldest son, then by his eldest grandson, and so on. That's the way it was supposed to be.

But something went wrong. My mother never gave birth to a son, and so her husband started a separate family with another woman. His coming and going between two families stirred up constant discord. Then, after Grandmother passed away, our family felt like a pick-up team without a coach. After a while, me and my sister both left, one after the other, and went to separate universities. Finally, my mother also decided to leave the family home. Only my grandfather stayed behind.

When my grandfather passed away, my father came back to our old home, but with his new family. That changed everything. The house, with a new and unfamiliar brother and sister, was no longer a place I could go back to. *I don't need a home anymore*, I told myself.

Three months ago, early in September, I returned from Tokyo to visit my mother. It was the first time I had visited her since my grandfather's death, seven years earlier.

When I told her I had rented a house, instead of moving in with her, my mother raised her voice—something she seldom did with me. "Are you serious?!" she said, then fell silent for a while. She rested her elbows on the table and covered her face with her hands. "You just got back, you know. Why on earth don't you want to settle in here for now?" she asked, dispirited. For me, it made little difference where I lived, since I had left home long ago. But I knew for sure it was too late to go back.

My mother did not try very hard to oppose my plan to live by myself. She may have had some sense about my unsettled lifestyle, as I had constantly moved from place to place, and had even strayed out of contact with her for extended periods. Still, I did not want her to worry about me too much. "It's only a stone's throw away—and anyway, I need space for my office," I said as I went out.

The ambulance passed in front of my house, with its red light blinking. The harsh red light flashed through the windows, then flickered behind my eyelids as I tried to go back to sleep.

It was unusual for a rainy night in December to be so still and cold; it made me nervous. In my mind's eye, the boundless sea expanded before me. On the sea, a boat was heading toward the horizon, leaving a white wake as it receded into the distance.

Suddenly I was wide awake. To be sure of where I was, I looked fixedly into the darkness outside. The unfamiliarity made me wonder how many places I had lived in since I left home. I counted on my fingers as I remembered their addresses and names.

Something magical about the sound of rain makes it easy to recall the past. Or maybe the smell of rain turns our thoughts inward…Gradually I found myself recalling unpleasant memories. To put them out of my mind, I closed the window, pulled the futon over me, and tried to go back to sleep. However, the smell of rain became heavier, more humid, and suffocating. I imagined the rain-soaked graveyard outside the house. I imagined the heavy rain falling through the trees and grasses, and into the ground. Does the rain soak ever deeper into the earth until it reaches an underground river or place far below the surface world?

For some reason, I found myself on the verge of calling out. I held my breath and looked around. I realized again that the house stood all by itself in the middle of the graveyard, and that I was alone. I had left the security of my mother's house to be here like this. "You have gotten used to living on your own. You have lived alone for almost twenty years, haven't you?" I said aloud, giving my thought a voice to calm my nerves.

Since I wasn't able to fall back to sleep, I decided to finish unpacking my household goods. I went downstairs, turned on the light, and opened the window. I again wondered at the fact that my new house was in a graveyard. The impression was even gloomier because the only street lamp was blocked by a thick clump of trees.

Outside, something white appeared from nowhere. A large dog passed just below the window. Startled, I felt my knees become weak.

It must be a stray dog, I thought, *foraging for food in the dawn.* With the dog were three, thickset puppies, their fur as white as their mother's. They rushed noiselessly, helter-skelter, like a scene out of a silent movie.

In a flurry, I ran outside. My intention was not to chase away the rain-soaked dog family, but to see those small, lovely creatures just a little longer, before they were gone. I thought it would make me even happier if I could touch them.

As I watched, two of the puppies ran across the street, climbed the curb, and reached their mother on the footpath. One puppy, however, was stumbling and tumbling and falling behind the others. The pavement was wet with rain and looked slick under the streetlight.

Finally the last puppy got across the street. But when it tried to jump up on the curb, it couldn't manage. Anxiously it paced back and forth in the gutter. In frustration, the puppy barked and whimpered. Its mother barked in return, which made the other puppies start to bark as well.

The yelp of the puppy was sorrowful. Again it failed to climb the curb and tumbled backward. It tried again and again. The sight of the puppy trying to scramble up to the footpath after its mother and siblings went straight to my heart.

Without thinking, I ran toward the puppy. My heart beat rapidly. It was as if every sound became muted. The three puppies' yelping and their mother barking—all faded away. My skin prickled. As I approached the sloping footpath and curb, the mother dog rushed at me, protecting her other two puppies. She retreated, then ran at me again.

Even though she might spring on me, I thought, *I still want to hold that poor puppy in my arms.* The mother dog's bewildered state, now charging and retreating, made me long for the puppy even more.

At last, I caught the puppy and lifted it into my arms, though it frantically tried to get away. Through its wet fur, I could feel its racing heartbeat and surprisingly warm body. As if in sympathy with the puppy's heart, my own heart thumped so hard I thought it would burst.

Grasping the puppy firmly in my arms, I ran to the house without looking back. *Is this how it feels to be a kidnapper? Or, to be a thief?* I wondered.

Inside, I washed the puppy in a basin of lukewarm water. The water turned murky with dirt in no time, and I had to change it again and again. The puppy kept struggling to pull itself from my hands. With its wet fur sticking to its skin, it looked almost naked. The sight was both funny and pitiful, and somehow made me want to cry.

I wiped the puppy with a bath towel, dried off its wet fur, then set it on the floor. Over and over, it shook itself to get the water off. Then the puppy went looking in the corners of the room, at the closed doorway, and up at the windows. There was no place it could go to get away.

After I bathed myself and changed in to dry clothes, I found the puppy hiding behind a curtain, its tail between its legs and only its rump poking out. I searched for food in the fridge, but could not find anything good for the puppy. I wished there was milk, but it was rare for me to have any dairy products around. With no other choices, I boiled water in a pan and put in some pieces of bread. Contrary to my expectations, the puppy gobbled up the bread so hurriedly it nearly choked several times.

I held the puppy on my lap. It did not try to escape from me any longer. Once it had dried, its fur was long and fluffy. The color had seemed white but now I saw there was some brown in it as well. And probably it was a boy. Looking closely at his face, I saw some of the hair around his eyes had fallen out, leaving patches of bare skin. It made his eyes appear to be set very wide. "You've got the smooth face of a piglet," I said to the puppy, and gently rocked him in my arms. His eyes suddenly looked wild and he gave a yelp of terror.

Alert now, I heard dogs barking outside. My hands began shaking. The barking of the mother dog caused a chain-reaction of barks from the neighborhood dogs. *They must have compassion for a mother who has had her puppy stolen and can do nothing but bark continually. They must be trying to pressure me to let it go,* I thought. *I had only wanted a cuddly puppy; how did I get myself into such a mess?*

It was three o'clock in the morning when I went back to the bedroom upstairs. I put the puppy in a cardboard box I had lined with towels. The puppy whimpered restlessly and tried to climb out, which in turn made me uneasy and anxious. I couldn't tell if he was looking for his mother. I picked up the puppy and drew him onto the futon with me. The pleasure of holding a warm, fluffy creature brought back nostalgic memories.

Outside the window, the puppy's mother was still barking. Listening to her barking, full of accusation, was hard to bear. I felt unable to breathe. *Is she going to keep barking like this all night?*

Some time later, the puppy dozed off beside me. Watching him sleep, I also sank into a slumber. Even while I slept, however, the mother dog's barking in the darkness lingered in my ears.

In the morning, the yelp of the puppy startled me awake. I had mixed feelings. It was pleasant to be needed, but I also felt guilty for having caused the puppy's suffering.

What had happened in the night was not a dream. With the puppy in my arms, I looked through the window. The rain, pouring harder now, blown by the wind, looked white. The trees surrounding the house were swaying in the strong north wind, their leaves twisted upside down.

The rugged surface of the cliff appeared to have moved closer to the house. I knew that on the other side of the cliff was the sea, and if I looked to the east from there, I would be able to see where my mother and sister lived. Farther to the east was my father's house. It was hard to believe that in this small town the two families were separated and yet both faced the same sea. This incessant rain was pouring on both their houses. *Rain, rain, harder and harder:* I remembered the words from my childhood.

The puppy was yelping in my arms. "From now on, you are my family. Give me a second, I'll cook something yummy for you," I said. Probably because I now had something warm in my life, I was overcome by sentiments I had not felt in a long time.

It wasn't usual for me to be out doing early-morning shopping, caring for the puppy, and so on. The hours flew by. In the afternoon, after eating its fill, the puppy nestled up to me and fell asleep. The warmth of the puppy stirred in me an emotion that long ago had settled to the bottom of my memory, out of reach.

Feeling the puppy near, I, too, became drowsy and fell asleep. Just then I heard a knock on the door. Nobody knew I was here, and anyway, I had just moved in. Wondering who it could be, I opened the door and saw a man in a work uniform standing as close as possible to the door in order to get shelter from the rain. I remembered that I had made an appointment today to have my telephone installed.

Seeing that I was at home, the workman waved to his co-worker in the van to come. The other man soon barged in with a bundle of coiled electrical wire on his shoulder. The steamy warm air of the entrance hall mingled with the odor of the men's bodies and their wet uniforms.

"Well, then, please take care of things," I said. Stepping back from the stuffy smell, I led them to the place where I wanted the phone to be installed.

Though the house was two stories high, it was not very big. The inside had been refurbished. The entrance opened onto a wooden-floored room, a one-mat tatami room faced the south, and a kitchen faced the west. On the second floor, there were a six-mat tatami room and a spacious veranda. I had decided to set up the phone in the hallway by the stairs.

The men got to work right away. "Will it take you long?" I asked. Although I tried not to sound as if I was hurrying them, the older, chubby worker looked up sullenly. He was probably offended.

"The old wiring from the previous phone is still in place, so there's no need to bring any new cable. We just need to extend it into the hallway and connect it," he replied. He looked away from me and went back to pulling a squeaking wire out of a small hole in the wall, like a magician pulling an endless scarf out of his pocket.

"Do you live alone, ma'am?" asked the other worker nonchalantly. He was much younger than his colleague. I didn't want anyone prying into my private life, and in any case before I could speak the puppy began barking. He had planted himself at my feet. Bracing his front paws, he barked so furiously that his floppy ears stood up.

"Damn it, you startled me!" the young worker said, shaking his fist at the puppy. He didn't seem to like dogs very much.

It was the first time I had heard the puppy really bark, and not just yelp. I couldn't keep from smiling at his brave behavior, which I took to mean that a kind of family bond had developed between us.

"Sorry. He hasn't adjusted to living here yet. He must have surprised you," I said, smothering a laugh. I picked up the growling puppy, feeling very affectionate toward him.

"Startled is right. I didn't expect to see a dog in here."

"Hey, even if you don't like dogs, there's no reason to be scared of a puppy."

Turning away from the workmen, who spoke in colorful Okinawan, I began to straighten up the downstairs room to use as my office. I had gotten rid of the household appliances I'd been lugging around, paring my life down to a fridge, a TV, and a word processor. I now had only essential furniture: an office desk and a bookshelf. I unpacked some books from a cardboard box and loaded them on the bookshelf. The puppy had followed me into the room but was now asleep behind the boxes.

I could overhear the workmen chattering. "I've done construction for this house before. Ten years ago, or even longer, when I was a cub like you."

"When was that? I was probably in elementary school. Man, you are even older than I thought."

"Idiot. Anyway, I remember it was Mr. X who brought me here."

"You mean the man I was just reading about in the paper?"

I hadn't meant to listen to their conversation. I was startled.

"Hasn't he been found yet?"

"Not yet."

"They've searched all over the place, checking his hangouts and up and down the shoreline. Even the rescue helicopter couldn't find him. Maybe his boat overturned and he was just swallowed up by the waves."

Mr. X was the man who, according to the news, had gone fishing and never returned. I realized the company name stitched on the breast of the workmen's uniforms was the same as the name of the company where the missing man was employed.

"Even the boat was not found?" I asked, leaning toward them, before I could stop myself.

"You know him?" In unison, the men turned to look at me.

I hastily shook my head, but in fact I was really upset. "It has been already three days, hasn't it? I wonder if he sailed out to sea." I didn't know why I felt so concerned. However, an image rose in my mind of a boat breaking up on the dark surface of the sea, even as it receded more and more over the horizon.

"What do you mean 'out to sea'? He knew better than anybody what would happen if he crossed the reef in that tiny boat." The younger worker's harsh, mocking tone was meant to make my words seem ridiculous.

"Well, he really might have gone out to sea," the older workman sighed, without looking up from what he was doing.

Higa Yasuo: Maternal Deities

Inviting and Greeting the Gods (Kami-nkē)
Kudaka Island, Kabēru, Hītachi
1977

"You're kidding. How could he have?" the younger man asked.

"Even if Mr. X didn't mean to cross the reef, he could have been dragged away by something…" The older man was stuck for the right word.

"A *majimun*, a demon spirit, is that what you mean?" the young man said in a teasing tone, showing his white teeth. His tanned face became even more childlike when he laughed.

The *majimun!* I stared at the man's face. It was an Okinawan word I'd forgotten while living in Tokyo. To hear the word alive in the vocabulary of a young man like him made it sound even stranger.

"I hear the day he vanished it was the anniversary of his mother's death. People say you're not supposed to go to sea on that day. I heard that his wife even tried to stop him from going, but he went anyway."

"So, that's how he became captured by his dead mother's spirit?" The young man laughed, obviously struck by the absurdity of the idea.

What the workers said reminded me of something. Maybe I'd just imagined it, but I remembered that once after she had died, I thought I'd heard my grandmother's voice.

My hometown extends in a gentle slope from the foot of the mountains—which are situated in the middle of the island—downward to the sea. Looking through our front gate and down a hill, I could see the ocean right in front of me. My grandmother disliked the idea of small children going to the shore without an adult. But often, at sunset, I was so involved in playing with the other children who lived by the seaside that I was oblivious to the passage of time. "Hey, hey!" my grandmother would call out and rush toward me with a furious expression. She would grab my arm so hard that I was afraid she was about to slap me. She said, "In the sea, there is something that can catch you." She asked me over and over if I wanted the *majimun* in the ocean to get a hold of me. Her grip on my arm was so tight that it really hurt. I would look up at her and see that her eyes, deep in her high cheekbones, were like two small black holes. I remembered that I had thought that her face at that moment was far scarier than any *majimun* could be.

One day, we were playing at the beach, running along the shore, making sculptures in the sand. As quickly as we piled up the sandhills, the waves would sweep them away, one after another. Engrossed in piling up sand, we didn't notice that the warmth of sunshine had gone and the wind had become chilly. The number of children grew fewer. One by one they were called home. Suddenly I found myself the only one on the beach. It was at that moment that I heard my grandmother call me. Involuntarily standing up, I immediately realized that it could not be her calling me, as she had recently passed away. The light grew dimmer. My grandmother's warning not to play near the sea after dark pierced me through the heart.

Suddenly terrified, I started running. Again I heard her calling me, more distinctly now. Her voice seemed to be part of the shady, humid darkness, and sounded uncanny, as if it were coming from the very bottom of the sea. For the first time I really felt the presence of something alien, frightening, and mysterious.

In my mind's eye I could see vividly the sheen on the night ocean, and the man caught in its grasp. The sea has a savage nature, which calls to us and captivates our souls.

"So, was Mr. X taken away by a demon?" The young man, who moments ago had been smiling derisively, now looked and spoke in awe.

"He might have gone away on his own," said the older man, as though withholding a secret. Strangely enough, he sounded almost cheerful. He then said abruptly, "At last! It's done," and turned the dial on the phone. While he was testing the equipment, the young man, still wearing a dissatisfied expression, gathered up their scattered tools to leave.

I opened the door and thanked them for their work. The rain showed no sign of stopping. The older man looked up and into the distance, where the rain came from, and his face grew serious. "The boat, at least, should have been found, you know," he muttered. Then the two men rushed out into the rain as quickly as they had come.

I was left with a strange feeling, impossible to describe. The puppy was barking incessantly at the men's retreating figures.

I urgently needed to talk to someone, anyone, though I couldn't explain why. Lonely and apprehensive, I dialed a number, then realized it was my mother's, and hung up quickly. Pausing for breath, I dialed again. This time it was the office number of a man I had met recently, though I wasn't sure if I had dialed correctly. Someone in the office picked up the phone, and I asked her to put me through to the man.

"I'm afraid Mr. Inoha is away at the moment," she said, flatly. I left my number and a message with her, and hung up. Then I dialed a couple of my close out-of-town friends and business associates to give them my new address and phone number.

Having gone a few days without a telephone, I felt a lot more cheerful knowing that I was connected to the outside world again. Tomorrow I would get back to my work as a freelance journalist and editor. I had already arranged to take on a job for a publisher who did his own printing. But first, I had to finish unpacking and tidying up my new office.

I glanced out the front window and saw the figure of a white dog on the footpath across the street. Drenched by the unrelenting rain, it stared fixedly in my direction. It was her. Once our eyes met, she began growling. I wondered whether I was seeing a continuation of the scene from last night, something I wasn't supposed to see. A sense of guilt went deep into my heart, like a splinter.

What made me do such a thing? I thought. At the same time, I had none of the regrets that normally arise after a shameful act. *It's merely a stray dog's puppy, which survives by scavenging furtively in the rubbish,* I thought. I startled myself that I was regarding it in that way. I sensed that something in my past was on the verge of being exposed, that it had just begun to emerge, and that it would eventually show itself entirely.

When I had visited my mother, after not seeing her for seven years, she had said in a hushed voice, "He must have grown up a lot, I guess?" The subject that she could not bring herself to mention all these years was finally out in the open.

"Oh, you mean Ikuji? Yeah, he would be in junior high school by now, right?" I had quickly answered her question with another question to keep us both from being uncomfortable. Ikuji was a name I hadn't had on my lips for years. Unprepared, I was becoming upset by this unexpected turn in our conversation.

The fact was, I had divorced my husband and let him take custody of our child, though my son was only one and a half years old at that time. While I was away, the boy would have grown up here. I could understand the troubled expression on my mother's face.

My husband's name was Higashihara Ikurō. I had known him since our student days, and married him when I worked in a small newspaper office, publishing a trade paper in Tokyo. Although he was from the same province as myself, his parents only approved of our marriage because I became pregnant. Soon afterward, I gave birth to a baby boy.

"Let's go back to our home village," Higashihara urged me more and more after Ikuji was born. He took it for granted I tacitly understood that, as the eldest son, he would succeed his father as head of the family.

"No, I won't go back," I said. To go home with him meant going back to a place I had escaped. I simply didn't want to return.

I began to feel repulsion toward him for planning to blindly follow the path predetermined for him—even though it meant abandoning the life he and I had built in the city—merely because it was expected of the eldest son. He reminded me of a certain someone who had turned his back on his wife because she didn't give birth to a son, and made another woman pregnant in order to secure an heir. The whole thing aggravated me more and more.

The thought of being a member of Higashihara's family—where his parents, grandparents, and siblings lived together—made me queasy. I had come from a broken family. I was afraid my negative feelings and my hatred for my father would make it impossible for me to be part of a new family.

I would bang the dishes as I washed them, vacuum the rooms noisily and often. I even raised my voice to him. "What kind of woman would just follow you back home! You're selfish. No, actually you're not being selfish—you're just spineless. That's why you are totally under your parents' thumb. If I had known this, I wouldn't have married you. You act like an old man. If you want to go, then go by yourself."

Turning to the baby, I asked, "Ikuji, my darling, you don't want to go, do you?"

By this point in our marriage, Higashihara was in the habit of not even replying when I spoke. Ikuji had not yet learned to speak and merely opened his eyes wide and stared at us. His lips were tightly pressed together and his mouth was drawn to one side. He often made this expression, which made him look like he was about to speak, and more grown up.

Not long after this, Higashihara left for his parents' home, taking Ikuji with him, although Ikuji was only eighteen months old. Higashihara had stopped asking me to come along. He was mainly concerned with protecting himself and Ikuji, with the single-mindedness peculiar to an eldest son. In his opinion, that was the proper way. If you left somewhere, and your family asked you to come back, that should be reason enough to return.

I saw Higashihara and my son off at the airport when they left Tokyo. Holding his father by the hand as they walked toward a boarding gate, Ikuji looked back at me and abruptly stopped. He must have thought that I was coming with them. Still holding his father's hand, he stamped his feet, uttered an incomprehensible cry, and stretched his other hand out to me. He had been growing without any problems; he was large for his age, and had begun walking early. But for some reason, he was still not even trying to talk. He wasn't making baby talk. His reluctance to speak caused me all the more to feel that I was abandoning him. I didn't want to be apart from him. "Don't take him away, Higashihara," I cried out. But my husband averted his eyes, destroying my last faint hope. Lifting Ikuji in his arms, he hurried to the boarding gate. Ikuji was crying and crying, nearly throwing himself off his father's shoulder. I turned my back and blended into the crowd of people in the lobby. This was the way my son and I became strangers to each other. When I looked again, father and son had disappeared through the boarding gate. That was more than ten years ago.

"I suppose we wouldn't recognize each other if we met on the street," I said in as casual a tone as I could muster.

"Don't you have any desire to see him?" my mother asked, her eyes cast down. She clearly blamed me for being a failure as a mother. She sighed deeply, wondering why I ended up divorcing, in spite of all the effort I had gone through to give birth to a boy.

Just at that moment, a certain memory came back to me. I remembered how proud I felt when I had delivered Ikuji. It was, I think, like my own mother's deep desire, which for both of us was mixed with grief.

"No way to go see him, is there?" I said aloud to the puppy at my feet, at the same time trying to ignore the barking of the mother dog outside.

The dog's supplicating bark was so distressing that I was on the point of screaming. She seemed to be saying, *Let my child go*, which upset me more and more.

And the more it rained, drenching the dog, the more furiously she barked. I felt pity and envy at the same time, for the desperate effort the dog demonstrated as she tried to get her puppy back. *No, I will never give him to you*, I thought, in a fit of jealously and vexation. Angrily, I opened a window.

"I'll make him happy, so stop worrying," I said aloud. I picked up the puppy and held it up to the window. Then, I waved the puppy's paw at its mother and said, "Bye-bye." I was being terribly childish.

"Say good-bye to your mum," I instructed the puppy. When I put the thought into words, I wondered if I had actually wanted to have a puppy when I picked up this one.

I closed the window and peered through the glass to see what the mother dog would do next. She kept barking for a while, but finally was giving up, her head drooping. She disappeared into the thick undergrowth along the footpath. Apparently, the dog and her pups lived in one of the tombs at the base of the cliff.

It rained for several more days. I wasn't used to living with something warm and fluffy. My old bachelorette's space was suddenly full of bustling activities. Looking after the puppy—feeding him, bathing him, and even helping him poop—excited me as if I were a new mother again.

I estimated that he was one month old. In the beginning, he spent most of the day curled up and asleep. Now, he followed me everywhere. Every detail about the puppy strengthened my attachment to him. I couldn't imagine that our coming together had been an accident.

I named the puppy Yu, one of the fifty Japanese syllables. When I called him, however, his name sounded more like "Yū," so I found myself calling him the English word "you," which amused me. Soon, I realized that I had in myself a hidden hunger for company, which made me smile.

One morning when the rain had stopped, I took the puppy outside for the first time. I had never intended to keep him inside the house. Even then, I didn't want to put him on a leash, so with pieces of scrap lumber I blocked the gate that led to the street and let the puppy run free in the yard.

"Okay, go play!" I waved him away. He looked up at me with his head cocked a little to one side, then dashed into a thicket. He came back right away, whimpered at me, and then jumped back into the thicket. He looked different now, so unlike that pitiful, unsteady little creature that had tried to escape from me one rainy night.

Because the backyard was overgrown with vines and weeds, the puppy could hide completely in the foliage. I decided to clear out the brush and plant flowers. Madagascar periwinkle would be good, since its flowers bloom in all seasons. Red hibiscus for a hedge around my house…but suddenly the image of my grandparents' grave, surrounded by a hibiscus hedge, came to my mind; my heart stood still.

Red hibiscus had been like a blazing fire at the gravesite when my grandmother passed away. It was the same when I visited the family grave after my grandfather's funeral. Why had I unconsciously chosen hibiscus for my house? The puppy was running around the thicket, probably chasing after a bug or some other small creature. The grass seemed fresher and brighter because of the rain. Watching him playing in the leaves and in the bushes, where his whole body was hidden, I suddenly felt anxious: Does he remember the night that I stole him from his mother? My anxiety about the puppy merged all at once with the memory of my own child. Does he remember me, his real mother? It was unendurable to think about.

My anxiety intensified. I thought when I couldn't see the puppy that he had vanished and would not come back. Impulsively, I blurted out, "Yū!" The puppy bounced out of the thicket and dropped something from his mouth onto the concrete step. It was a big, bluish-black earthworm, wriggling, twisting its half-transparent body from side to side, while the puppy sniffed at it, wanting to play.

"You naughty boy, leave it alone." I tapped his head, and he began playfully pulling at my socks and biting my hand lightly while I tried to push him aside.

"We need to get you a dog house, don't we?" He whimpered fawningly, as though he understood what I had said.

Thinking about a doghouse reminded me of the message to call me back that I had left at Inoha's office. I was confident he would help me make a kennel if I asked.

So far, however, there had been no call from Inoha, which annoyed me slightly. It had been four days since I had phoned his office. Did the office girl I spoke to forget to pass along my message to him? Though I had met him only recently, I felt it was all right to ask him to hang around, as he was about ten years younger than me. Usually I was the one who called if I wanted him to go out drinking. Was I vain enough to think his shyness around me, an older woman, was a sign of affection?

"Ha-hah," I laughed aloud bitterly.

The earthworm, once half-transparent and dark purple, was now lifeless and stiff as a dry twig. I pinched its shriveled body and threw it into the grass. I stood up. The puppy playfully tried to nibble the hem of my slacks.

"I have Yu now. I am not lonely, am I?" I said. I picked him up and nestled him against my cheek. He licked my face in response. High above, the sky was clear. Even though it was winter, almost the middle of December, the day was full of sunlight. When I looked toward the graveyard, I could see the evergreen leaves sparkling. The red hibiscus dazzled me.

Inoha was not the only one who had not called. I hadn't received a single phone call from anybody—the phone had been silent since the workers installed it. After some hesitation, I tried calling him again, conscious that I was beginning to depend on him. The same voice answered and said the same thing: he was away. I felt stung for a moment, but then reminded myself that our relationship was not so intimate he would pretend to be out just to avoid speaking to me. I asked her again to tell him to call me back.

Late that afternoon, I made up my mind to go out by myself. I had been putting off lots of little errands. As soon as I started the car, the puppy tried to jump from the passenger seat into my lap. "Oh well, are you a little scared?" I said and let him stay in my lap as I drove, one arm around him to keep him calm.

The bright colors of the sunset were about to fade. We drove along the gently sloping road, with thick brush on each side. It struck me how much the town had changed over time. Before long I reached a new shopping mall that was already decorated with advertising banners and festival lanterns, announcing a year-end sale and preparing for Christmas and the New Year. Even the puppy jumped up to look out the car window at the colorful decorations.

I stopped first at a pet shop that I had called in advance. I carried the puppy inside with me to buy dog food and a collar. Then I headed to a supermarket, where I discovered that pets were not allowed inside. I had no other choice but to leave the puppy in the car. When I got out and closed the door, he stretched up on his back legs and pressed his nose to the half-opened window, following me with his eyes. It was hard to tear myself away from him; his yelping almost made me go back to the car several times, but I had to get the shopping done today. Anyway, it would take only a few minutes. I forced myself to turn away from the puppy's imploring eyes and went into the store while he yelped behind me.

I shopped hurriedly, all the time thinking I could hear the puppy calling me. When I got back to the car, I was surprised that his face was no longer at the window, nor could I hear him barking. Oh, what a good boy, so well behaved, I thought. But when I opened the door, the puppy was not there. I checked under the seats, called his name, and asked passersby if they had seen a puppy. I gestured, trying to describe him. No matter how hard I searched up and down the rows of cars, I couldn't find him.

I had left the window half open to be sure he had enough air, but it would have been impossible for the small puppy to climb out of the window on its own. Just at that moment, I noticed a boy, probably a student at the junior high school, mounting his bicycle on the footpath near the store entrance. He was watching me. His behavior was odd, and he was silhouetted by the pale fluorescent light of the store sign.

"You stole him!" I said aloud. The boy said nothing, but his gaze became even more intent. When his large eyes met mine, he compressed his lips firmly to one side, which made him look angry. I was struck by the thought that I had seen that expression somewhere before.

It all happened in an instant. The next moment, the boy pumped the pedals of his bike and rode off at a furious pace. His actions and demeanor stung me, as though somebody close to me had brushed my hand away.

I went back to my car. *Shouldn't I stay here?* After all, this was the spot where the puppy disappeared. But what would be the point if he had been taken away? I had to start searching—but in what direction? I got in the car and pulled out of the lot, confused and uncertain. I figured I would start by searching the narrow alleys nearby.

The alleys were laid out in a grid and most of them were one-way. They held no clues that would lead me to the puppy, and I could only expect to find him if I heard him yelping. I first thought that if I called him he might hear me and bark. On second thought, I wasn't sure if I dared to call out in this quiet residential area. I drove slowly, listening closely at each house. They all looked alike. They were well lit, and I could hear people's voices over the loud sounds of their television sets. I felt miserable.

Inside one particular house, I glimpsed what appeared to be a happy family. A grandfather laughed and talked loudly. A grandmother was grumbling about something and paced around a room. A stern, crabby father sat beside a mother who looked reserved. Two little girls were romping around their parents like puppies. It was a classic domestic scene, like the pictures of typical happy families we had drawn when we were children.

A car behind me, probably in a hurry, flashed its lights and honked its horn. I quickly turned down the next alley.

My search for the puppy was in vain. He could have been anywhere by now, perhaps far away from here. There was nothing more I could do. Accelerating, I pulled onto a broad street.

Presently the rows of well-lit houses ended, and I found myself driving through a dark patch of woods. The shadows of the trees hung over the road. In order to see through the darkness, I had to brighten the car's headlights. Eventually, the road became a downhill slope. In front of my windshield the blackness gave me the sensation that I was driving into a gaping hole. I stepped lightly on the brake.

I could see my house up ahead, and that from this direction the silhouette of the power station's chimney in the distance looked as if it were part of my house, creating the illusion that the structure was a crematorium in a nightmare. The numerous tombs that surrounded the house rose up in the darkness like boulders on the bottom of an ink-black sea.

After a restless night, I set off the following morning to look for the puppy again. I felt driven to continue searching. After returning to the supermarket where I had been the evening before, I again tried to extend the range of my search. The children had all gone off to schools and day nurseries, so the houses in the alleys were completely quiet. The only sound was the groan of my car's engine.

An old woman, whose silver hair was bobbed in the fashion of a little girl's, was sweeping fallen leaves. When she noticed me, she stopped sweeping and waited till my car passed by. Because I was driving at a snail's pace, peering here and there, she looked at me suspiciously.

I decided to park along the main road and search the side streets on foot. It had been warm the past few days, and the sun was strong enough to make me perspire.

Here and there I heard a puppy's yelping. Once it was a noisy Spitz, and on other occasions it was a dog family or someone else's puppy on a chain.

By then, I had wandered far to the east of the supermarket. Listening only for my puppy's yelp, I walked along a gravel road, one of the few unpaved parts of the area, as if the contractor had simply stopped work at that point. Once in a while, huge dogs howled at me from the inside of gates as I passed. Some threw themselves against their restraints to get at me. I was being barked at by dogs while trying to rescue my dog. I felt slightly amused by the irony of it.

The puppy might never come back, I thought. Then I imagined what it would be like when I found him. But what if somebody had deliberately taken him to keep him as a pet? Worse still, what if my puppy had already become more attached to the thief than to me? Since the puppy wasn't wearing a collar, there was nothing to prove that he belonged to me. Even if I detailed what I knew about the puppy—like how the fur on his face fell out and grew back—it would be of no use as proof. As for the ownership of the puppy, I wasn't sure if I could confidently demand that he should be given back to me. I had misgivings about my competence to own a pet, since I am neither consistent nor responsible. I was responsible for nothing and no one—a person separated from her home and family.

Just then I stopped dead in my tracks. Before me was a house with a faded, red-tiled roof, surrounded by garcinia trees and a stone wall. The house was familiar to me. While the surrounding houses had been rebuilt and modernized into concrete structures, that old house had nothing going for it except its size. Somehow, however, it had the character of its owners.

Small, dark-purple flowers were blooming so vigorously that they almost covered the entrance gate. When I had passed through that gate for the first time it had been to exchange conventional wedding gifts. Meeting my ex-husband's parents had weighed heavily upon my mind that day because, until then, I had never even seen them, even though their son and I had been living together before marriage. Moreover, I was six months pregnant.

"A son first. Give birth to a baby boy," his parents said almost in unison, conveniently forgetting that they had been opposed to our marriage. It was the same thing that my mother had been told again and again. When I was a child, those phrases sounded like a magic spell hissed over my mother, like the whispering of the Devil. It must have scared my mother when she was young, and on the day I met my husband's parents it made me, another expectant mother, equally apprehensive.

Standing now in front of the house where I had once had so many ties, I was hopelessly bewildered and didn't know in which direction to turn. I expected someone to appear from inside at any moment. I had heard that my ex-husband had married again, and that he had a child by his second wife. In a flurry, I quickly retraced my steps.

Just moments before, the winter sunshine had cheered me; now it had the opposite effect. I felt utterly rejected by my past, and with a guilty conscience, I started walking faster.

After passing through a couple of alleys, I arrived at the road where I had parked my car. The face of the boy I had seen yesterday near the supermarket suddenly popped into my mind.

The encounter with him had been like a gust of wind that carried both a great nostalgia and an indescribable uneasiness. I felt impelled to see him again, just to make sure. A junior high school was in the upper part of the town, so instead of getting into my car, I walked past it toward the school. I was not sure what I wanted to confirm by seeing the boy, nor whether I would be sure of what I saw.

Near the school, I came across a bunch of boys in school uniforms. Stepping aside, I waited for the boys to pass. As they walked by, one boy's eyes looked daggers at me. With his visor pushed high on his forehead, his fair-skinned face was exposed to the harsh sunlight. Those large, penetrating eyes and his firm-set lips, drawn to one side, were undoubtedly those of the boy I had seen last night. I sensed that he had something to tell me. I strained my eyes, hoping to ascertain what it could be, but he abruptly averted his eyes as he passed.

That was my boy, I thought. I had thought so since seeing him yesterday. The last time I had seen my child was when he was only eighteen months old, so I couldn't know what his grown face looked like. But I felt certain about this boy. Not because he reminded me of his father or resembled how he looked as a baby. It was neither more nor less than intuition, something from the depths of my mind. The boy's meaningful expression was imprinted somewhere deep, far back in my memory. At the same time, it was very unlikely that a small infant would be able to remember his mother's face from so long ago. The more I thought about him, the more disturbed and agitated I became.

I woke up in the middle of the night to the sound of a telephone ringing. It had been part of my dream but continued ringing, neither real nor unreal for a time.

I wasn't expecting any calls. In fact, I had already given up the idea of receiving a call from Inoha. But since, there had been not even a single call from anybody, I had begun to think something was wrong with my phone.

A conversation I had had recently with a staff person from the publishing house crossed my mind. "Where have you been? We were trying to reach you all this time," he had said when he caught sight of me. He raised his voice, probably because he was accustomed to speaking above the din of printing machinery, I thought, and now even when the machines were turned off he was unable to speak in a normal tone of voice. "I phoned you again and again till I got weary of it."

His heated tone was clearly meant as an excuse for giving to someone else the freelance job he'd promised to me. "I called you many times! Your number is xxxx, isn't it? I called the right number, didn't I?" he kept saying.

But I had never heard my phone ring, even once. How come? Propping myself up, I tried to figure it out. Since I could make out-going calls with no problem, I figured my phone had been installed properly. It had gone from being strange to being creepy. I remembered the worker's statement that he had once before come to my house to install a phone. And then he and the other worker had talked about the man missing at sea, and the fact that the man had not been found yet. To make it easier to take care of the puppy, I had begun a while ago to sleep in the tatami room on the first floor. In this dark room, the passage of time now seemed to stop. Holding my breath, I became acutely aware that I was desperately waiting for something.

The sound of dogs fighting and puppies yelping came from a graveyard across the street. It made me think of scenes in my family's house in bygone days. A fragile family, broken up so easily. The image of my father's face came to me—a man I didn't want to call my father. But what about myself? Was I so different from him, abandoning one's own child for an undeniably selfish reason? The barks of the dogs became louder and more furious, as though they were responding to my tumultuous emotions.

The boy's eyes, glaring at me, were like the stagnant, cold air in the room. My gut feeling was that he must be my son, Ikuji, and that feeling had not diminished.

In the morning, I called the telephone company and explained the situation.

The person in charge kept me waiting quite a while. Finally he came back on the line. "Your number is dead," he said, as if it were nothing. He explained that "dead number" is slang for a disconnected number. "But I'll double-check it," he said, sounding optimistic. "In any case," he continued, "you should change your number."

By the time I hung up, I was not totally satisfied with his explanation. I looked at my gray telephone in silence. Of course, somebody made a simple blunder, but I couldn't help thinking there was something else going on. A kind of...something invisible...had mysteriously affected my telephone.

That gray lump of plastic with a dial and a receiver had changed into something ominous and uncanny. Just as I was thinking this, I sensed that someone was in the tatami room. Through the ground glass of the window I saw a human figure outside the house. I couldn't tell if it was an adult or a child by its size. The figure slowly moved around the house, to the floor-length window facing south. For a while, the figure was out of sight, then it reappeared outside the same window on the east side, and moved to the south again. *What is that person doing, walking around my house?* Hearing in my mind the ominous metaphor in the phrase, "your number is dead," I was assailed by a dark premonition: something was going to happen. With bated breath, I strained my eyes at the outline of the figure moving from window to window. It disappeared again and in an instant there was a knock at the back door. *Someone is contacting me directly, instead of ringing my disconnected telephone. Who can that be, calling on me at this hour of the morning?* I struggled to my feet to answer the door.

"Who is it, please?" I asked, trembling, afraid to open the door.

"Excuse me for interrupting you, but could you please open the door?" The low voice was of a women speaking in fluent Okinawan, and using the most polite form of address.

Opening the door, I saw she was thin, small, and old. Lit from behind, her face was in shadow. From her deep-set eye sockets, the part of her face in darkest shadow, I saw the glint of her quick assessment of me.

Grandma! The word almost jumped out of my mouth.

"This house has been unoccupied for a long time. Are you living here now?"

"Yes, I've just moved in. What do you want with me?" I was aware that I had spoken harshly to her, probably because I was still upset by seeing a mysterious figure prowling around my house.

"Excuse me, I am a woman who buys empty bottles. I came here to ask you if you have some." She must have sensed the reproach in my tone, so she spoke more diffidently, switching to Japanese. Probably it was not her usual way of speaking, as her words came across as somewhat awkward.

Feeling sorry for her, I put on a show of trying to search the house for an empty bottle, even though I knew I had none. After all, I had only just moved in. When I was about to explain this to her and ask her to leave, she lowered herself onto the step inside of the door, removed the scarf from her head, and began to speak about the former occupant of my house.

"The person who used to live here took out a lot of bottles," she said.

Her curly gray hair quivered. Because she sat with her back to the sun, her face was in shadows; still, I saw that deep wrinkles were engraved in her heavily tanned face. Her surprisingly full cheeks were bright. "All his children had gone on a journey, so he was constantly alone. He was strong and healthy and looked much younger than his real age. He drank a lot, and he would put large, empty bottles outside for me, right over there." Leaning to the side, the old woman motioned toward a spot next to the house. She seemed to cherish the memory of him, as if he had been one of her relatives.

I had no idea who the owner of the house was, let alone that an old man had lived in it alone. All my lease contracts had been made through a real estate agent. Considering that it was a two-story house, the rent was extremely low, so I had agreed to take it without a moment's hesitation. The realtor asked me a dozen times whether I was serious, each time looking straight into my eyes as if to question my sincerity. It was not until I signed the contract that he revealed that the property was originally for sale, but that he couldn't find a buyer—probably because the house was run down and near a graveyard. The rental agency had taken a lot of trouble to renovate the place, he added—including removing a Buddhist altar to make the interior larger. The rent was deposited in a specified bank account.

"Did he pass away?" I asked the old woman. She slowly shook her head. "He moved into an old people's home. Sadly, he pleads to come home— *let me go, I wanna go home*—people say he still phones home at least once a day."

"You mean he calls here?"

"Yes, he lost his mind and couldn't grasp the fact that the house was now empty."

Her tone was sympathetic. Then she closed her eyes for a moment, as if she were praying.

I could see in my mind the image of an old man, devotedly dialing the number to his old house every day. I felt the strange irony in the fact that the phone in this house never rang, no matter how many times someone tried to call. It was weird. The thought gave me gooseflesh, made me involuntarily fold my arms across my chest in terror.

"It is quite natural for a person to hope to die in his own bed," the old woman said, as though she was consoling herself. While speaking about someone else, she was actually pondering her own end, I realized, which no doubt was not far away. After a while, probably remembering her job of bottle collecting, the old woman stood up sluggishly.

Before leaving, she said that she would give me five yen per large bottle, and that she'd leave money on the window frame if I put bottles outside while I was away. She bowed deeply to me, and then left.

I could see her beyond the concrete wall pulling her handcart, slowly struggling up a gentle slope. *Is there a place for her to rest beyond that slope?*

I simply couldn't regard that old man, who was so eager to come home, as someone who had nothing to do with me. I felt sad and lonely. My mind was in confusion at the way everything had been muddled up. Maybe I just wanted to cry—like a child deserted by her father, like a mother deprived of her child…

Later that afternoon, I drove around as usual to search for the puppy. I longed to hold it in my arms again. I had no idea how or where to look for him. Without meaning to, I found myself driving by the junior high school. Once I realized where I was, I felt it was where I had intended to go from the outset. I wanted to see that boy. When I admitted to myself how I was feeling, other emotions that I had suppressed until now rose up in me like a tsunami. I parked the car near enough to the junior high school to have a full view of its gate, but far enough away so that he wouldn't notice me watching. I waited for the boy to come out.

Eventually, merry bunches of pupils in uniforms emerged from the school, one after another. But I couldn't see him among them. There is another junior high school in the town, but I was absolutely sure that this was the one he attended. I waited and waited. Still he never appeared.

I had no alternative but to leave, so I drove around to the other side of the school and onto the main street. A hearse crossed the intersection in front of me, and immediately I imagined it was part of a funeral procession for the man missing at sea, and that his boat was hidden somewhere among the line of mourners.

"The boat was found!" someone called out. I opened the door of my house and went out. Cars were lined up on both sides of the street. Obviously the cars were connected to the fresh grave and the four funeral flags that had been set up at each corner of the graveyard. Around the gravesite were bunches of imitation flowers. The long, white funeral flags hung slack, making it difficult to read what was written on them. I was reminded of the day I had finally managed to visit my grandfather's grave, after I had missed his funeral. The hibiscus flowers around the grave were blooming in all their glory, and seemed somehow excessive for such a sorrowful occasion.

Although there was no one nearby, as far as I could see, I heard a number of people saying, "He's home." That was what the telephone worker had said: "He might have gone back." Somehow, I felt a kind of relief, as if my doubts and anxieties had been lifted from my shoulders. I thought I was alone, but all at once I caught a glimpse of two girls near the thicket of hibiscus. Holding hands, they were staring fixedly at the man's grave. *Are they his daughters?* In those two girls I saw my sister and me as little children, waiting patiently for our always-absent father. Just then, I sensed that I was being watched. I turned around. There stood the boy, with the puppy in his arms.

Just as I thought—it was you—you stole my puppy! I almost said it, but checked myself before the words came out of my mouth. I felt daunted by something about him, something like an inflexible, obstinate will. Even the puppy in his arms seemed to embody the boy's will. He stood still in dead silence and stared at me, but his eyes said everything.

I woke up with a choking, claustrophobic sensation. *Was that a dream or was it real?* The blazing red of the hibiscus flowers, too magnificent and vital for a grave, was vivid in my memory. Is their scarlet color, like blood, symbolic of the life force of the deceased? Our houses, our lives, will eventually decay, but this vivid red will last forever.

Dogs barked somewhere around the graveyard. It must be her—the puppy's mother. Will her voice penetrate the darkness, cross over the cliff, and finally reach a distant place where her puppy is waiting?

Translation by Nagadō Madoka and Frank Stewart

Higa Yasuo: Maternal Deities

Inviting and Greeting the Gods (Kami-nkē)
Miyako Island, Nishibe, Yūkui
1995

Okinawan Shaman Songs

The following are two kinds of traditional songs sung by female shamans in Okinawa. The first is *fusa* (trance song), sung by sixteen shamans from four shaman lines on the southern Okinawan island of Myāku (Miyako). The song is part of the winter festival that commemorates the island's settlement by communicating—through the original "timeless time" that the song reconstructs—with the first great mothers who founded the settlement. In this *fusa*, which is part of a cycle of ceremonial songs, the shamans assert a woman's right to control the house she lives in (including its hearth, its songs, its stores, and its economic surplus) even if that right is not recognized by Japanese civil law. Although males pray at the borders of the sanctuary where the song is sung, they are not permitted to take part in the trance or singing. (Only recently has a version of the song been transcribed by male researchers.) The *fusa* is a difficult song whose subjects seem to be simultaneously singular and plural—though they are translated here as plural—and human and divine. It is said to have been passed down from the timeless time of the island's beginning, and the singers are believed not to be possessed by the gods but, rather, to be accompanied by them. Part of a dance, the song is sung by the shamans for themselves as well as for the great mothers. In the ceremony, the older shamans transfer their trance and song power to younger women, who are their nieces either by blood or by designation.

The second kind of song is *omoro* (shamanic "desire-song"). The ones translated here are from the *Omoro-sōshi* (Book of Desire-songs), an anthology of medieval Ryūkyūan shaman songs collected and transcribed by courtiers in 1531 and 1613. They are the oldest recorded Ryūkyūan songs and, though apparently edited by court officials, are regarded by most modern Okinawans as the classics of non-Japanese Ryūkyūan culture.

SONG OF THE MOTHERS: A VILLAGE TRANCE SONG

The gods peaceful
the householders gentle
descending from the original village

descending from divine Shiraji
the great gods want our song
they desire the god-shamans' trance song
pushing, pushing, coming down
descending to this earth
descending to Myāku Island
since they all have come down
since all the gods have gathered
Machimi of the true house
master of a hundred trance songs
thanks to the mother gods
thanks to the awesome gods
blessed by their permission
blessed by being filled
let us dance a hundred trance songs
let us dance to countless songs
let us dance a hundred dances
let us dance to countless songs
let us dance a hundred dances
let us dance countless dances
let us step to trance songs and then return
let us step to the dances and then return
we householders and mothers
we god-strong and mothers
because we are child gods
because we are born into a line of gods
thanks to the mother gods
thanks to the awesome gods
blessed by their permission
blessed by being filled
to the voices in our original mouths
to the voices of gods
let us sound our voices
may those around us speak their names
we householders and mothers
we god-hearted and mothers
are as in the sky
are as in the upper place
and having no fine child
and having no beautiful child
we have received Machimi of the true house
we have received our precious nieces
as children born
as children from inside us
receiving each from Mishima Shrine

receiving a hundred trance songs
receiving each from Shiraji Shrine
receiving countless songs
to Machimi of the true house
to our precious nieces
singing, passing to each
a hundred trance songs
telling, we are passing to each
countless songs
we householders and mothers
we god-minded and mothers
because we are born into a line of gods
thanks to the mother gods
thanks to the awesome gods
blessed by their permission
blessed by being filled
to the voice in our original mouths
to our true god's voice
we have been accompanied by gods
we have been together with gods
we have gained past power
we have spoken as the root stands

OMORO 729

A fine man, a stunning groom
a wonderful son-in-law
    Fafiya, O groom Fafiya
we really thought you were our son-in-law
we truly thought you were our son-in-law
we took you in, gave you treasures
we gave you our ancestral robes
you took the treasures and ran off
you took the robes and disappeared
poison grass of a son-in-law
floating weed of a son-in-law

Apparently respectable and common in early times, matrilocal residence
was a custom in which, due to the influence of maternal relatives, husbands
spent only their nights with their wives and children, returning during the
day to their mothers' homes. In this *omoro*, a mother and householder—
perhaps along with her sisters—is expressing her opinion of the young man
Fafiya, who went to live in his bride's house. Fafiya apparently absconded
with the valuable items he was given or entrusted with in the house, which
either belonged to his mother-in-law or were provided by his wife's family.
He may have been a slow or lazy worker and thus unpopular with his wife's

Higa Yasuo: Maternal Deities

Inviting and Greeting the Gods (Kami-nkē)
Miyako Island, Shimajiri, Jūrukunichi
1977

relatives, or he may have lacked the spiritual power to assist female shamans in trances, or he simply may have been unsatisfactory to his wife, the householder. The lines indented in this *omoro* and those that follow were probably refrains.

OMORO 987

Singer Yachikima of Onna
singer Yachikima of Afuso
    how painful to think of
the daughter of the head of Awa Village
the daughter of a father who worries for her
she's been in the hills for three months
she's been praying for power for three months
bitten by mosquitoes
bitten by horseflies

The spiritual leadership of women in village life probably accounts for the failure of the Buddhist equation of the male with the spiritual and the female with the physical to take hold in Ryūkyūan society. "Yachikima" is the name of a singer invoking a woman who, in preparation for an Awa Village festival, has been practicing austerities and training for trances with her fellow shamans for three months.

OMORO 1041

In the trance place of shining sun
the great shamans pray, rubbing their palms
    present tribute to Shō Shin,
    King helped by his mother
in the trance place of Sonto
the lordly shamans pray, rubbing their palms

In this *omoro*, the power of the Shō king to collect tribute is linked with the power he receives from female shamans. Indeed, the king's power had to be constantly renewed in court ceremonies: the female shamans would transmit their power to him by rubbing their palms in trance.

OMORO 40

Great woman sun god below sea's far edge
young shaman-god of the eastern sky
    show your bright power from the great depth
the king, who rules this island

the supreme male, who rules this land
has built a shrine above the cooking fire
tries to capture the sun in his castle hearth
he calls on the huge-hearted shaman-god Kikoe
she presses her hands together, concentrating
shining, in the southwest corner of the castle
incandescent inside the castle shrine
feeling true joy
taken by deep ecstasy
the red-mouthed fire god moves in response
the woman shaman of the hearth sways in reply
they carry the prayer to the sun god far below
they carry the longing to the sun god in the east
the ancient woman Amaniko hears the prayer
the old ancestress Kesaniko accepts the prayer
the sun god below the earth chooses a strong day
and comes toward the central fortress
comes toward the heart of Shuri Castle
toward the place of dance in the golden castle
toward the trance-ground in the towering castle
arriving on the beach at Ayako Harbor
arriving on the beach at Shitsuko Harbor
in the trance-hall the sun enters the shining shaman-god
in the hall through her eyes into those of the king
in his heart he feels the power
in his heart he is born once again
King, descended from King Eiso
King, descended from the sun
as long as the sun god rules below the earth
as long as the sun god rises in the east
your central fortress will prevail
Shuri Castle will remain on earth
the great sun shaman-god will protect it with night
the young sun shaman-god will watch it with daylight

Here, in the maternal Niruya Kanaya zone (the divine dimension), shamans rub their hands, concentrate, and communicate through the male fire god–shaman with the female sun god–shaman ruling beneath the earth. The sun god–shaman then visits Shuri Castle.

OMORO 514

Mount Sayafa, sacred peak
    eyo, e, pull, push
Mount Sokonya, sacred underground shrine

a god-horse in the three holy chambers
a god-horse in the three inner rooms
hooves the color of snow
hooves of pure white
tying on a golden saddle from Kyoto
tying on a silver saddle from Kyoto
attaching a glistening crupper
attaching a glistening breast harness
fastening a cinch of hemp thread
fastening a bridle born of clouds
the great shaman now mounting
the country's protector now riding
descending to Yonafa Harbor
descending to Baten Harbor
sailing out past bays
sailing out past capes
walk on toward the east
walk on toward the sun-birthing hole

This *omoro* may have been performed during the accession ceremony for a new supreme shaman in a cave shrine on Sayafa Hill, a distance from Shuri Castle. The song is a vision in trance time of the supreme shaman's actual journey toward the sun: with more than two hundred shaman attendants, she is to proceed down the mountain to the harbors, then to Kudaka Island in the east, where she will sail smoothly or, as the song says, "walk" on the ocean toward the "sun-birthing hole" on the eastern horizon. The sun is believed to be reborn every dawn in the womblike Niruya Kanaya zone below the horizon. There she will be reborn as the new supreme shaman.

OMORO 893

Eagle-fish of the east
    flying fish leaping eastward
    surely female god-shamans protecting us
    let us be at peace, protected
eagle fish of the sun-birthing hole

The sun-birthing hole often seems distinctly female. In this song, anxious sailors on the open sea are relieved to see fish leaping above the waves, a sign that the spirits of their shaman relatives have passed through the hole and been reborn in fish form to lead them to safety. The fish are referred to as *kami* (god-shamans). The song was probably sung on land by the shamans, who in singing it created a space and time in which their lovers and relatives far away at sea could find peace and safety.

Higa Yasuo: Maternal Deities

Inviting and Greeting the Gods (Kami-nkē)
Kudaka Island, Kabēru, Hītachi
1976

OMORO 1167

The superb people of Taira
    climbing up Akafanta Hill
    when they gaze out over Ofotabaru
    fields swelling with white rice
the renowned, outstanding people

Until the early twentieth century, the shamans of some rural areas would climb the highest local hills and stare down in *shimami* (viewing ceremonies intended to invest their villages with power and fertility). In this *omoro*, probably sung around the time of rice planting, the leading villagers—the shamans—climb the highest hill and in timeless time view the fields of newly planted rice. Their trance gaze seems to stroke the young rice like wind; present, future, and timeless time engage in a dialog, much as the shamans' eyes are engaged by the horizon and the fields.

OMORO 993

Beautiful-legged brother protected by the shaman-god
    beloved brother
graceful-legged brother protected by the shaman-god
when my brother travels to Shuri
when my brother goes up to the city of lords
I will fly ahead of his ship
I will be a bird and lead him

In this *omoro*, the sister singing about her love for her brother may be the shaman–god in the song or someone who is simply adding her protection to that of a powerful shaman. A mixture of shamanic and secular faith, the song stems from the belief that in relation to their brothers all sisters are *onarigami* (gods) and thus able to enwrap the men in a wide, invisible cloak of spiritual affection and protection.

OMORO 965

My sister, a shaman-god
    come to protect me
    ah, yes
my sister, become a shaman-god
turning into a beautiful butterfly
turning into a mysterious butterfly

The shaman in the *omoro* above sings about a brother on a ship that has lost its way or is struggling in high waves. The butterfly the man desires to be near is both an island and his sister.

OMORO 1000

The great shaman of Itokina
   giving her child straw sandals
   climbing the holy peak
   when she sees the god-ship
   she thinks so hard it hurts
   about her younger brother's safe voyage
fourth-month hail falling
   sleeves like fine dragonfly wings
   raising her face, wet
   when she sees the god-ship

Romantic love and spiritual communication sometimes mix in *omoro*. Following a village-viewing ceremony, a woman gazes out at a ship, which is simultaneously a god and a shaman like herself. Because it is a shaman-ship, it is a part of her spiritual body. On this ship is her lover, who, being male, is also her younger brother. With her spiritual gaze, she surrounds and protects the ship from harm.

Maternal Deities and the Ancestry of Humanity:
The Life and Photography of Higa Yasuo

The child of Okinawan parents who emigrated to the Philippines, Higa Yasuo was born on Mindanao Island in 1938. His father was drafted into the Japanese army and died during World War II. With his mother and two siblings, he remained in the Philippines until 1946, when the family returned to Okinawa.

Three years later, Higa's mother died. Raised by his grandmother in Koza City (now Okinawa City), he graduated from high school in 1958. But because his family was poor, he could not pursue his dream of going to college. Instead, he took a job with the police force and was posted at the Kadena Police Station, near the largest American military base in all of Asia. Assigned to the crime scene investigation unit—which mainly handled cases involving American servicemen—Higa learned to use a camera, and for the next ten years he worked as a forensic and documentary photographer.

In 1968, while on duty at the police station, he witnessed a fully loaded B-52 bomber crash shortly after take-off on a mission to Viet Nam. The experience was a turning point in Higa's life: he decided to leave the police force and become a professional photographer.

He moved to Tokyo and enrolled in the Tokyo School of Photography, graduating in 1971. That year, the first exhibition of his work was held. *Umarejima Okinawa* (Okinawa, Land of My Birth) was shown at the Ginza Nikon Salon in Tokyo, then travelled to Osaka, Naha, and Koza. Photographs from the exhibition were featured in the magazine *Kamera mainichi,* and the following year, in 1972, the Tokyo School of Photography published a collection of his work as a textbook. Through his photography, Higa was able to explore and rediscover his native island, Okinawa.

In 1973, he was commissioned by a magazine to photograph Miyako, an island about two hundred miles southwest of the island of Okinawa. While in Karimata Village on Miyako, Higa witnessed the Uyagan matsuri (Ritual of Ancestral Deities), an experience so intense that it launched him on a life-long exploration of the sacred ancient rituals of the Ryūkyūs.

Higa Yasuo: Maternal Deities

Worshipping the Gods (Kami-agami)
Miyako Island, Karimata, Uyān
1974

In 1975, Higa travelled to Kudaka Island, regarded since ancient times as sacred. There he met the *noro* (female shaman) Shizu Nishime. This meeting was another critical moment in his life. In the following months, Higa visited Kudaka Island over a hundred times, and through Shizu Nishime he was able to observe and photograph the ancient ritual known as Izaihō. In 1978, the ritual was discontinued: the shaman priestesses had dwindled in number, and there were not enough young women on the island to replace them. Before the demise of Izaihō, Higa carefully studied and recorded the rite. The collection of photographs he produced, *Onna, kami, matsuri* (Women, Deities, and Rites), won the thirteenth Taiyō Award. His efforts also resulted in such important works as *Kamigami no shima: Okinawa Kudakajima no matsuri* (The Island of Gods: Rituals of Kudaka Island, Okinawa) and *Ryūkyūko: onnatachi no matsuri* (The Ryūkyū Arc: Rituals of Women). In 1980, he won an *Okinawa Times* Encouragement Award for the exhibition *Kamigami no shima Kudaka* (The Island of Gods, Kudaka).*

Higa's documentation of shaman rituals in the Ryūkyūs was the beginning of a journey that took him from the spiritual roots of his homeland to the rituals and ceremonies of minority people elsewhere in Asia. By comparing female shamans of ethnic minorities worldwide—such as *noro* of Kudaka Island, *mudang* of Cheju Island, and *itako* and *gomiso* of Aomori Prefecture—Higa gained an international perspective and a profound understanding of the subject. By the 1980s, he was thus regarded as more than a fine photographer. As he fused photography with careful research in ethnography and anthropology, scholars in those fields began to acknowledge the great significance of his work.

In 1990, Higa was invited by Okinawa University to lecture in Naha and in Hirara, a city on Miyako. The following year, he gave a series of lectures at the Meiji Gakuin University in Tokyo, and the university made him an affiliate lecturer. By 1992, after his photographs were exhibited in a number of major cities, a collection of his early work was published. *Umarejima Okinawa: Amerika yū kara yamato yū* (My Native Island Okinawa: From American Rule to Japanese Rule) featured photographs taken from about 1968 to 1975.

After years of study, Higa produced a twelve-volume series: *Kamigami no kosō* (The Ancient Origins of the Gods). In 1987, he had presented the first part of the series, *Kamigami no kosō: Uyagan* (The Ancient Origins of the Gods: Uyagan), at exhibitions in Naha and Hirara. The entire twelve volumes of *Kamigami no kosō*, published in 1993 by Niraisha Publishing, received numerous awards: the twelfth Regional Culture and Landscape Research Award from the Japan Place Name Research Institute; the Photo-

---

* Kudaka Island is the setting of *Umi no Tenzakai* (Gods beyond the Sea), a modern *kumi odori* by Ōshiro Tatsuhiro in this volume.

graphic Society of Japan Award; the Koizumi Yagumo (Lafcadio Hearn) Award; and the fourteenth *Okinawa Times* Publication Culture Award.

Also in 1993, a two-volume set from the larger series was published in Tokyo by Daiichi Shobō: *Kamigami no genkyō: Kudakajima* (Kudaka Island: The Ancient Home of Gods). These volumes continue to be the seminal resource for research on Kudaka Island.

As if declaring that his work on Kudaka and ancient rituals was complete, in December 1993 Higa held a new exhibition in Naha and Nago entitled *Jōmin* (People of Compassion), comprising portraits of Okinawans from throughout the islands. A year later he moved to Miyako Island. He lived there by himself, once again photographing and studying intensively the ancient rituals. No doubt he intended to publish a book on the Miyako island group.

Higa's last exhibition, *Hahatachi no kami: Ryūkyūko no saishi sekai 95 Miyakojima* (Maternal Deities: The World of Rituals in the Ryūkyū Arc, 1995, Miyako Island), was held in Naha in March 1998. A dozen years later, the exhibition entitled *Higa Yasuo: Hahatachi no kami* (Yasuo Higa: Maternal Deities) was displayed at the Okinawan Prefectural Museum & Art Museum, in Naha, from November 2010 to January 2011, and at the Izu Photo Museum, in Shizuoka Prefecture, from January to May 2011.

Higa Yasuo passed away in May 2000. He was sixty-one years old. I wish he had lived longer. A great photographer, ethnologist, and anthropologist, he has left a huge legacy and makes us aware that there is still much work for us to do and many responsibilities to shoulder on his behalf.

Translation by Katsunori Yamazato and Frank Stewart

Higa Yasuo: Maternal Deities

Worshipping the Gods (Kami-agami)
Miyako Island, Karimata, Uyān
1989

WESLEY IWAO UEUNTEN

Nothing Can Compare:
A Selection of Okinawan Folk Songs

The traditional music of the Ryūkyūs—both classical (for the court) and folk—can be traced back to ancient times, possibly to ritual chants *(omoro)*. The chants were passed down orally, and though much must have been lost over time, 1,248 *omoro* were collected in the twenty-two–volume *Omoro-sōshi*, printed in three parts—in 1531, 1613, and 1623. Volume eight seems to establish the link between *omoro* and traditional court music and folk songs. Both *omoro* and classical music were composed with verses primarily in the *ryūka* form (three phrases of eight syllables followed by one of six syllables).

From at least the early fifteenth century, Okinawan music was strongly influenced by the kingdom's contact with China. Beginning about 1404, Chinese investite envoys to Okinawa were entertained with annual arts festivals *(ukansen-odori)* that included folk music (refined when performed at court) and dancing from all the provinces. Thus, royal court entertainment and folk music evolved together.

After the Satsuma invasion in 1609, classical and folk traditions and instrumentation were influenced by the Japanese. However, it was in the interest of the Satsuma clan that the Ryūkyūan kingdom maintained the appearance of independence, and thus indigenous music continued to be sung and composed. Following the Meiji annexation of Okinawa in 1879, the Japanese embarked on a campaign to create a uniform and united nation. With the strict imposition of mainland Japan's culture and language in Okinawa, indigenous music and dance suffered a period of decline: performers were no longer employed at court, and young people were encouraged to regard Japanese cultural practices as superior to their own. Today, the resurgence of Okinawa's distinct cultural identity is being reinforced through music, from traditional *ryūka* lyrics to pop and hip hop.

The following songs reflect changes in the social and political situations in Okinawa over several hundred years. Some were traditionally sung as part of *kumi odori*—court dance-and-music entertainments—at community festivals. I have also included a lullaby and work songs. The selection concludes with a song about twentieth-century Okinawan immigration to North America. Each song is followed by a brief explanation.

KAJADEFŪ BUSHI

> To what can I compare
> The happiness I feel today
> It is like a budding flower
> Bejeweled by morning dew

"Kajadefū (Kageyadefū) Bushi" is said to have been composed by an official in the Ryūkyūan court: during a dispute over the succession to the throne, the official advocated for the mute royal son, who suddenly was able to speak. The song continues to be sung by Okinawans throughout the world at the beginning of celebrations and auspicious events.

UNNA BUSHI

> A sign posted on the Unna pine
> Says, "Rendezvous are forbidden!"
> Do they think a sign
> Could prevent us from loving?

Along with "Kajadefū Bushi," "Unna (Onna) Bushi" is one of the five important court songs sung before the Ryūkyūan king. It is now part of the repertoire of classical Ryūkyūan songs performed and preserved throughout the diaspora. Nabī, a woman of the commoner class in Unna, is said to have composed the words to this song, which expresses defiance of the vertically structured patriarchal government that developed across Okinawa during Satsuma rule.

NAKAFŪ BUSHI

> Is this not a floating world
> with only one true meaning?
> Why is it then
> That our words do not meet?

The lyrics for this version of "Nakafū Bushi" were said to have been written by court musicians for the last Ryūkyūan king, Shō Tai. It was a period of much strife. Factions differed over what the kingdom should do in response to events such as the Opium Wars and the arrival of Commodore Matthew C. Perry to the Ryūkyūs and Japan. King Shō Tai was deposed by the Meiji government in Tokyo in 1879.

CHIJŪYĀ BUSHI

[verse 3]
We are separated by a vast ocean
But the same moon shines upon us
Are you gazing
At the same sky tonight?

[chorus]
On the beach, the plover sings,
   "Chui chui"

"Chijūyā Bushi" (also known as "Hamachidori Bushi") was composed after the nineteenth-century annexation by Japan propelled Okinawans into the modern economic system. Unable to pay family debts, many Okinawans were forced to leave home to work: sons were sold to fishermen as indentured servants, and daughters were sold into prostitution. "Chijūyā Bushi" is said to reflect the feelings of a son sold to fishermen.

KIJOKA LULLABY

Count one, then two
Three and four are next
Then come five, six, and seven
Eight, nine, and ten

[chorus]
Hoi, hoi, hoi
Stop your crying
Hoi, hoi, hoi

This good rice is for
Number one son
Sweet potatoes are good enough
For numbers two and three

[repeat chorus]

Send a child of thirteen
To faraway Japan
Build a bridge of gold
For them to cross

[repeat chorus]

This is part of "Kijoka Lullaby." Kijoka is in the northern part of Okinawa and is well known for the weaving of *bashō-fu*, or banana-fiber cloth. As Okinawa became integrated into Japan's economic structure, young women who once did the tedious weaving of *bashō-fu* began migrating to mainland Japan for better-paying work. They tried to save part of their wages and send money home, hoping to build a "bridge of gold." Ironically, most of these young women, who would traditionally have been learning to weave by hand, ended up working in textile mills in Japan.

ASHIMIJI BUSHI

Nothing can compare
To the sincere joy
That the working person
Feels when he sweats hard

[chorus]
Surayō, sura
to work we go!

Fifty *jū* per day
Five *kwan* in fifty days
Can one lose by saving?
So says the old adage

Working morning and night
The money that I save
Like a young pine tree
Will grow with the years

For the sake of everyone
For your own sake as well
With high spirits
Render good service

"Ashimiji Bushi" was written for a 1929 "Thrift and Savings Campaign" that was conducted in Okinawa on the occasion of the Shōwa emperor's accession. While ostensibly written for the emperor, the song does not encourage service to him, but to one's community and oneself. The emphasis on one's labor being one's own property is perhaps a manifestation of the song having been written during the era of union activities in Okinawa. "Ashimiji Bushi" became popular among Okinawan immigrants in Hawai'i, who struggled for labor unions on the plantations, and is still sung at *bon* dances in the state.

Higa Yasuo: Maternal Deities

Worshipping the Gods (Kami-agami)
Ikema Island, Yūkui
1974

HIYAMIKACHI BUSHI

[verse 1]

Uchinā is an island of great treasures
Making a name for itself
Come together in one spirit and rise up

[chorus]

Hey, hey, hey hey hey
Rise up, come on, rise up!

[verse 2]

A bountiful harvest
Is a sign that good times have come
Keep your spirits up! You can do it!

[verse 3]

Music blooms beautifully like a flower
Let the world know
About our Uchinā

[verse 5]

I'm a fierce tiger
And if you give me wings
I will cross the great Pacific

[verse 6]

Fall seven times and jump up eight
Let the world know
About our Uchinā

Shinsuke Taira was an Okinawan immigrant to Los Angeles. In 1953, he returned to Okinawa and wrote the lyrics to "Hiyamikachi Bushi" with the aim of giving hope and encouragement to the people enduring the hellish aftermath of the Battle of Okinawa. At the 2010 National High School Baseball Championship, this song was played when Okinawa's Kōnan High School defeated all its mainland Japanese opponents to win the tournament. In that context, the song affirmed Okinawa's dignity within Japanese society.

Ryūka: Okinawan Lyric Poetry

Ryūka is a form of Okinawan lyric poetry sung to the accompaniment of the sanshin. When written, ryūka have thirty syllables, arranged as three phrases of eight syllables followed by one of six. The form and rhythm of ryūka are deeply embedded in Okinawan culture. For many of the following poems, the authors are unknown; some poems are attributed to certain authors based on a lyric's style and sentiment.

No sign of you yet.
Are you late or not coming?
Still I wait throughout the night.
Even the moon's sad face abandons me.
(YUSHIYA CHIRŪ)

We lay together so sweetly.
Your face shining and lovely.
Near midnight I woke to see the moon
Slipping away over the hill.

In the long days we work
In separated garden plots.
Meet me at night, please,
No matter how briefly!

Hey, butterfly, heading east.
Hold up a moment. On your
Winding errands take this message
From me to my beloved.

The newly formed buds of grain
Are as plump as girls of twenty.
So fresh and golden. I give to you
The pick of spring's first harvest.

I've crossed off the days
Until your return.
x after x makes me tremble,
Dreaming of your arms around me.

I count the pebbles on the beach.
Each is a day since you've been gone
Counting and waiting.
Counting and waiting for your return.

Mount Unna blocks the way
Between your village and mine.
If I could only sweep it aside to make
The distance to your village closer!
(UNNA NABĪ)

The bridge of Hija hurts me.
Someone heartless built it.
And I must cross over and leave home
to work in that shameful district.
(YUSHIYA CHIRŪ)

I am neither the newly ripened millet
Nor the freshly plump rice grains
Yet the greedy sparrows circle me
And tear at my tender places.

Others must have their reasons
But I am ashamed to cling
Like a coward to my wretched
Interminable life.
(YUSHIYA CHIRŪ)

If you love me, dear one,
Come quickly to the flowering village,
Ishado, in Nakagushiku,
To ask for my hand.

Translation by Taira Buntarō, Frank Stewart, and
Katsunori Yamazato

Higa Yasuo: Maternal Deities

Worshipping the Gods (Kami-agami)
Iriomote Island, Sonai, Shitsu
1974

Gods Beyond the Sea

"The sacred sites of Kudaka Island are bare, unadorned, yet eternally filled with *something*," the renowned contemporary Japanese painter Okamoto Tarō once remarked. I imagine this invisible *something* to be love. When the real fifteenth-century King Shō Toku was driven from the throne of the Ryūkyū Kingdom, I think it was not because he wasn't a strong king, but because the gods conspired to let him meet his true love on Kudaka Island. I believe this is the reason the love story between Shō Toku and Kunikasa is still told centuries later.

In *Gods Beyond the Sea* I wanted to depict how the history of Okinawa reflects the gradual dismantling of cultural practices in which the female element is held to be supreme, embodying the virtues of intuitive, selfless love. These cultural values are defeated by male cultural practices, in which logical thinking is the ultimate virtue.

I witnessed the Izaihō ritual of Kudaka Island many years ago. Soon after, the ritual was discontinued, but I believe the people's religious spirit has not died. The chant, *Ēfai, Ēfai*, still lives in my ears, and as long as I keep hearing those voices, the praying heart of Kudaka will not die away. Those voices encouraged me to write this play.

Cast of Characters

KUNIKASA, head priestess of Kudaka Island

SHŌ TOKU, king of the central government in Shuri

ASATO, priest and advisor to Shō Toku's rival, Kanamaru

FIRST MAN

SECOND MAN

THIRD MAN

FIRST SHAMAN

SECOND SHAMAN

THIRD SHAMAN

The stage is dark. The song gets louder as a moving image of a white horse appears on a screen behind the actors. The horse is galloping toward the audience from the horizon.

SONG (CHIN BUSHI)

A white horse emerged from the horizon
And it entered the island and myself.

As the stage lights come up, we see Kunikasa and King Shō Toku holding hands.

KUNIKASA   I am Kunikasa, a shaman of Kudaka Island.
              Last night I dreamed of the horizon:
              Beyond the deep blue water, beyond the infinite space
              From the far-off world of uneasiness,
              A white horse came galloping toward us,
              Its mane bristling,
              Toward this island, toward myself, as if attacking…

SHŌ TOKU   I am none other than King Shō Toku.
              The gods at Chūzan, Shuri Castle,
              Instructed me to seek the gods of *Nirai Kanai*—
              Following a white bird.
              Who knew we would be shipwrecked by a typhoon?
              My life was saved on Kudaka Island,
              Saved by the father and brother of Kunikasa
              And Kunikasa tenderly cared for me.

KUNIKASA   Although you are a king
              Your life was saved on Kudaka Island.
              The depth of care only I know.
              Our meeting was planned by the gods themselves.
              I will protect you throughout your lifetime.

              SONG (AGISHICHISHAKU BUSHI)

              Fragrant is the wind of Kudaka,
              Beautiful are the tender feelings between them.

Kunikasa and Shō Toku dance happily together. Exit Shō Toku. Enter Asato.

ASATO   I am Asato,
              Residing in Asato Village.
              I am a shaman and diviner.
              Fortune brought me to the side of Lord Kanamaru
              And I divined the future of the kingdom.
              I've come here because I saw the spirit
              Of the King falling onto this island
              And saw it trapped in lust, chasing after women.

KUNIKASA	An unexpected visitor Bringing to this island political turmoil from Shuri Castle, A hateful man upsetting our King's peace. On Kudaka, women are endowed with great spiritual power. I will take care of the King and I ask that you Return to Shuri immediately.
ASATO	The spiritual power of this island is known throughout the kingdom, But for the future safety and prosperity of the kingdom I will not trust women's spiritual power.
KUNIKASA / ASATO	Because we do not trust one another A test of our spiritual powers is unavoidable— On a different day, in a different place. SONG (YUNABARU BUSHI) Gods of the Horizon, give us life. Two shamans—a woman and a man— will engage in spiritual competition.

Kunikasa and Asato express their antagonism in dance and then exit. A drum beats, heralding a battle. Dancers in black enter and fight one another, then exit. King Shō Toku, Asato, and Kunikasa enter.

SHŌ TOKU	I am Shō Toku, King of Shuri. We have now arrived on Kikai Island At the northern boundary of the kingdom. Because the islanders have evaded paying taxes, Using bad weather as an excuse, I have decided to wage war on this island. Tell us, my counselors, How we should attack the island.
ASATO	My Lord, Assault the island With fiery arrows From our warships. Make the islanders suffer our maritime power, Then we will attack by land.
KUNIKASA	My Lord, How brutal and destructive. It is easy enough to burn up the whole island, But it will incite hatred among the islanders And will provoke the wrath of the island's gods, Which could bring calamity to the King himself.

ASATO	Impertinent woman! What will happen to the kingdom if we hesitate in such a matter?
SHŌ TOKU	Wait, Asato, Let us hear what else Kunikasa has to say.
KUNIKASA	My Lord, Your ships are pointing toward the place on the horizon From which the sun rises, and to which we give prayer. Though the island's harbor is in that direction, A King should not draw a bow at the sun. In a vision I see that many large rocks are scattered in the north. Let our soldiers use them to cover a tactical advance And encircle the village from the back—
ASATO	My Lord! Surrounding the village from the back Will lead to a protracted battle with the villagers.
SHŌ TOKU	That is enough, Asato! Kunikasa's strategy is the superior one. Soldiers, begin the encirclement immediately. Go around to the northern side; attack from there.

MUSIC (TACHIUTUSHI)

Soldiers in black dance, waging war. During the battle, Kunikasa prays and Asato stares at her. An image of a white horse appears on the screen behind them. The battle is won, the soldiers exit.

SONG (SHŪRAI BUSHI)

The spiritual power of the white horse is great.
With the help of the gods we return victorious.

Shō Toku and Kunikasa exit.

ASATO	Impertinent female shaman of Kudaka Island! How loathsome she is, so arrogant in victory. I cannot let her diminish my high prestige as diviner. Oh, that unforgivable woman! I cannot cast off my hatred. I will choose a favorable day And ruin her.

Three men of Kudaka Island enter.

FIRST MAN	Kudaka is a good island. Gods live in every corner of our land.

Higa Yasuo: Maternal Deities

Worshipping the Gods (Kami-agami)
Miyako Island, Shimajiri, Pāntu
1975

SECOND MAN	Kudaka is a good island. The hearts of the King and the shaman are one.
THIRD MAN	Though Kudaka is a good island, We sometimes meet bad people.
FIRST MAN	There is news from Shuri! I heard Lord Kanamaru has killed the King.
THIRD MAN	But there are others who say The King escaped from the castle.
SECOND MAN	Where did he go?
THIRD MAN	If I knew, I could be the island's diviner.
FIRST MAN	Speaking of that, What has happened to the male diviner?
SECOND MAN	I am very curious too. Rumor has it that he fled to our island. Has anyone seen him?
THIRD MAN	If I see this man, I will trample him.
FIRST MAN	Oh, talk big and you'll be sorry later. Your big words will fly all the way to Kikai Island.
SECOND MAN	If the King comes and hides himself on this island, What would you do?
FIRST MAN	Nothing. What can we fishermen do?
THIRD MAN	We could take him far away from here.
SECOND MAN	What lies in the sea beyond the horizon?
FIRST MAN	*Nirai Kanai* maybe…
THIRD MAN	*Nirai Kanai* could be the answer for every question.
SECOND MAN	Here comes Mr. Evil from *Nirai Kanai*.
THIRD MAN	It's time we left.

The three men exit. Enter Asato.

SONG (KUDUCHI)

Being a man
I mean to triumph in every battle.
That is why I walked up the slope of the sea,
That is why I crossed the ocean to this island.

The female shamans of the island enter. They gather around him and Asato whispers to them. The shamans exit.

ASATO   Crossing the sea so swiftly, without incident,
               Foretells the success awaiting me.
               I planted rumors among the shamans
               To make them jealous of Kunikasa's love for the king.
               They will grow hostile toward Kunikasa
               And thus I will use them to avenge myself.

Kunikasa, followed by three shamans, enters. Asato hides himself.

               SONG (YŪSHAINŌ BUSHI)

               The horizon is so far away.
               Our hearts are so fathomless.

FIRST SHAMAN   Being a shaman of Kudaka,
               Kunikasa is forbidden to pledge her love to the King.
               Today let us confront her.

SECOND SHAMAN We will test Kunikasa on this auspicious day
               On the seven sacred bridges.
               If she is innocent,
               She will cross the bridges safely without falling—

THIRD SHAMAN   Kunikasa,
               Does the white horse from the horizon
               Still visit you?
               Cross the seven sacred bridges there
               And prove your innocence.

KUNIKASA   I am a woman, I miss the King.
               The white horse will run today and tomorrow.

               SONG (SANYAMA BUSHI)

               I am a woman, I miss the King.
               The white horse will run today and tomorrow.

Kunikasa begins to cross the bridges.

ASATO   Is the spiritual power of the Kudaka shaman still intact
               Though the King has passed away?

Kunikasa, shocked by the news of Shō Toku's death, falls off the bridge and dies.

FIRST SHAMAN   On this distant island we had not heard of the King's death.
               Please tell us what has happened in Shuri.

ASATO   The King had always been ineffectual,
               And his government had always been irresponsible.
               So Lord Kanamaru finally seized the throne.

SECOND SHAMAN	O gods! Please tell us more about this grave news.
ASATO	Your island has nothing to do with this matter. You women and children should ask no more about it.
FIRST SHAMAN	Do not insult us as women of a remote island.
SECOND SHAMAN	We cannot forgive you for telling us lies about Kunikasa.
THIRD SHAMAN	We will drown you in the sea like a poisonous insect.

The three women dance to drive Asato away.

SONG (SENSURU BUSHI)

Even though a disturbance breaks out in Shuri,
Life in Kudaka remains intact.
Even though a revolution takes place in Naha,
It does not interfere with life in Kudaka.
With protection from *Nirai Kanai*
We will enjoy a rich life in Kudaka.
We will wash poisonous insects and diseases into the sea.

Having driven Asato away, the women exit. Shō Toku enters. At the same time, a white horse runs forward on the screen.

SHŌ TOKU	I am the spirit of Shō Toku, King of Shuri. Having fallen into Kanamaru's snare, I escaped Shuri Castle and set sail to Kudaka. But, alas, I shipwrecked and died on my way here. Though I am now a spirit, the fate of Kunikasa Weighs heavily on my heart, And thus I have come to Kudaka Island. Oh, Kunikasa, hear my lament. Rise and let us go to the other world, To *Umi nu Tinzakai*—the world beyond the horizon.

Shō Toku, holding Kunikasa's dead body, sings.

SONG (AGARIE BUSHI)

Wake up, Kunikasa, let us go, you and I
To *Umi nu Tinzakai*,
To the other world beyond the horizon.

Translation by Katsunori Yamazato and Frank Stewart

Higa Yasuo: *Maternal Deities*

Worshipping the Gods (Kami-agami)
Kume Island, Nishime, Umachī
1990

Possessed by Love, Thwarted by the Bell: An Overview of *Kumi Odori*

Kumi odori is an aristocratic dance-drama developed in 1719 by Tamagu-suku Chōkun as part of Okinawan court performance for the ritual investi-ture of the monarch. *Shūshin Kani'iri* (Possessed by Love, Thwarted by the Bell) was written for this court presentation and has remained one of the most frequently performed works. This essay gives an introduction to *kumi odori* based on the practice of Kin Ryōshō, an important twentieth-century master of the form. A translation of *Possessed by Love, Thwarted by the Bell*, with stage directions reflecting Kin Sensei's choreography, follows this essay.[1] The essay and translation were originally published in *Asian Theatre Journal*, 22:1 (spring 2005) in a slightly different format.

Kumi Odori's *Historical Context and Performance Practice* [2]

Okinawan (or Ryūkyūan) *kumi odori* ("combination dance"),[3] a form that combines dance, dialogue, music, and song in creating its play's dramatic effect, had its debut in 1719 at a banquet in the Okinawan capital city of Shuri, for the purpose of entertaining the Chinese envoys to the Okinawan kingdom. Its period of growth and development ended with the dissolution of the kingdom by the Japanese government in 1879. A few artists who had access to this tradition through their aristocratic birth preserved it. There was a revival of interest in this dance-drama form in the mid-twentieth cen-tury, culminating in its designation by the Japanese government in 1972 as an "important intangible cultural asset" (Tōma 1986: 266). This valuation now places *kumi odori* in the same category as the traditional Japanese per-forming arts, such as ancient court music (*gagaku*), puppet theatre (*bun-raku*), *nō*, *kabuki*, and *gidayū* chanting. In 2004 the National Theatre Oki-nawa in Urasoe city near Naha opened, marking another step in official recognition of this important cultural genre (Thornbury 1999: 230–247). However, despite this recognition, the social base that gave birth to *kumi odori* is gone and the revival is still largely a case of cultural conservation. The *kumi odori* repertoire has not grown significantly since the demise of the kingdom, and practitioners focus on replicating past masters rather than developing new performance practices.

Between 1719 and 1879, however, the form flourished in the court, reflecting the taste and refinement of the aristocrats who were the audience, actors, and authors of the genre. One can turn to the Okinawan tradition of religious dances (*kami ashibi*) and chants (*umui*), night meetings that allowed the young people of the village to sing, dance, and socialize (*mō ashibi*), or to the *chondarā*, a slow religious dance related to the *nembutsu odori* of Japan, for distant antecedents of the form (Origuchi 1929: 1–23; Ōura 1974: 11–19).

But for more germane information, one must consider the situation of the court at Shuri, with its refined aristocrats, to appreciate how they utilized music and dance while playing the delicate political game of balancing their islands' tenuous economy by keeping good relations with their more powerful neighbors, China and Japan (Kerr 1975 [1958]). To ensure itself a position in Chinese trade, Okinawa was more than willing to acknowledge the suzerainty of China. The culture flow that resulted stimulated the development of art and ethics in Okinawa. The *sanshin* (Jpn.: *shamisen*; a three-stringed plucked instrument) came from China in the fourteenth century and was adopted as the major musical instrument, the Chinese classics became required readings for the educated man, and Confucian ethics affected the moral code. The way the hero of *Shūshin Kani'iri* flees a woman and seeks protection of a monk reminds us of the young scholar of the Chinese white snake legend who seeks asylum in a Buddhist monastery, as well as Japanese stories, discussed below, that may be related to this Chinese legend. Chinese models impressed the authors of *kumi odori* performance.

King Satto of Chūzan in central Okinawa inaugurated the tribute system with China in 1372, during the Ming dynasty in China. The system continued under his successors, who united the entire island under their rule, and through the three centuries of Satsuma control of Okinawa, until the abolition of the Ryūkyū Kingdom in 1879. As a part of the tribute system, the emperor of China would confirm the succession of the Okinawan king by sending envoys to perform investiture ceremonies. For this event (*ukwanshin*; "crown ship" ceremony), envoys would arrive in the spring when the prevailing winds blew toward Okinawa and return five or six months later when the winds again turned toward the mainland. During the interim, the Chinese officers were entertained with music and dance. It was for one such *ukwanshin* performance that *kumi odori* was first presented (Ihwa 1974b: 412–422).

The influence from Japan to the north also played a role in the development of Okinawan *kumi odori*. Since the early seventeenth century, Japan was officially closed to foreign trade, except for a small number of Chinese and the Dutch in Nagasaki. The lords of the Satsuma domain in southern Japan had taken advantage of this fact to engage in a profitable smuggling trade. From 1609 onward, when Satsuma took control of Okinawa, the

Japanese supervised the political affairs of Okinawa, so that the trade riches that poured into Okinawan harbors passed north to enrich Japan.

Artistic influences from Japan meanwhile flowed south to Okinawa. Tamagusuku Chōkun (1684–1734), who was to create *kumi odori*, had made five trips to Japan before 1715, visiting both Kagoshima, the seat of the Satsuma clan, and Edo, where he studied and viewed the Japanese arts of the period (Thornbury 1999: 232). There is no doubt that he borrowed from *nō* in devising this art form that would impress the Chinese envoys who came for the *ukwanshin* investiture of King Shōkei in 1719. At the Chōyō banquet on the ninth day of the ninth month of the lunar calendar, the chrysanthemum viewing festival day, two *kumi odori* were performed: *Nidō Tichiuchi* (Vendetta of the Two Sons) and *Shūshin Kani'iri* (Possessed by Love, Thwarted by the Bell) (Ihwa 1974b: 420). Tamagusuku had been appointed to the post of *udui bugyō* (minister of dance) as early as 1715. This office was first held by Tansui Uwekata (1622–1683) and had become a regular court position, the major responsibility of the office being the preparation of the *ukwanshin* entertainments.

Despite the skepticism of those who found a dancer speaking ludicrous, Tamagusuku had undertaken the creation of this dance-drama form following his reappointment as *udui bugyō* in 1718 (Ihwa 1974b: 413). Tamagusuku is the author of the first five *kumi odori*, namely, *Nidō Tichiuchi* (Vendetta of the Two Sons), *Shūshin Kani'iri* (Possessed by Love, Thwarted by the Bell), *Mekarushī* (Master Mekarushi), *Kōkō nu Maki* (Filial Piety), and *Unna Munu Gurui* (The Madwoman). These plays are generally shorter than the later ones written in the genre, lasting about thirty minutes in contemporary playing time, compared to the two hours and forty minutes required for the longest *kumi odori*.

A number of similarities between *kumi odori* and *nō* are apparent to those who know both genres. Tamagusuku was acquainted with *nō*, and the choices he made in his performances for the 1719 investiture ceremony reflected Japanese models. The pared-down physical setting of the stage resembled *nō*. The legends and folklore material selected for presentation, the structure of the plays, the refined dance, the subdued chant, and the use of travel songs (*michiyuki*) are all links that point back toward *nō* antecedents. Since Tamagusuku's work is strongly influenced by *nō*, it is possible to find equivalents for his pieces in the *nō* repertoire. *Shūshin Kani'iri*, for example, is clearly related to *Dōjōji*, as both concern an enamored woman who transforms into a demon and enters a bell (Ihwa 1974a: 65–66; Yokomichi and Omote 1963: 137–141; Keene 1970: 245–250; Majikina 1974: 335–341).

However, the borrowing is not straightforward: in the case of *Shūshin Kani'iri*, for example, the first part of the play has strong resemblance to the *nō* play *Kurozuka* (Black Mound), also called *Adachigahara* (The Adachi

Field).[4] The legend of *Dōjōji* has a long history in Japan, going as far back as the twelfth-century Buddhist tale collection *Konjaku Monogatari* (Tales of Times Now Past). At the same time, however, Tamagusuku had an Okinawan legend that told a tale similar to *Dōjōji* available to him, so his treatment of the material is quite different. Avoiding the *nō* tendency toward a remembrance of things past, he opted instead for a presentation of things present. In *Dōjōji* we see the spirit of a woman revisiting the scene of her past, passionate love, while in *Shūshin Kani'iri* we have a real woman falling in love and then transforming into the demon as we watch. Where *nō* remembers a past event, *kumi odori* shows the real action.

There are other differences as well. For instance, the principal actor (*shite*) in the *nō* play wears a mask, whereas his counterpart in *kumi odori* does not do so routinely: hence, in *Shūshin Kani'iri* only the demon wears a mask, while the woman wears none. The philosophical background of the two traditions also differs. In *nō*, Buddhism is ever present, preaching the impermanence of all things and salvation through renunciation. In *kumi odori*, the philosophical background is Confucianism, which is oriented toward this world and teaches moderation as an ideal in all human activities. As the woman attempts seduction, Wakamatsi answers:

> If one is born a man,
> unless he holds reason and intellect as his standards,
> he will indeed create chaos
> in society. (*Shūshin Kani'iri*, lines 77–80)

Such pragmatism is reflected in the scripts. While *nō* refines the spirit toward enlightenment, helping viewers cast off earthly emotion and dross in an apotheosis of chant, music, and dance, *kumi odori* advocates Confucian moderation.

Tamagusuku used the *ryūka*, a form in classical Ryūkyūan (i.e., Okinawan) poetry, with three lines of eight syllables followed by one of six, as his verse. He used selected words from old *omoro* (or *umui*) religious chants and employed classical music in creating the songs, which highlight the important moments of the play. Gesture came from the classical court dance with its clean, spare movement style. While the folk music and dance of the island are lively, quick, and expressive, the court aesthetic is subdued, slowed down, and restrained. *Kumi odori* is austere and chosen—each gesture, sound, and word feels crafted by a master artist. For performers, Tamagusuku used male aristocrats, for whom ability in music and dance was considered a mark of good breeding.

Kumi odori plays, after being created for these rites of investiture, were performed at important social gatherings of the aristocrats. Between such performance occasions, texts were kept alive in the audience's mind through recitation. For example, when women gave birth it was common to keep watch with the mother through this dangerous period, and, during the evening, the men would recite *kumi odori*. As a result of this custom, when a performance came, the audience might know the text as well as the actors.

The dissolution of the kingdom in 1879 threatened to bring about the dissolution of *kumi odori*, because the aristocrats lost the income that had allowed them the leisure to devote their lives to music and dance. The few musicians who continued to work in the genre eventually chose one of two directions. Around the turn of the twentieth century some performers attempted to establish a *kumi odori* theatre in Naha, but by 1919 popular taste had forced this group's *kumi odori* to be transformed into *shibai*, a popular theatre genre that continues into the present.

The other direction was more conservative: in the homes of some former aristocrats, the music, dance, and *kumi odori* tradition continued to be passed from father to son. The master *kumi odori* performer Kin Ryōshō (1908–1993) learned from his father, Kin Ryōjin (1873–1936), who learned from Amuru Pechin, an important performer in the last *ukwanshin* in 1866.[5] Mr. Kin, in turn, taught dance and *kumi odori* in his studio to both men and women in Naha in the second half of the twentieth century, training his son to follow him. In such recitals as those given by his students and his students' students, *kumi odori* continues though the social and historical conditions that fostered it have long since vanished.

Since the return of Okinawa to Japan in 1972 there has been revival of the art. In recent years Nōhō Miyagi, who studied under Genzō Tamagusuku, has taught it at the Okinawa Kenritsu Geijutsu Daigaku (Okinawa Prefectural University of the Arts). Through teachers such as Kin and Miyagi the art continues, but the major teachers are aging and few new artists have entered their ranks: in 1996 the forty-eight acknowledged master artists averaged sixty years in age (Thornbury 1999: 243). Recent developments include the 18 January 2004 opening of Japan's sixth national theatre, the National Okinawa Theatre. *Shūshin Kani'iri* was on the opening program.

The long-term success of the revival may be unclear, but there is no doubt that the art, along with music and dance, is seen by proponents of indigenous culture as an important icon of Okinawan identity in the face of both American and Japanese cultural presences. The island was occupied by the United States from 1945 until 1972, and American military bases remain, despite the resentment of locals against the constant onslaught of American culture. The austerity of *kumi odori* is about as far as one can get from MTV aesthetics, a fitting antidote to global culture. Tourism has developed. The art is a sign of local difference, which can be touted on Web pages to international tourists and presented to visitors.

Likewise, proponents of Okinawan language and culture conservation in the face of Japanization have embraced the art: aurally, visually, and aesthetically it keeps Okinawan culture alive. To perform, the now languishing local language must be learned. To costume the performers, the traditional fabric art of *bingata* must be maintained. To appreciate the genre, understanding of the aesthetic of the palace is required. A living *kumi odori* is Okinawa's proof of a glorious past, celebrating the people's complex ability to navigate waters between China and Japan, politically and artistically.

Kumi odori was born of cultural diplomacy in 1719, and now, at the beginning of the twenty-first century, it continues a cultural mission. The new national theatre, Japan's sixth, should bring Okinawan cultural capital to national attention. Recent innovations have included revivals and the creation of new scripts. *Gosamaru,* the story of the fifteenth-century lord of Nakagusuku Castle, was performed in 1995 at the site of the castle—a gap of forty-three years since the last production at the site. The producer's intentions seemed to combine touristic performance with bolstering local cultural awareness (Nakagusuku Castle Site Cooperative Management and Consultation Committee, n.d.). Five new *kumi odori* written by Ōshiro Tatsuhiro were published in 2001 (Yonaha 2003). While it is not clear that Ōshiro's productions will last, they are the first major attempt to expand a repertoire that Kin Ryōshō saw as "complete" in 1976.

The Stylistic Context

Kumi odori is a form of drama that combines movement, speech, and music in the acting out of plays. To understand the stylistic context of the genre, each of these components is examined below.

Play

According to Kin Ryōshō, the repertoire of *kumi odori* consists of forty-four extant pieces. These works are classified according to their subject matter as *sewa mono* ("domestic plays," including fourteen pieces) or *jidai mono* ("historical plays," of which there are thirty pieces). The latter (which are sometimes called *kataki-uchi mono* or vendetta plays) often deal with revenge motifs, and have stock characters such as the *aji,* or lord; the *waka-aji,* or young lord; and a proud *ufunushi,* or general. Stock scenes of parting and reunion recur in them.

The *sewa mono* are plays that focus on poignant human emotions such as love or filial devotion. *Shūshin Kani'iri,* with its love-consumed heroine pursuing her reluctant young man to the monastery where he seeks sanctuary, is an example of the latter group of plays. There is an Okinawan proverb that a woman in love becomes a serpent if she broods too deeply on her emotion, and in *Shūshin Kani'iri* we see this process happen before our eyes (Ōta 1974: 379). But, if the plot takes the proverb quite literally, the style of performance is far from realistic.

Movement

The movement style of *kumi odori* is the highly stylized classical dance form. Movements are clear and simple, but this very simplicity is part of the difficulty of the form. The general image is somewhat reminiscent of *nō*. In the characteristic walk, the foot slides straight forward on the floor with the toe springing up and away from the ground at the last moment.

The face registers little overt expression. Kin Ryōshō liked to compare the face of the *kumi odori* dancer to the mask of the *nō*. A lowered head may signify sadness; a backward glance may indicate fear. The eyes, however, are alive and precede any body movement, focusing the direction and destination of the coming move. The vitality of these eyes in a face that emulates a neutral mask (one that has no particular expression) exemplifies the way in which violent emotions are contained in this refined dance-drama form.

Classical dance is traditionally divided into three categories: *wunna*, or woman's; *wakashū*, or young man's; and *nisu wutuku*, or male. These types found in classical dance of the court can be compared to, but do not exactly correspond to, the types of *nō*. For example, the *wunna* and the *onna* in *nō* seem equivalent, the *wakashū* correlates to the *kokata* or child role, and the *nisu* role has equivalencies to male roles in *nō*. But even though it is linked to *nō*, the art has been modified by an Okinawan aesthetic.

There are variations in stance and posture for each of the three types, but the basic movement patterns are related. The most striking variable is the degree of effort used for the moves, from the flowing style of the woman to the abrupt mode of the man. The young man's style is a mean between these two extremes. In *Shūshin Kani'iri* we see this range of styles in the woman (*wunna*), Wakamatsi (*wakashū*), and the demon, whose dance uses elements drawn from the male style. The four priests do not fit precisely into any of the three categories, and their movements are a bit more natural, but there is a high degree of stylization as they pantomime hitting each other or falling asleep. The function and style of these priests can be compared to the *kyōgen* roles in a *nō* performance.

Although all movement in the performance is considered *odori*, or dance, it is possible to distinguish three levels. The first level is the performance of realistic actions in the dance style and includes such activities as sitting, standing, and running from another character. These movements establish clearly the basic plotline of the story. A second level can be seen in which realistic movements are intentionally heightened to reveal the emotional life of the character. Thus, the woman in *Shūshin Kani'iri*, searching the temple for her lover, suddenly breaks from her walk and performs a series of swirling turns that express her passion, presaging the imminent transformation into the demon. The third level is dance in the strict sense of the term and includes travel dances (*michiyuki*), dances that express an emotion, dances that tell the story (fighting, courting), and dances within the play (as when one character asks another character to perform). In *Shūshin Kani'iri* we encounter two *michiyuki* dances (the young man's and woman's), and a story dance in the battle between the priests and the demon at the very end of the play.

Only men performed this art before the fall of the kingdom: all were aristocrats who fulfilled court duty and found personal pleasure in performing. The casting was done with attention to body type: the age and build of the dancer would be appropriate to the character that he portrayed. Body type and the clean style worked together toward a fine physicalization of character. Today women are trained in the art, learning and performing both female and young male roles.

Speech

The dialogue and songs that comprise the text are in classical literary Okinawan and display both a high level of formality and a significant use of metaphor. The delivery of spoken lines is stylized throughout, but has variations appropriate to the emotional situation of the character. As with *nō*, there are two styles of delivery: *kyōgin* or *tsiyujin* (strong singing), which is employed by strong male characters such as a lord; and *wagin* or *yuwajin* (soft singing), used by women and young men. There are slight differences in speaking style between woman and young man, but to the untrained ear both sound similar, rising softly through the first two lines of eight *morae*, or syllables, with a slight dip at the end of the second line, then floating up again for a sharper descent at the end of the fourth line, which completes the verse.

In *Shūshin Kani'iri*, as in many *sewa mono*, *wagin* is the sole style, since its softness is appropriate both to the characters and the love theme. Variations do occur within the basic contour that the chant affords, allowing sharp contrasts that highlight moments of emotional agitation. Thus, in *Shūshin Kani'iri*, Wakamatsi delivers a short, sharp reprimand to the woman as he rejects her overtures of love. He begs the chief priest for assistance in a breathless tone that varies from the normal style (8-8-8-6 *mora*) and indicates his agitation (in 7-5 *mora*). Good vocal production is an important quality for an actor, since it is felt that much of the emotional life of the play is conveyed by the voice. Still, the main aural feature of the production—the singing, which is performed at the most climactic moments of the play—is reserved for the musicians.

Music

The instruments of *kumi odori* consist of the *sanshin* (Jpn.: *shamisen*; a three-stringed plucked instrument), the *kutu* (Jpn.: *koto*; a thirteen-stringed zither), the *kūchō* (a three- or four-stringed bowed instrument), the *hansō* (a flute), and two drums, one large (*ōdaiko*) and one small (*kodaiko*). The *sanshin*, imported from China in the fourteenth century, is the primary instrument and is used in almost all *kumi odori* music. The *kutu* was introduced from Japan and is a secondary instrument that was probably not employed in *kumi odori* until the nineteenth century. The *kūchō* and *hansō* are, likewise, secondary instruments.

The drums have a variety of functions: first, for dramatic emphasis, as in highlighting the rising of the bell and the poses of the demon in *Shūshin*

Kani'iri; second, to accompany the entrance of certain personages, such as a lord or general; and third, to accompany dance. The drummer adds further accents by giving *yagwi* or drummer's calls, as in the demon dance of *Shūshin Kani'iri.*

The songs, which are sung by the *sanshin* player or players, use tunes drawn from the classical repertoire, with lyrics of *ryūka*. A tune has one *honka* (main text), but may have many other texts that are also sung to it, so one melody may be found in many different *kumi odori*. Certain tunes are associated with certain kinds of emotions or types of scenes, as we can see in examining the songs of *Shūshin Kani'iri*. For example, the "Chin Bushi," a tune that is used as Wakamatsi's travel music, is employed with twenty-four poems collected in the *Ryūka Zenshū* (Shimabukuro and Onaga 1968: 30–34); most of these poems are *michiyuki* (travel songs). "Hwishi Bushi" (Song of the Shoals), which is used when the singer expresses the woman's thoughts in the meeting scene, is associated with sadness and used mainly for love songs. "Shichishaku Bushi" (Song of Seven Feet), or in a variant reading "Nanayumi Bushi" (Song of Seven Bows), the woman's travel song, is used with songs of unhappy love, and "San'yama Bushi" (Song of Scattering Mountain, or Dirge), the final tune of *Shūshin Kani'iri*, is associated with parting and death (Shimabukuro and Onaga 1968: 26, 30, 32).

The importance of the songs in this play cannot be overemphasized. The *ryūka* poems from *Shūshin Kani'iri* listed in the *Ryūka Zenshū* collection comprise as much as one-fourth of all the *ryūka* attributed to the playwright Tamagusuku Chōkun. Thus, one may state that the songs establish the scene and direct the action of the play. In the climactic moments, the dialogue of the actors ceases and the musicians essentialize the characters' emotions in song.

Performance Context

By examining such aspects of *kumi odori* as staging and program, we can begin to understand the atmosphere in which it was and is performed. This allows clearer understanding of the effect the form has on its audience.

Staging

Until the demise of the kingdom, a stage modeled on that of *nō* was used. The eighteen-foot-square platform had a bridge (*hashigakari*) leading on from stage right (*shimote*). Another entrance was from stage left (*kamite*) from behind the edge of the *bingata* hanging that formed the backdrop for the entire stage. This hanging was called the *himatsi*, after the pine tree with a red sun design it portrayed. It is possible that the musicians as well as the actors awaiting cues sat behind this drop during the performance, since it was easy to see and hear through it. The other alternative was to have the musicians onstage on the stage-left side.

At present, *kumi odori* is done in auditoriums on modern stages with the musicians seated stage left or in the wings. But a symbolic use of stage space that *kumi odori* shares with *nō* remains evident despite the proscenium. In *Shūshin Kani'iri* the stage is bare as Wakamatsi enters and announces he is on a country road. A few moments later we are in the house where he seeks shelter, and, later, after he makes a circuit of the stage, the same space has become the monastery. Set pieces and props are few (a lamp or a stick) and are often left onstage even when the scene has changed to a distant locale. The actors and audience focus on the essence of the action, rather than becoming entangled in external details.

The props that are used often indicate ideas, rather than realistic objects. Thus, the walking stick that Wakamatsi carries does not reach the ground, but still cues the audience that he is on a journey. The bell used in *Shūshin Kani'iri* is one of the few significant set pieces in *kumi odori*. Modeled on the bell of Enkaku-ji Temple in Okinawa, it plays an important part in the play as the hiding place of Wakamatsi and the place where the woman metamorphoses into the demon. But even in this scene the stage is essentially a bare space for the enactment of symbolic action, rather than an area filled with realistic detail.

Program

The first *kumi odori* program included two plays and was performed during the *ukwanshin* investiture of King Shōkei in 1719. Previous "crown ship" performances may have been more clearly memorials for the dead monarch. Tamagusuku's innovative production this year provided a more secular entertainment with Confucian themes. As time went by, the program became standardized and the number of occasions on which *kumi odori* might be performed grew. As the sixty-first, seventy-third, and eighty-fifth birthdays of the chief priestess were important occasions, the king himself might perform for these celebrations. She was always a relative of the king and served an important shamanic function in religion (Lebra 1966: 95–114). Although *ukwanshin* performances continued to be the major ones, the aristocrats did not wait a generation between plays.

The *ukwanshin* performances took place in the afternoon and lasted approximately five hours without any intermission. Plays were performed with dances before and between. Ihwa Huyū (1929) lists a program for the twelfth day of the eighth month of the lunar calendar in 1838.[6]

1. "Omoro Koneri" [*Umui* Chant]
2. "Iriko Odori" [Team Dances Medley]
3. "Sensu Odori" [Fan Dance]
4. *Nidō Tichiuchi* (Vendetta of the Two Sons) [a *kumi odori*]
5. "Onnagasa Odori" [Women's Flower-Hat Dance]
6. *Shūshin Kani'iri* (Possessed by Love, Thwarted by the Bell) [a *kumi odori*]

7. "Kakko Odori" [Drum Dance]
8. *Chūshi Migawari nu maki* (The Story of a Loyal Retainer Who Dies in His Master's Stead) [a *kumi odori*]
9. "Karabō" [Chinese Stick Dance]
10. "Mari Odori" [Ball Dance]

We see that two *jidai mono* are balanced by a *sewa mono*, making a total of three *kumi odori*. Kin Ryōshō noted that the dances that interspersed the plays would be appropriate to their place on the program and that a vendetta play ordinarily came after a *sewa mono*, since it was a stronger way to end a program.

At present *kumi odori* are presented at schools of dance such as the Jinpūkai run by Kin Ryōshō's son and successor, Kin Yoshiharu. Once a year, a program that lasts about three hours is performed. Normally two plays are chosen, one from each category, with dances between. In such performances, students of master artists join the lineage that stretches back to Tamagasuku, as *kumi odori* continues in a context that emulates its original program.

Conceptual Context

In approaching *kumi odori*, it is useful to grasp some of the concepts that lie behind the form. This helps us appreciate some of the standards by which a good performance is judged. The first prerequisite is a good text. The language should have *hin*, which may be translated as grace or refinement. The concept of *hin* is also applied to a performance, meaning the grace with which a scene is done. This does not come by chance but is the result of long years of correct work by the performer and full concentration on what he is doing in the specific performance.

Two qualities that the performers should have are *kan* and *konashi*. *Kan*, the ability to put life into a performance, is largely intuitive. Someone who has *kan* will learn things quickly, but more important than this is *konashi*, the accumulation of experience that allows one to master the essence of a scene. If we put *kan* on the intuitive side of the scale, *konashi* is more toward the learned side of it. An actor who has *konashi* has mastered timing and has the ability to put his body and mind in the right place during a performance.[7]

If one has *konashi*, it seems to follow that one has *kan*, but not vice versa. To be a good performer one must have both, and to have a good *kumi odori* performance, all the performers should have these qualities. In a good performance, all the elements should be in balance, with nothing too strong and nothing too weak. This occurs when the *kan* of all the actors and musicians unites to create the essence of the piece, which lies in the feeling rather than in the words. Then *hin* is achieved and the audience participates in the moment of grace.

Two centuries of careful selection of the best way to create a particular moment lie behind *kumi odori* performance. Although change is not sought after, this is not a changeless form. "When something becomes too rigid, it is dead," said Kin Ryōshō (1976). Innovation is accepted when it contributes to the dramatic life and truth of the piece. Kin Ryōshō tells the story of Ukubara Pēchin, who was a major performer of the late kingdom period. He changed the way in which the woman in *Shūshin Kani'iri* moved the lamp when looking at Wakamatsi on her first entrance. As his wife helped him search a closet, he noticed that, to see most clearly, one should hold a lamp so that the light falls at an angle.

This story shows both the conservatism and the flexibility of the form. To a hearer from a more change-oriented culture, it seems a slight alteration and almost surprising that it should be cited as an example of the importance of being open to a more truthful way of doing things. Yet the story affirms that improvement, rather than repetition, is the value. The anecdote shows that if things do not often change, it is because the performers feel that improvements have already been made by their predecessors. Kin Ryōshō himself claimed that he has not initiated any innovations, but recreated the form as he learned it from his teachers.

Formerly, the concept of *ūsū-hūkū*, or service to the king, lay behind the performance of *kumi odori*. The high seriousness with which the actors considered their work is reported by Kin Ryōshō in stories given below.[8]

> While Tawata Pēchin was playing the lord of Tanora in *Ūkā Tichiuchi*, his house went up in flames. Although he heard the report of the fire from the comments of the audience, he did not halt since "performance for the king came first."
>
> Ukuhara Pēchin was practicing the role for *The Madwoman*, a play about a missing child. His wife laughed at him and he chased her out of the house—"to this extent you must be serious."

Today the concept of service to the king is gone and, along with it, the dedicated core of aristocrat performers whose seriousness about their art created the form. *Kumi odori* now depends on recognition of its artistic merits to draw performers and audiences to it. The number of people who study and perform in the genre is growing, but most lack the dedication and economic base that enabled some of the artists of the kingdom period to undertake their all-consuming study of classical music, dance, and *kumi odori*.

But the story of this genre is far from over. An art form that personified refinement and reified class differences is now seeking to become an icon of Okinawan ethnicity in the face of globalization and assimilationist influences from Japan. The "combination dance" created to theatricalize the power and refinement of the Shuri court moves on as artists culturally navigate new tides and present shoals.

NOTES

1. This introduction is based on interviews with Kin Ryōshō in the context of production of *Shūshin Kani'iri* produced under the leadership of Barbara Smith and Judy van Zile at the University of Hawai'i Music Department in the summer of 1976 during the Institute on the Performing Arts of Okinawa. James Hanashiro and Earl Ikeda, students of Kin Ryōshō, were instrumental in explaining the many ideas. Kimiko Ohtani and Etsuko Higa provided additional help in translation and clarification during the workshop. Cheryl Yoshie Nakasone dancing the role of the hero in the play and now carrying on Kin Ryosho's style in Hawai'i should also be thanked (see *Ryūkyū Geino: The Legacy of Kin Ryosho,* 2008). The strengths of this introduction derive from these people, and the weaknesses belong to myself (Kathy Foley) alone.

2. The form is called *kumi udui* in Okinawan, but present scholarly work uses the Japanese name.

3. The language of the Ryūkyū Islands, of which Okinawa is the principal island, is considered to be related to Japanese and to have separated from the Japanese of the mainland sometime between the fifth and the tenth centuries. There are complex rules about the phonetic differences between Okinawan and Japanese; however, the major difference is that Okinawan has three vowels (*a, i,* and *u*), compared with five vowels (*a, i, u, e,* and *o*) in Japanese. The Japanese vowel *e* becomes *i* and *o* becomes *u* in Okinawan. There are more consonants in Okinawan than in Japanese, including *kw, gw,* and *hw,* as well as such consonant-vowel combinations as *tsi, ti, tu, di,* and *du.* Instead of *ki,* Okinawan uses *chi.* Thus, *kumi odori* is pronounced *kumi udui* in Okinawan. See Sakamaki 1964: 11–13.

4. In the *nō* play, traveling monks arrive at a house in the Adachi Field after dark and ask for lodging; the woman of the house initially refuses but in the end allows them to stay overnight. However, the monks discover that the woman is actually a demon who devours human beings. The monks run away and the demon chases them. The play ends with an exorcism, which dispels the demon. See Yokomichi and Omote 1963: 369–373.

5. Kin Ryōshō was one of the master performers of *kumi odori,* which was designated as an important intangible cultural asset in 1972. See Naha Shuppansha Henshūbu 1992: 164.

6. This is in Ihwa 1929: table of contents, 1–2. The table of contents in this edition has its own separate pagination.

7. It might be useful to further explore these concepts and see how closely they follow *nō* aesthetics: *yūgen* might be compared to *hin,* and *kan* to *hana* (Sorgenfrei 2004).

8. This was stated by Kin Ryōshō (1976). See also Kin Ryōshō 1965: 72–96.

REFERENCES

Ihwa Huyū. 1929. *Ryūkyū gikyokushū* (Collection of Ryūkyū Plays). Tokyo: Shun'yōdō.

———. 1974a. *Ryūkyū gikyokushū* (Collection of Ryūkyūan Plays). In *Ihwa Huyū zenshū* (Complete Works of Ihwa Huyū), vol. 3, ed. Hattori Shirō, Nakasone Seizen, and Hokama Shuzen. Tokyo: Heibonsha.

———. 1974b. "Ryūkyū sakugi no biso Tamagusuku Chōkun nempu" (Chronology of Tamagusuku Chōkun, the Originator of the Ryūkyūan Playwriting). In *Ihwa Huyū zenshū* (Complete Works of Ihwa Huyū), vol. 3, ed. Hattori Shirō, Nakasone Seizen, and Hokama Shuzen, 402–429. Tokyo: Heibonsha.

Keene, Donald, ed. 1970. *Twenty Plays of the Nō Theatre*. New York and London: Columbia University Press.

Kerr, George H. 1975 [1958] *Okinawa: The History of an Island People*. Rutland, VT: Charles E. Tuttle.

Kin Ryōshō. Lecture. 1976. Class lecture for MUS 477H (Musical Cultures: Okinawa). University of Hawai'i at Mānoa, Honolulu, 6 July.

———. 1965. "Recollections of Shuri." In *A History in Pictures: Okinawa, Then and Now*, ed. Taira Shōjirō, trans. Nashiro Masajirō, 72–96. Naha: Gakken Okinawasha.

Lebra, William P. 1966. *Okinawan Religion: Belief, Ritual, and Social Structure*. Honolulu: University of Hawai'i Press.

Majikina Ankō. 1974. "*Kumi odori* to nōgaku to no kōsatsu" (A Consideration of *Kumi odori* and *Nō* Plays). In *Ihwa Huyū zenshū* (Complete Works of Ihwa Huyū), vol. 3, ed. Hattori Shirō, Nakasone Seizen, and Hokama Shuzen, 323–356. Tokyo: Heibonsha.

Naha Shuppansha Henshūbu, comp. 1992. *Ryūkyū geinō jiten bessatsu: Ryūkyū geinō jitsuenka sōran* (Dictionary of the Ryūkyūan Performing Arts—Supplement: Comprehensive List of Ryūkyūan Performing Arts Practitioners). Naha: Naha Shuppansha.

Nakagusuku Castle Site Cooperative Management and Consultation Committee, n.d. "Restoration of the Gosamaru Legacy at Nakagusuku Castle," <www4.ocn. ne.jp/~knaka/ncastle/ncastlee3.html>, accessed 19 April 2004.

Origuchi Shinobu. 1929. "*Kumi odori* izen" (Before the *Kumi odori*). In Ihwa Huyū. *Ryūkyū gikyokyushū* (Collection of Okinawan Plays), 1–23.

Ōta Chōbin. 1974. "*Kumi odori* 'Shūshin Kani'iri.'" In *Ihwa Huyū zenshū* (Complete Works of Ihwa Huyū), vol. 3, ed. Hattori Shirō, Nakasone Seizen, and Hokama Shuzen, 379–380. Tokyo: Heibonsha.

Ōura Miyo. 1974. "Characteristics of Ethnic Dances of Okinawa." *Joshi taiiku* [Women's Physical Education] 16 (2): 11–19.

Ryuku Geino: The Legacy of Kin Ryosho. 2008. *The Performing Arts of Ryūkyūs as Presented by Jimpu Kai USA Kin Ryosho Ryukyu Geino Kenyusho, Hawaii Shibu*, ed. Trisha Aragaki and Charlene Gima. Honolulu.

Sakamaki Shunzō, ed. 1964. *Okinawan Names*. Honolulu: East-West Center Press.

Shimabukuro Seibin and Onaga Toshio. 1968. *Ryūka zenshū* (Complete Collection of Classical Ryūkyūan Poems). Tokyo: Musashino Shoin.

Sorgenfrei, Carol. 2004. Personal communication with Kathy Foley, 10 April.

Thornbury, Barbara E. 1999. "National Treasure/National Theatre: The Interesting Case of Okinawan *Kumi odori* Musical Dance-Drama." *Asian Theatre Journal* 16 (2): 230–247.

Tōma Ichirō. 1986. "Kumi odori no seiritsu" (Development of *Kumi odori*). In Nihon minzoku kenkyū taikei (Japanese Folk Studies Series), vol. 6: *geinō denshō* (Performing Arts Transmission), comp. Nihon Minzoku Kenkyū Taikei Henshū Iinkai, 265–282. Tokyo: Kokugakuin Daigaku.

Yokomichi Mario and Omote Akira, eds. 1963. *Yōkyokushū—ge* (Collection of *Nō* Plays, Part Two). Nihon koten bungaku taikei, vol. 41. Tokyo: Iwanami Shoten.

Yonaha Shōko. 2003. "Okinawan Drama; Its Ethnicity and Identity under Assimilation to Japan," <www.geocities.co.jp/Hollywood-Screen/9455/eng08.html>, accessed 19 April 2004.

Possessed by Love, Thwarted by the Bell

Written around 1719 by Tamagusuku Chōkun, Shūshin Kani'iri (Possessed by Love, Thwarted by the Bell) *is one of the earliest* kumi odori *and continues to be one of the most frequently performed. For the 250 years following the development of* kumi odori, *the most important performances were in the context of* ukwanshin, *entertainments for the official envoys sent to the Ryūkyū Kingdom by the Chinese emperor. With the demise of the Ryūkyūan court in 1879, the genre languished until it was designated as an important cultural asset by the Japanese government in 1972. This translation of a version of* Shūshin Kani'iri *includes stage directions and choreography based on the practice of Kin Ryōshō, an important twentieth-century master of the traditional form.*

Cast of Characters

WAKAMATSI, a young aristocrat
WOMAN, a village girl
DEMON
CHIEF PRIEST
FIRST NOVICE
SECOND NOVICE
THIRD NOVICE

Wakamatsi's Travel Song: "Chin Bushi"[1]

The SINGER, *who plays the* sanshin, *is accompanied by flute* [hansō] *and drum* [kodaiko]. *He expresses* WAKAMATSI's *thoughts as the character enters from upstage right in the slow, stylized walk of classical dance.* WAKAMATSI *wears a salmon pink* bingata *kimono that is pulled up, revealing his red leggings and tabi. The short stick he carries and the wicker hat* [hana amigasa] *signify that he is on a journey.*

SINGER	Even when the shining sunlight in the west
	has become slanted to the length of a cloth,[2]
	I am going alone, to Shuri
	because of court service.

Wakamatsi moves a few steps in one direction, turns and tries another. Finally halting in confusion, he faces the audience and introduces himself, his voice rising and falling in the gentle chant of wagin *delivery.*

WAKAMATSI	I am Wakamatsi of Nakagusiku.
	As I must serve at the court
	I am going up to Shuri.
	In the dark night of the twentieth of the month
	I have lost my way.
	The mountain paths are especially
	heavy with dew.

He looks at his sleeve, indicating weariness, then glances toward his right.

	Toward the light at the edge of that village
	I shall go, and there ask
	for a night's lodging.

He moves upstage right and halts, facing the wings.

	Is someone in this house?
	May I ask for your assistance?
	The day set while I was traveling,
	and I have lost my way.
	Have pity on me
	and let me stay this night.

WOMAN	[*Offstage*] Who is this that wants to have lodging
	so late in the evening?
	Because my parents are away,
	I cannot do such a thing on my own.

WAKAMATSI	In this world even the dew borrows
	its lodging on a flower.
	Please have mercy on me
	and provide me with lodging.

WOMAN	If I let someone stay for the night
	while my parents are out,
	it will become known to others
	and rumors may arise.

WAKAMATSI	When you have said your parents are away
	and you cannot act on your own,
	it is hard for me to repeat my request.

Tamagusuku . *Possessed by Love*   99

But I am Wakamatsi of Nakagusiku.
As I have service at the court,
I am going up to Shuri.
In the dark night of the twentieth day,
I cannot see the way to the capital,
I do not know the way to return.
So I have been at a loss.
Please have pity
and let me stay overnight.

Song: *"Hwishi Bushi"*[3]

The SINGER *accompanied only by his* sanshin *sings the* WOMAN'*s thoughts as she enters from upstage right and circles behind* WAKAMATSI. *She pauses and moves the lamp back so that she can see his face more clearly, then circles behind to survey him from the other side. Her pink* bingata *kimono is untied since she is at home and reveals her red and pink half-kimono, white skirt, and red* tabi *that she wears underneath.*

SINGER   Now that I realize it is you
why should I refuse your request for lodging?
Through the long winter's night
let us have conversation.

As she turns away WAKAMATSI *moves and both kneel on the floor. As she puts down her lamp, he places his traveling hat and stick carefully on the floor.*

WAKAMATSI   In the dark night of the twentieth,
I was lost.
At your merciful house
I shall rest awhile.

WAKAMATSI *lies down. The* WOMAN *gazes at him intently, then blows out the lamp. As she speaks, she moves to the sleeping boy, kneels, and waves her hand gently above him to awaken him.*

WOMAN   This is indeed a rare meeting.
Wake up, wake up, dear one.
I wish to talk with you
if only for a moment longer.

She returns to her place as WAKAMATSI, *startled, kneels up.*

WAKAMATSI   Tonight is our first encounter.
I do not think there is anything to talk about.

WOMAN   A meeting by previous arrangement would,

She raises her hand and looks toward her sleeve clasped in her other hand.

of course, signify a bond between people.
But even our encounter,
which is like a touching of sleeves by chance,
perhaps signifies the bond between us.

WAKAMATSI   I do not know such things as bonds.
Nor do I know the ways of love.
I am only waiting
for the white clouds of dawn.

He turns away from her.

WOMAN   As a mountain warbler in spring
seeks flowers and sucks their nectar,
so is the custom between a man and a woman.
Do you not know it?

WAKAMATSI   I don't know!

Agitated, he sharply cuts off her last phrase and snaps his head toward her.

WOMAN   Even if one is born a man,
if one does not know love,
he is like a jeweled cup
without a bottom.[4]

WAKAMATSI   [*Regaining his composure, he returns to his normal chant.*]
If one is born a man,[5]
unless he holds reason and intellect as his standards,
he will indeed create chaos
in society.

Song: "Hwishi Bushi"

The WOMAN *and* WAKAMATSI *sit motionless with bowed heads as the* sanshin
player sings the WOMAN's *disappointment.*

SINGER   If I had known from before
that my loved one was unattainable,
why would I have tied my sleeve
to an ill-fated love?

WAKAMATSI   I do not care if you tried
to tie my sleeve to an ill-fated love.
As for myself, I have the court service
and I am going to Shuri.

He stands and starts to leave.

Song: "Hwishi Bushi"

SINGER   We are now tied in an ill-fated love.
How can I ever let it go?
If he leaves me,
there is only one way left to take,
to die together.

The WOMAN's *head rises; seeing that* WAKAMATSI *is going, she rushes to him and reaches for his shoulder. With a sweeping motion, he throws off her arm. She falls back, but tries again with the other hand. He casts her off once more, dropping his hat and stick in the process. She recoils, then runs offstage right as he continues his progress, glancing back over his shoulders to show his apprehension. The drum starts to beat almost imperceptibly. As the song ends, the drum builds and* WAKAMATSI *breaks into a run that circles around the stage toward upstage left, where he will seek sanctuary in the monastery. At the same time a large bell is lowered upstage right.*

WAKAMATSI   [*His words pour out breathlessly.*]
Hello! The Reverend Priest!
Please save my life
precarious as the dew.

CHIEF PRIEST   [*Enters from the curtain at upstage left. He wears a purple robe and white* tabi. *A brocade sash with the red of the Shingon sect crosses his chest and he carries a priest's fan and a Buddhist rosary or* ojuzu *of clear glass.*]
At such a late hour of the night
there is a voice of a child.
It is very strange.
I will hasten to hear him.

WAKAMATSI   [*Falls to his knees and clings to the* CHIEF PRIEST's *waist.*]
A woman at a house
where I stopped for the night
would not release the bond
of an ill-fated love.
Finally in desperate passion
she wanted us to die together
and has pursued me
to take my life.
I have come to seek refuge
in this temple in Suyiyushi
with its name of good omen.[6]
Please save my life!

CHIEF PRIEST   Oh, what a perilous lot has fallen on you!
Since she is throwing away life

and concern for shame,
and comes to seek you,
this is no ordinary matter.
Do not think lightly
of a woman's passion for love.
If she has set her heart upon it,
she might even risk a life.
There is no place to hide you.
But it is hard to say no,
because the look in your eyes
makes me feel pity and compassion.

He puts his arms around WAKAMATSI *protectively.*

WAKAMATSI [*His voice returns to the normal* wagin *or soft pattern as he becomes calmer.*]
There is no other place for me to go.
I came here, relying on your goodwill.
Please have mercy and save my life.

CHIEF PRIEST I wish somehow to find a place
to hide your flowerlike face
and to protect your life
precarious as the dew.
There is no other way to take
but to give her the torture of love.

Putting his fan in the back of his collar, he takes WAKAMATSI's *hand and leads him to the bell.*

I will hide you under the Bell of Dawn,
which signals the break of day.
Come now.
Here, go inside the bell.

WAKAMATSI *enters the bell. The* CHIEF PRIEST *lowers it and moves to center stage.*

CHIEF PRIEST I will call the novices
and have them guard him.
Novices! Novices!

NOVICES Here.

The NOVICES *enter immediately from upstage left and wait obediently in a line to hear his order. They wear light-blue kimono and white* tabi *and carry black rosaries.*

CHIEF PRIEST Open your ears
and listen carefully.
If a woman in the flower of youth

comes to seek someone,
you must not carelessly admit her
into this temple, which is closed to all women.
Even if she might happen to
search inside the temple grounds,
carefully guard the vicinity of this bell.
Watch carefully.

He gestures emphatically with his fan as he leaves upstage left.

NOVICES   Yes, Master.

FIRST NOVICE   [*Takes up a crossed-arm position downstage right.*]
What a meddling and annoying priest he is!
But when he goes out of the temple,
it will be pleasant to talk
about the things of the world with that young man.

SECOND NOVICE   [*Moving downstage, crossing his arms.*]
Such a beautiful boy in the flower of youth
should not be left alone.

THIRD NOVICE   [*Takes up position by the* FIRST NOVICE, *crouching so that he can look up into his face.*]
Only if there is a mutual bond,
will the flower send its fragrance toward that person.

FIRST NOVICE   Oh, what a saucy fellow!

The FIRST NOVICE *hits the* THIRD NOVICE *for his freshness. All move back to guard the bell. The* FIRST NOVICE *and the* SECOND NOVICE *seat themselves cross-legged and cross-armed in front, and the* THIRD NOVICE, *resting his head on his hand, stands behind. The seated ones doze off, and the* THIRD NOVICE, *seeing his chance for revenge, hits the* FIRST NOVICE, *who wakes with a jerk but finds no culprit since the* THIRD NOVICE *has mimed sleep. He nods off again as the* THIRD NOVICE *peeks up and strikes the* SECOND NOVICE, *who looks up in surprise, but sees only his sleeping companions. Delighted, the* THIRD NOVICE *prepares another blow for the* FIRST NOVICE, *but quickly feigns sleep as his victim wakes. As soon as all is quiet again, the* THIRD NOVICE *grabs the heads of the other two and bashes them together. His comrades turn to repay his blows, but are interrupted by the entrance of the* WOMAN.

Song: "Shichishaku Bushi"[7]

The WOMAN *enters from upstage right as the* SINGER *expresses her emotions. Her kimono is tied with a purple sash and she carries a peony hat [hanagasa] that signifies she is traveling. The three* NOVICES *stand in alarm and extend their arms in front of them to prohibit her entrance.*

WOMAN	In this transitory life ephemeral like the dew,
	rather than being unable to attain my desire,
	I shall seek out my dear one,
	and together we shall leave this world.

| SECOND NOVICE | Women are prohibited here. |
| | Go back, go back! |

Song: "Shichishaku Bushi"

Determined to enter the temple, the WOMAN *waves the* NOVICES *aside with her hat. They regroup and follow her in a line.*

WOMAN	The fence that surrounds and prohibits
	access to my dear one
	is of no account.
	For a butterfly flying to a flower,
	there is no barrier.

As she pauses in emotion, the NOVICES *attempt once more to deter her.*

FIRST NOVICE	It is a time-honored custom that
	women are forbidden to enter temples.
	What has caused you
	to come looking for someone?

WOMAN	I have come to search for my beloved,
	because I have set my heart on him
	who is twice seven years of age.

FIRST NOVICE	The loved one whom you seek
	I have never seen, even in a dream.
	Hurry and go back,
	young woman.

The NOVICES *gesture once more to stop her.*

WOMAN	In this world, even the insects
	have feelings of affection.
	How hateful is a man
	who does not understand such things!

FIRST NOVICE	[*Moving across the stage, he takes up a crossed-arm position down right.*]
	When I hear her reproach,
	I see reason in it.
	Let us pretend that we have not noticed her
	and admit her into the temple.

| SECOND NOVICE | [*He too breaks the line of resistance. He gestures to his shaved head as he speaks of it and assumes a crossed-arm position downstage left.*] |

Even if one has shaved one's head,
if he does not know compassion,
he is like a lifeless stone
or a stick of firewood.

THIRD NOVICE   [*Circling behind, he crouches accusingly by the* FIRST
NOVICE.]
You have forgotten
the orders of the chief priest.
Why do you carelessly admit her
into the temple?

FIRST NOVICE   Oh, what an impertinent fellow!

He drives the THIRD NOVICE *away with a blow.*

THIRD NOVICE   [*Nursing his head, he retreats.*]
Even though they have taken tonsure,
they are being lured by the fragrance
of a woman in the flower of youth.
How amusing!

Gesturing to his shaved head, he circles to the SECOND NOVICE *to make his comment.*

SECOND NOVICE   [*Hitting the* THIRD NOVICE.]
Oh, what an impudent fellow you are!

FIRST NOVICE   This woman is as beautiful
as the cherry blossoms of spring,
or perhaps she is more like
the fragrance of the plum blossoms.

The FIRST NOVICE *and* SECOND NOVICE *point to each other in agreement.*

Song: "San'yama Bushi" [8]

The NOVICES *go behind the* WOMAN, *clasping their hands nervously. As the song of the musician progresses, the* WOMAN *starts to walk slowly, searching the temple grounds. She pauses to show her agitation, then continues as the* NOVICES *follow with crossed arms. Anxious to see her, the* SECOND NOVICE *leans on the shoulders of the* FIRST NOVICE. *As the* THIRD NOVICE *leans on the* SECOND NOVICE *to see over his head, the* FIRST NOVICE *trips under the combined weight and almost hits the* WOMAN. *He turns to the* SECOND NOVICE *and threateningly raises his arm. The* SECOND NOVICE *cringes, then starts to hit the* THIRD NOVICE, *who ducks. The* THIRD NOVICE *turns to strike the fellow behind him, but stops, realizing there is no one there to hit.*

WOMAN   In this life there can be
no fulfillment with my loved one.

I am desperately involved in unrequited love
and I feel as if I am going to die.

The drum starts a low roll expressive of the WOMAN'*s rising passion. The drum
accompanies her movement as she breaks her walk, stamps her foot, and rushes
from one side of the stage to the other. She spins twice, swinging her hat wide, leaps
and lands in a sitting position with her hat in front of her face. Meanwhile the*
NOVICES *huddle together with clasped hands and, keeping their distance, scurry
from one edge of the stage to the other.*

CHIEF PRIEST	[*Entering from upstage left, he helps* WAKAMATSI *from the bell and rushes him off stage left.*] Oh, something terrible has happened. You must get away quickly. Hurry!
WOMAN	[*Removes the hat from her face, which is now covered with red makeup, showing how her passion has consumed her.*] Even now, that suspicious bell!

*She flings her hat at the bell and rushes under. At this point she enters the bell and
becomes a* DEMON *spirit.* 9

CHIEF PRIEST	[*Reenters from upstage left and faces the* NOVICES, *who spread out in a line stage right.*] Well, what happened? What happened?
FIRST NOVICE	The demon, the demon…
CHIEF PRIEST	[*Waving his fan to calm them.*] What is the matter?
SECOND NOVICE	The bell, the bell…
CHIEF PRIEST	What is the matter? What happened?
FIRST NOVICE	Though hard we tried to deny her admission and stop her, we could not stop that woman who came searching for the youth. She looked for him inside the temple, and when she did not find him out of bitter resentment she became possessed by a demon and clung to the bell.
CHIEF PRIEST	There, I have told you so! You have carelessly neglected my orders, and have done such a thing.

What shall we do?
Well.
Since it has already happened,
talking will accomplish nothing.
Let us invoke the power of prayer,
and endeavor to exorcise the evil spirit.
Come now.

NOVICES   Yes, Master.

The CHIEF PRIEST *puts his fan in the back of his collar and goes to the bell as the*
NOVICES *fall into line behind him and, emulating him, clasp their hands and*
kneel. They pray, chanting.

NOVICES   We pray to the five great *vidyarajas* to subdue the evil
          spirits.[10]
          In the east is Trailokyavijaya, the conqueror of the three
          realms,

Drum starts.

          in the south is Kundalin, the ambrosia king,
          in the west is Yamantaka, of awe-inspiring virtues,
          in the north is Vajrayaksa, the thunderbolt guardian,
          and in the center is the Great Holy Acalanatha, the
          Immobile one, the chief of the great kings.
          Pay homage to Samantabhadra, Mahavairocana, and
          the Yaksa kings,
          Who destroy all terror and strengthen the Word.[11]
          He who listens to what I teach will attain to Great
          Wisdom.[12]
          He who knows my Body will attain to Buddhahood in
          this world.

The CHIEF PRIEST *emphasizes the last words of the prayer and continues to repeat*
it in an undertone as the flute enters with its piercing tones. The THIRD NOVICE
quakes fearfully, peering over those in front of him to see what is happening. The
SECOND NOVICE, *too, starts craning to see. The drum builds and the bell rises,*
revealing the DEMON *that hangs from its lip, striking forceful poses. She wears a*
horned hannya *mask and an off-white half-kimono with a silver triangle design*
that represents serpent scales, a white skirt, and red tabi. *A heavy black wig with*
hair askew is on her head, and the bingata *kimono is pulled up.*

The bell lowers and rises once more, and now the DEMON *emerges, stamping her*
feet. The kimono is tied around her waist and she holds the red bell striker in her
hand as if it were a weapon. A dance battle ensues, in which the choreography
physicalizes the power of prayer fighting the fury of the DEMON. *The* CHIEF
PRIEST *and* NOVICES *have risen and the* DEMON *forces them back again and*

again, but each time they push back with prayer. The NOVICES *quake with fear and hide behind the* CHIEF PRIEST. *The* DEMON *quivers and the strain of the battle is visible in her raised arm as the* CHIEF PRIEST *sends her swirling off stage right with the final words of his prayer.*

The CHIEF PRIEST *and* NOVICES *circle and exit stage left, but the curiosity of the* THIRD NOVICE *draws him back. He looks around furtively and, reassured that all is calm, he starts a sigh of relief. The offstage call of the* CHIEF PRIEST, *with an accompanying drumbeat, sends the* THIRD NOVICE *leaping into the air before he rushes off stage left.*

Translation by Nobuko Miyama Ochner with stage directions by Kathy Foley

NOTES

1. A travel song *(michiyuki uta)* is a lyrical description of the travel of the main characters and is sung by the musicians. *Michiyuki* is used not only in *kumi odori* but also in *nō, kabuki,* and the medieval ballad-drama called *kōwaka*. "Chin Bushi" is one of the classical songs contained in the *Kunkun-shii,* the books of music that use a tablature system of notating Okinawan music, invented by Yakabi Chōki in the eighteenth century. There are twenty-four poems that may be sung to this melody, the largest number of which are the travel songs for *kumi odori;* other poems deal with the loneliness of mountain regions, love, the task of gathering sea water to make salt, and so on. The melody and the lyrics are both tinged with gentle sadness and melancholy. See Tōma 1992: 259.

2. The "length of a cloth" (Ok.: *nunu daki;* Jpn.: *nuno dake*) is an epithet to describe the state when the setting sun nears the horizon, signifying the shortness of something (Shimabukuro and Onaga 1968: 32).

3. "Hwishi Bushi" is a melody set to fifty *ryūka* poems, almost all of which express the sadness of love (Shimabukuro and Onaga 1968: 232).

4. "A jeweled cup without a bottom" refers to the following passage from chapter 3 of the medieval Japanese *zuihitsu* (literary miscellany) titled *Tsurezuregusa* (Essays in Idleness; ca. 1330) by Yoshida Kenkō (1283–1350): "A man may excel at everything else, but if he has no taste for lovemaking, one feels something terribly inadequate about him, as if he were a valuable winecup without a bottom." Translation by Donald Keene (1967: 5). See also Ihwa 1974: 57.

5. "If one is born a man…" is an alteration of the Ihwa text in which is given: "If one is born a woman." The change here was made according to the performance tradition of Kin Ryōshō, who was the primary resource person for this text. Both in the Ihwa text and in the Tōma text, which is based on Ihwa's, the term used is "woman." Ihwa explains the passage in this way: "If one is born a woman, unless she has reason and propriety, she is certainly a prostitute." Ihwa's reason for this gloss is that the author borrowed the Japanese term *jigoku* (Ok.: *juguku*), which colloquially meant "prostitute" (Ihwa 1974: 57). However, Tōma Ichirō rejects Ihwa's theory and he suggests that instead of "prostitute" the term means "a horrible state of having

lost one's reason and strayed from normal human morals" (Tōma 1992: 260). Kin Ryōshō contends that an innocent young boy of fourteen would not use such a word as prostitute. According to Kin, the Okinawan term *jiri* (Jpn.: *giri*) has the meaning of *richi* (intellect) and *risei* (reason). In this context, *jiguku* would mean "a terrible disorder in society."

6. The temple name Suyiyushi (Jpn.: Sueyoshi) functions as a "pivot word" in classical poetry. Pivot words have double meaning: one in connection with the words that precede it and another in combination with the words that follow it. One meaning of the phrase is *yuku suyi yushi,* which means "the future will be good"; the other meaning of the phrase is a place name, as in "this temple in Suyiyushi."

7. "Shichishaku Bushi" is also called "Shichiyomi Bushi" (or its variant reading "Nanayumi Bushi") according to the compilers of *Ryūka Zenshū* (Shimabukuro and Onaga 1968: 26). There are sixteen poems set to this melody, most of which sing of young women's single-minded devotion to love, unhappy love, the suffering of love, and the sorrow of parting (Tōma 1992: 261).

8. "San'yama Bushi" is used for poems describing grief at the death of a parent, child, brother, sister, spouse, or other dear one (Tōma 1992: 261). Forty-two poems in *Ryūka Zenshū* are set to this melody (Shimabukuro and Onaga 1968: 30, 139). From the second half of this poem, the woman becomes deranged (Shimabukuro and Onaga 1968).

9. This notation is one of the few original stage directions contained in the Ihwa text (Ihwa 1974: 66).

10. This prayer is of the esoteric Shingon Sect of Buddhism, and it is borrowed from the *nō* play *Dōjōji.* "The five great *vidyarajas*" are called *godaimyōō* in Japanese. They are the five divinities with fierce appearances whose function is to protect Buddhism and Buddhists from harm. These divinities are called upon in the esoteric Buddhist rite of exorcism. Trailokyavijaya is the Sanskrit name of the deity called Gōzanze Myōō in Japanese. Kundalin is the Sanskrit name of the deity called Gundari Myōō in Japanese. Yamantaka is the Sanskrit name of the deity called Daiitoku Myōō in Japanese. Vajrayaksa is the Sanskrit name of the deity called Kongō Yasha Myōō in Japanese. Acalanatha is the Sanskrit name of the deity called Fudō Myōō in Japanese. See Nakamura 1975; *Japanese-English Buddhist Dictionary* 1965; Inagaki 1989; and Ono 1977.

11. The two lines here are a paraphrase of *darani* (Skt.: *dharani*), that is, "that by which something is sustained or kept up." Often regarded as the quintessence of a sutra, the *dharani* is a set of mystic syllables believed to embody mystical power that keeps up the religious life of the reciter (*Japanese-English Buddhist Dictionary* 1965: 44–45). The paraphrase of the *dharani* in this play was provided by the Reverend Fujitani Yoshiaki, the Bishop of Honpa Hongwanji Mission of Hawai'i, in August 1976, for the Japan Studies Institute on the Performing Arts of Okinawa. Samantabhadra (Jpn.: Fugen Bosatsu) is a bodhisattva; Mahavairocana (Jpn.: Dainichi Nyorai) is a manifestation of Buddha; and Yaksa (Jpn.: Yasha) is the term for fierce, angry deities who protect Buddhism.

12. The last two lines of the incantation are in classical Chinese style, with parallel construction. This is also a set phrase in the esoteric Buddhist exorcism used in the *nō* plays, such as *Dōjōji* and *Kurozuka.* See Yokomichi and Omote 1963: 141, 373.

REFERENCES

Ihwa Huyū. 1974. *Ryūkyū gikyokushū* (Collection of Ryūkyūan Plays). In *Ihwa Huyū zenshū* (Complete Works of Ihwa Huyū), vol. 3, ed. Hattori Shirō, Nakasone Seizen, and Hokama Shuzen. Tokyo: Heibonsha.

Inagaki Hisao. 1989. *A Dictionary of Japanese Buddhist Terms: Based on References in Japanese Literature*. Union City, CA: Heian International.

Japanese-English Buddhist Dictionary. 1965. Tokyo: Daitō Shuppan.

Keene, Donald, trans. 1967. *Essays in Idleness*. New York: Columbia University Press.

Nakamura Hajime. 1975. *Bukkyōgo daijiten* (Dictionary of Buddhist Terms). Tokyo: Tōkyō Shoseki.

Ono Kiyohide. 1977. *Shingon mikkyō seiten* (Sacred Writings of Shingon Esoteric Buddhism). Tokyo: Rekishi Toshosha.

Shimabukuro Seibin and Onaga Toshio. 1968. *Ryūka zenshū* (Complete Collection of Classical Ryūkyūan Poems). Tokyo: Musashino Shoin.

Tōma Ichirō, ed. 1992. *Ryūkyū geinō jiten* (Dictionary of the Ryūkyūan Performing Arts). Naha: Naha Shuppansha.

Yokomichi Mario and Omote Akira, eds. 1963. *Yōkyokushū—ge* (Collection of Nō Plays, Part Two). Nihon koten bungaku taikei, vol. 41. Tokyo: Iwanami Shoten.

Mabuigumi

Uta was sitting in the open veranda, gazing at the brilliance of her dew-drenched garden, growing brighter in the morning sun, when the calisthenics music from the radio in the community center nearby began to play. She sneered *humph* and sipped her tea through a chunk of raw sugar in her mouth. For generations the elderly had started the day with a cup of tea before getting to work. But in early April the Senior Citizens' and the Children's Associations had begun encouraging morning calisthenics in front of the community center. They claimed the sessions were good for such things as bringing together children and seniors, and for an "Early to Bed, Early to Rise" campaign. A month after the sessions began, members of the Senior Citizens' Association had begun wearing exercise outfits totally innapropriate for their age, and merrily making their way to calisthenics. Naturally, they urged Uta to join them. No matter how hard they tried, however, she curtly responded, "I won't go," and continued with her morning tea.

At the beginning, the music for calisthenics was blasted through a large loudspeaker on the roof of the community center. Uta had stormed into the center's office to complain about the excessive noise. Kawakami, the chubby, middle-aged president of the Children's Association, had just smiled at her from under his baseball cap and paid no attention to her complaint. So Uta had gone home, retrieved a reaping sickle from under the eaves of her house, and returned to the community center. She then barged through the children exercising in the public square, and started climbing the telephone pole to cut the wire to the loudspeaker. In a panic, Kawakami jumped up quickly and turned the speaker off. Thereafter, the music played from a radio, not through a loudspeaker. Although the noise continued to disrupt Uta's peace in the morning, she compromised out of regard for the children and left the matter at that.

Only children had showed up in the beginning. About a week later, however, five or six older folks started coming. By the end of the second week, children and seniors alike filled the public square. One of the former teachers who had personally encouraged the elderly to participate was Ōshiro, a retired principal on the board of education. On the way home from calisthenics one day, he collapsed in front of his house and passed on to *gusō*, the

Okinawan afterlife. *That's what happens when you don't listen to people*, Uta thought to herself as she stood at the edge of her garden watching the line of cars crawl down the narrow hamlet road toward the crematorium.

She expected Ōshiro's death to bring an end to the calisthenics, and for a while there was a decline in attendance. It wasn't long, however, before even more people were coming, and the sessions were thriving. She could understand why her fellow seniors would want to be around young children, who reminded them of their grandchildren. Like her, half of the elderly participants lived alone and therefore enjoyed the company. Nevertheless, she continued her boycott.

The music for the calisthenics radio program was just changing to the second set when Uta's neighbor, Fumi, came rushing through the entrance in the stone fence surrounding Uta's home. Going around an old pile of stones that was the *hinpun*—a barrier to keep out bad spirits—Fumi cried out, "Big Sister!" and grabbed Uta.

Surprised to see Fumi on the verge of tears, Uta asked her, "What in the world's the matter, this early in the morning?!"

"Big Sister, please, I need you to come to my house."

"Okay, okay. Wait until I at least have another cup of tea," Uta replied, and began pouring.

Fumi grabbed Uta's hand and began dragging her off the veranda. "What are you doing? I haven't even put on my slippers yet," Uta protested.

As Uta scrambled to put on her yellow rubber sandals, Fumi held her harder by the wrist and started off down the street, kicking up white sand as she went. Fumi's house was less than twenty meters away, and they arrived before they could exchange another word. Fumi went first through the front door, pulling Uta behind her and into the inner part of the house.

"Grandma!" In front of the closed door to the back room, Kentarō and Tomoko sat looking anxiously at Uta. The brother and sister were in elementary school, in third and first grade, and Uta loved them as if they were her own grandchildren. When she saw the looks on their faces, Uta became serious. Fumi let go then and slowly opened the door.

The sliding shutters were closed and a fluorescent light dimly illuminated the space. In the middle of the four-and-a-half-mat room lay Kōtarō, snoring lightly, a terry-cloth blanket over his abdomen.

"Did he have a stroke?"

Fumi silently shook her head. Uta sat down next to Kōtarō's head and placed her hand on his forehead. Temperature and pulse were normal. Although there was a little sweat on his brow, the expression on his sleeping face was peaceful, and nothing seemed to be out of the ordinary.

"What is it? What's wrong?"

Fumi sat silently, her eyes filling with tears. Uta was becoming annoyed. As she looked at Kōtarō's peacefully sleeping face, Uta silently cursed

Fumi, thinking how helpless she was for someone in her forties with two children, and especially considering how proud she was that her ancestors had been members of the Shuri privileged class. Kōtarō's hair was thinning noticeably for someone in his early fifties, yet the ruddy complexion of his face was good health itself.

Just yesterday, Kōtarō had brought Uta some freshly caught *gurukun* and spoken with her for close to an hour. Kōtarō, a farmer-fisherman, had lost his parents in the war when he was an infant, and been raised by his grandmother, Kamadā. Living next door, Uta had always treated him with affection. She had no children, and her husband, Seiei, had disappeared during the war. For all those years she had lived alone, and she thought of Kōtarō as her own child. Kōtarō, sensing this, thought dearly of Uta and returned her affection.

Uta rubbed his cheek as she looked him over, thinking to herself, *He's lost his* mabui *again, hasn't he?* As a toddler, Kōtarō had often lost his spirit. He would be startled or overwhelmed with fright by the slightest thing. And when his spirit fled his body, he would lapse into a kind of listlessness. This would happen five or six times a year. It might happen when he had fallen from a tree or nearly drowned in the ocean. Either Kamadā or Uta would have to perform a *mabuigumi* to return his spirit to his body. After he reached adulthood, it happened less frequently. But even so, every two or three years Kōtarō would lose his *mabui* and Uta would be called.

"It looks like Kōtarō's lost his *mabui* again," she said to Fumi while lightly shaking her head. *So don't make such a big fuss out of nothing*, she thought. Right when she was about to say "I wonder what caused it," she realized that something black was sticking out of Kōtarō's nostrils. At first she thought it might be nose hair, but then it jerked in all of a sudden. Next, it poked out from between his lips about three centimeters, making small probing movements toward his cheek and jaw, as if searching for something. As Uta looked on in astonishment, two eyes the shape of matchstick heads jutted out of Kōtarō's mouth. A purplish-gray claw wrenched open his mouth, and a large *āman*, a hermit crab, about the size of an adult's fist, popped out. Startled by the sight, Uta reacted without thinking. Trembling, she grabbed a nearby fly swatter and swung it with all her might. The *āman* moved like lightning. By the time the swatter snapped against Kōtarō's face, it had already dived back into his mouth. He stopped snoring, and the skin around his nose and jaw turned red in a mesh-net pattern.

"Big Sister!" Fumi called out to her.

When their eyes met, Fumi bowed her face to the floor and wept bitterly. Uta let her cry for about five minutes and then asked her to describe what had happened.

Kōtarō was rather fond of liquor and playing the *sanshin*. After warming up with a few drinks during supper, he would frequently go down to the seashore by himself to play his *sanshin* and sing Okinawan folk songs.

Because he was the *utasā,* the singer, for the Eisā Bon Festival and the village dance that took place once every four years, many of the villagers looked forward to hearing his sweet voice floating into their hamlet through the *mokumaō* grove.

Kōtarō had gone down to the shore to sing the night before. When Fumi heard the music stop, sometime after ten o'clock, she went out to the beach to get him. As usual he had fallen into a comfortable, inebriated slumber. Fumi had hoisted her slender husband—who weighed only half the typical man—on her back and carried him home. She had put him to bed in the back room, which they used as a bedroom, and although she had slept next to him, it wasn't until the following morning that she realized something was wrong.

When she woke up, she had glanced over at him and had seen a black lump perched on his mouth. Still drowsy, she couldn't quite make out what it was, even though sunlight was coming through the slits in the sliding shutters. She had sat up, rubbed the sleep from her eyes, and taken a good look. Two tiny eyes, the shape of matchstick heads, had met her gaze. Fumi had frozen for a moment, then leapt backward in alarm. She kept backing away, her bottom sliding on the floor, until she bumped into a pillar. She had clung to it, risen to her feet, and rushed to open the shutters. Exposed to a shaft of light sparkling through the dusty air, the *āman* had disappeared into Kōtarō's mouth. But before long, it had appeared again, waving its feelers.

"This is terrible!" she cried. Fumi had gingerly reached out for the light cord dangling directly over her husband and pulled. The *āman* had held its two pincers over its eyes as if to shade them, and looked at Fumi. Afraid it might run loose, she had quietly moved along the wall to the door and then dashed from the room, straight to Uta's house.

While Uta was listening to Fumi struggle through tears to tell the story, she watched the *āman*. Its feelers were constantly moving, and its claw hovered over Kōtarō's lower jaw. The creature seemed to be some kind of hermit crab, but was two or three times larger than the common *āman* that could be seen dragging their spiral-shaped African turban shells through *adan* thickets and fields near the seashore. The common *āman* were no bigger than a child's fist, and their thick claws were just strong enough to snap a pair of disposable chopsticks. Surely, she reasoned, with such a large body, this one must have had a hard time finding a big enough shell. Even so, to force itself into a person's mouth seemed rather brazen.

"Come now, you're an adult. Don't cry. You've got two kids, you have to be strong," Uta said, taking a flannel handkerchief out of her pocket and handing it to Fumi. "Thing is, Kōtarō has lost his *mabui*. Since he couldn't protect himself, that *āman* was able to climb into his mouth. Don't worry, though. When his *mabui* returns to his body, the *āman* will leave right away. It won't be long before I bring his *mabui* back, so just hang in there." As she said this, Uta began to remove Kōtarō's T-shirt. Fumi nervously helped her while keeping one eye on the *āman* as it scurried back into Kōtarō's mouth.

The *mabuigumi* ritual, which had long been passed down in the village, wasn't very complicated. First, the priestess performing the *mabuigumi* goes to the place where the *mabui* fell out, taking with her a piece of clothing the person had been wearing when it happened. After offering prayers and placing three small stones in the clothing, the priestess brings the bundle back home, offers another prayer, and puts the afflicted person's clothing back on. Then, the "lost" *mabui* would return to its original body, and the exhausted and dazed person would regain his or her vitality.

Uta removed Kōtarō's pale-blue T-shirt, which reeked of sweat and was stained with fish blood and soil. She carefully folded it, put it under her arm, and stood up. She confirmed with Fumi where Kōtarō had been sleeping on the beach and left the room. Sitting by the entrance, hugging their knees to their chests, were Kentarō and Tomoko. Uta patted the two on the head and gave them a reassuring smile, then urged Fumi to make their breakfast and send them off to school.

Uta went straight home after leaving Fumi's house. In her kitchen she gathered up the items she would use as an offering—*sake*, rice, and a tray—and bundled them up in a square cloth. She boiled more water for tea, and placed some as an offering on the family Buddhist altar. She then lit and placed incense on the altar, put her hands together in prayer, and drank two cups of tea. After feeding the chickens and the goat, she grabbed her cloth-wrapped bundle and headed for the beach.

The narrow road between the *fukugi* trees and the stone fence was covered with white sand. It led to a grove of *mokumaō* growing along the seashore for about a hundred meters and acting as tidewater control. Between the tree trunks she could see an ocean so blue that it looked as if it had just been born that morning. When Uta reached the grove, with its abundance of noisily chirring cicadas, she turned towards the sea. Stepping out from under the shade of the trees, she brought her hands together. She walked on the dazzling white sand until she came to an *adan* thicket just beyond the end of the *mokumaō* grove. In front of the thicket grew a lone *hamasūki* tree, its branches graceful as those of an old pine tree. Its swaying leaves were shaped like rabbit ears and felt like velvet. The shade of the *hamasūki* was just right for an afternoon nap, and Kōtarō frequently sat under the tree and played his *sanshin*.

As Uta approached, she saw a solitary figure sitting in the shade, wearing a pale-blue T-shirt. As she stared at his profile she thought, *It just might be him!* When she got closer, she saw that indeed it was Kōtarō's *mabui*. She sat down next to it, sighed deeply, and let the breeze blow in through her collar.

Though the ritual was called *mabuigumi*, it was usually nothing more than a few words of reassurance to ease someone's anxiety. In most cases, the words were spoken as a charm to restore a child's vigor after he or she was startled or tired out. Every once in a while, however, older persons lost or became detached from their *mabui*. This time, she suspected a serious detachment had occured, considering that an *āman* had entered Kōtarō's body. She was nervous. It had been a while since she had last seen a *mabui*, and besides, this one belonged to Kōtarō.

Kōtarō's *mabui* was gazing at the ocean with a blank expression. His face was suntanned from working out at sea and in the field, and his close-trimmed hair and stubby beard were streaked with gray. He had drawn his knees to his chest, and his arms hugged his legs. Unlike Kōtarō, who typically wore a perpetual smile and had a pleasant demeanor, the *mabui* looked sad.

Uta gazed out over the ocean with Kōtarō for a while. She didn't see anything unusual, just the dazzling white of sunlight on the sea.

"Hey, Kōtarō. Fumi, Kentarō, and Tomoko are all worried about you. Hurry up and come home already."

Though she called out to Kōtarō this way, he didn't respond. She spread out the square cloth she had prepared, put a small helping of rice on the tray, and filled the *sake* cup with *awamori*. With a disposable lighter, she lit some sticks of incense, stood them upright in the sand, and sat erect. Bringing her hands together and staring intently at Kōtarō's profile, Uta intoned a prayer in a faint, murmuring voice.

Channēru riyū no ari shika wa wakaranu shiga, Kōtarō no mabui no ochite yā ninju no shiwashiteoru kuto, mura no kamigami nkai taisuru uyamē, ugwansu ni taisuru achikēde susō no aibiraba, sugu ni nōsu kuto, datin, Kōtarō no mabui wo mudushite kimi sōre…

I don't know why, but Kōtarō has lost his *mabui,* and his entire family is worried. If there are oversights in our reverence for the village gods or treatment of the ancestors, we'll correct them immediately, so please return Kōtarō's *mabui* to his body…

Repeating these words over and over again, Uta prayed to the gods of the *utaki* and the ancestral spirits everywhere watching over the village. When she finished, she hung the T-shirt over the shoulder of Kōtarō's *mabui* and tried to get him to stand. But the *mabui* refused to budge. When she reached out, all she felt was a faint sensation in her fingertips, as if she were touching water. Uta had performed *mabuigumi* hundreds of times, and until now all of the *mabui* had obediently listened and, for the most part, done as she asked. She was bewildered; Kōtarō's *mabui* made no attempt to move, and just remained as before, gazing at the sea.

"Is there something out in the ocean?" She squinted and looked again, but nothing seemed out of the ordinary. For an hour or so, Uta continued trying to persuade the *mabui* to return to Kōtarō's body. When nothing changed, she became exhausted and plopped down onto the sand. As she studied the side of his face, Kōtarō's *mabui* faded in and out with the sunlight filtering through the leaves. From behind her, someone called out, "Big Sister!" Standing there were Fumi and the ward chief, Shinzato Fumiaki.

"How's the *mabuigumi* going?" Fumi asked uneasily.

Look, his mabui *is sitting right there in front of you,* Uta was about to respond. Then, realizing that the two of them couldn't see it, she just shook her head in silence.

"It's not going well, is it?"

"No need to get alarmed. Kōtarō's *mabui* seems to have strayed from his body, but it'll come back soon," Uta responded, irritated with Fumi. She then looked at Ward Chief Shinzato.

Shinzato was in his second term in office. Three years ago, he had become the chief of the ward, right after retiring from his position at town hall. When he had gotten into mischief as a child, Uta had often given him a licking. To this day, he had a hard time looking her in the eye.

"Big Sister Uta, it's pretty serious, isn't it?" Shinzato crouched down to be in the shade of the tree and wiped his face with the towel hanging around his neck. "I just had a look at Kōtarō, and well, what in the world is that thing?"

"An *āman.*"

"That much I can tell. What's an *āman* doing in Kōtarō's mouth?"

"How am I supposed to know? All I know is that when Elder Sister Gujī was *nīgami* high priestess long ago, she once said that bad things can happen to you if you lose your *mabui* and your body grows weak. That's what's happening to Kōtarō, and why I was just praying for his *mabui* to return to his body."

Shinzato muttered an ambiguous *hummmh* as Uta turned her back to him and Fumi. In a low voice she again urged Kōtarō's *mabui* to hurry back to his body. Even though Fumi had come, nothing changed. Kōtarō's *mabui* didn't even seem to be aware that the three of them were standing right there. It continued staring off into the ocean, making no sign of moving. Unable to do anything for the moment, Uta folded up the T-shirt and tidied up the liquor and the tray. "I'll try again later," she said, indicating to Fumi and Shinzato that they should leave with her for the time being.

After returning to Kōtarō's house, Uta and Shinzato went to the back room and sat on either side of Kōtarō. Fumi brought out breakfast, but with the *āman* popping in and out of Kōtarō's mouth, right before her eyes, Uta had lost her appetite and could barely touch the food. Shinzato, however, had already eaten three extra helpings of rice. As he picked up a piece of broiled fish with his chopsticks, Shinzato carelessly held it out near Kōtarō's face. Quick as lightning, the *āman* snatched the fish with its pincers and drew back into Kōtarō's mouth.

"You careless fool, what do you think you're doing?!" Uta whacked Shinzato on the head with the fly swatter, and he apologized profusely. The room was unbearably hot, even with the electric fan on. Seeing that Kōtarō was incapacitated for the foreseeable future, Uta understood why Fumi needed to make arrangements with the ward chief for assistance. Deep down, however, she was disappointed that Fumi hadn't waited until she had finished the *mabuigumi*. After Fumi had cleaned up the dishes, she returned to the back room. Shinzato then brought up the subject of his assistance.

He began by insisting that the incident be kept a secret, within a very small circle, and that it absolutely had to be kept from people in other villages. Since the ailment was not something doctors handled anyway, they would also keep it a secret from the Ōshiro Clinic, and work to help Uta succeed with the *mabuigumi*. Shinzato said that he would take responsibility for looking after Fumi and the kids until Kōtarō recovered. Fumi expressed her gratitude repeatedly, bowing over and over. "When things get rough, we stand together," Shinzato said with a sheepish grin. Though Uta was feeling repulsed by Shinzato, she went along with his suggestion.

Shinzato had decided to hold a meeting later in the evening, so he departed to round up the top three officers of the Senior Citizens' Association, the president of the Men's Association, and other prominent members of the community. Uta consoled Fumi for a while, then she also left and returned home. Though Kōtarō's lost *mabui* weighed heavily on her mind, Uta lived alone and had several things she had to take care of every day, such as working in the field and looking after the goat.

In the afternoon, after doing fieldwork and having lunch, she rested for about two hours before cutting grass for the goat. It was a little past five o'clock by the time she was able to go back out to the beach. Kōtarō's *mabui* was still sitting in the same place and in the same position as before. As the sunlight softened, a faint glow enveloped the sea. A white moon floated beside a towering thundercloud on the horizon.

"Hurry up and come home." Uta repeated these words once more in a soft voice. She even placed herself directly in front of the *mabui*, bringing her hands together in prayer. Still, it made no reply. She gave a sigh of despair. It felt as if the Kōtarō who had always called out to her upon seeing her from afar, and had treated her like his own mother, had somehow forgotten who she was. For half an hour or so, until Fumi came to get her, Uta sat silently and intently gazing at Kōtarō's profile and the ocean. She scooped up the sand and let it spill from the palms of her prayerful hands.

When Uta arrived at the community center, the presidents of the Senior Citizens' Association, the Men's Association, the Young Adults' Association, and the Women's Association were waiting for her in the tatami-floored room next to the office. It was apparent that Ward Chief Shinzato and the men had already opened several cans of beer. As they stuffed their mouths with the rice balls and sashimi that had been set out, the men were talking about the village council election to be held in three months. There was a rumor that Furugen Sōsuke, president of the Men's Association, was going to be a candidate. At the sight of Furugen tapping Kinjō Hiroshi—the president of the Young Adults' Association—on the shoulder and offering him a beer, Uta grew irritated. The atmosphere of the meeting seemed inappropriate considering Kōtarō's condition.

"Furugen, you counting your votes already?" she asked sarcastically. As she sat down, an awkward smile floated across Furugen's face, confirming his guilt.

"Not at all, Big Sister, not at all." He was about to pour soy sauce into a small plate for Uta, but she brushed his hand aside and poured it herself. Matayoshi Tsuru, the president of the Women's Association, held out a pair of chopsticks for Uta as she bowed to her.

When Shinzato saw Uta put her chopsticks down after placing two pieces of sashimi in her mouth, he addressed the group. Shinzato didn't waste any time getting to the point. Apparently, everyone had gone to see Kōtarō before coming to the community center. While Uta was surprised at how well informed everyone was, she also had a bad feeling.

"In any case, what I'm most concerned about is how this matter might affect the hotel construction plans by the company from mainland Japan," Shinzato said.

Uta was shocked. This was rather different from what he had told her earlier.

"After all, we're dealing with Yamato people, from mainland Japan, you know. And if they hear rumors about an *āman* entering someone's body— why, this would really alarm them! It might even spook them into canceling the plans for the hotel. And with other areas in Okinawa trying to attract hotel construction and investment, if word gets out about Kōtarō, then rumors will start spreading about our village. People will get the impression that strange things will crawl into your body if you stay here overnight. And as you all know, Yamato people get nervous about things like this, not to mention that most of them are prejudiced against Okinawa. So as you see, our bid for the hotel that we worked so hard for could go to ruin. And that's why, in this case, I feel we absolutely have to keep Kōtarō's condition a secret."

"Is that all the sashimi we have?" demanded Shimabukuro Genpachi, president of the Senior Citizens' Association, hardly waiting for Shinzato to end his speech.

"Okay, okay, I'll bring some more out right now," Kadena Miyoko— who worked in the community center office—replied in a cheerful voice. She promptly brought out a tray of sashimi and a half-liter bottle of *awamori*. Although she was only twenty-five years old, Miyoko had already been divorced twice and had three children. She had a carefree personality, though, and had always assisted Uta enthusiastically with religious rites and rituals. Consequently, Uta was rather fond of her. After Miyoko had filled the women's cups with tea and returned to the office, Shinzato again asked for everyone's cooperation.

"On the other hand, Ward Chief...," said Kinjō, president of the Young Adults' Association, as he raised his hand. Apparently not expecting any resistance in the matter, Shinzato looked displeased. "On the contrary," Kinjō continued, "don't you think it might generate good publicity if word gets out there's a person here with an *āman* stuck in his mouth? I'm betting just about everyone would want to see something as strange as that. If it hits the newspapers and makes the TV news, my guess is people will be coming to our village in droves."

Shinzato looked like he was about to say something to get things back under control, when Uta shouted at Kinjō, "You rotten little brat! What're you trying to do—turn Kōtarō into a freak show?"

Kinjō half rose to his feet, ready to bolt away from Uta, who, from the fury in her face, looked as if she was about to leap over the table to get her hands on him.

"Big Sister Uta, please try to calm down. This youngster doesn't know what he's saying." In a flurry of confusion, Shinzato and Furugen did their best to restrain her.

"For the president of the Young Adults' Association, you sure don't understand how people feel. You can't just go spouting off as you please." Uta struck the table with her hand and sat down. Fumi, sitting next to her, hung her head, her shoulders trembling. Tsuru, the Women's Association president, placed her hand on Fumi's shoulder and glared at the men.

After watching both Shinzato and Furugen apologize, Genpachi finished off his cup of *awamori* and barked, "What is this? Giving in to the women like that. How pathetic!"

"*You, keep quiet already!*" roared Uta, causing Genpachi to fall silent immediately.

Despite the quarrel, in the end everyone agreed to go along with Shinzato's suggestion. Until Uta finished the *mabuigumi* and the *āman* left Kōtarō's body, everyone was supposed to keep the situation a strict secret, not discuss it with anyone outside of the group, help Fumi with the kids, and for the time being stick to the story that Kōtarō had gone to a relative's house in Naha to take care of a family matter.

While the men continued to drink and party at the community center, Uta left and walked Fumi home. Then she went back to the seashore alone. By the light of the white, budlike moon, she had no trouble seeing her way without a flashlight. She listened to the sound of the waves breaking on shore, and felt the velvety sand give way beneath her feet as she walked to the *hamasūki* tree. In the faint blue shadows, Kōtarō's *mabui* was staring at the sea. Uta sat down next to it and looked out at the ocean, watching the moonlight flicker on the surface of the water.

In her youth, she and the other young people used to gather on the beach in the evenings and stay out late moon-gazing, drinking liquor, and singing to the accompaniment of the *sanshin*. They would sing songs to each other while everyone listened closely, passing on the best lyrics. Those who sang with feeling and sentiment were swooned over by everyone. It was during the many evenings spent in this fashion that she and Seiei had become acquainted. It was also the way Kōtarō's parents, Omito and Yūkichi, had first fallen in love.

Uta thought she could hear a *sanshin* accompanied by young voices singing from somewhere on the beach, and she felt an ache in the depths of her heart. She couldn't recall how long it had been since she had last come out to the shore at night by herself. Seiei, Omito, and Yūkichi had all died during the war, leaving her the only one to grow old. As she sat on the beach with these thoughts, she was overcome by a sudden loneliness, and called out to Kōtarō's *mabui*. "What is it that you're gazing at?"

There was no reply. As the moon drifted, concealing itself behind a cloud, and the moonlight grew fainter, Kōtarō's *mabui* seemed to fade.

"Kōtarō, let's go home," she said, and rose to her feet. Though the faint *mabui* continued to stare at the ocean, trembling as if in the gentle breeze, the figure appeared to tilt its head to one side, ever so slightly. The movement may have only been due to the flickering shadows of the swaying leaves, but Uta felt as if she had somehow, even just briefly, gotten through to Kōtarō's *mabui*. She put her hands together in prayer and left the beach.

From then on, Uta performed the *mabuigumi* in the shade of the *hamasūki* four times a day: in the morning right after her tea, around noon after finishing her work in the field, at dusk, and in the evening. Nevertheless, Kōtarō's *mabui* continued to sit motionless and stare out to sea. Uta grew more and more impatient, and by the third or fourth day, with a growing sense of helplessness and frustration, she was having trouble eating properly. She wasn't the only one growing thin. The departure of Kōtarō's *mabui* had left him listless; to make matters worse, his body was withering away because the *āman* was intercepting and consuming the food and the liquids meant for him. While Kōtarō withered, the *āman* grew larger day by day. It had grown so big that now it was nearly as large as the coconut crabs of Miyako and Yaeyama Islands. Whenever it popped out of Kōtarō's mouth, it practically dislocated his jaw. Everyone avoided talking about the *āman* in front of Fumi, but the mere thought of what it might be doing inside of Kōtarō's body made them all shudder.

On the evening of the fifth day, all those who were at the previous meeting gathered again in the back room of Fumi's house and sat around Kōtarō, discussing what to do next. In the middle of the conversation, the *āman* pried open Kōtarō's mouth and lumbered out, revealing its entire body. It got a pincer caught in the tatami mat and tried to free itself, scraping at his quilt with one of its legs, which was over fifteen centimeters long. Kōtarō was lying on his side, and his head fell from the pillow. The *āman* made a grating sound as it bent its grayish-purple leg, and Kōtarō's body twitched ever so slightly right before everyone's dumbfounded eyes. Fumi screamed, Uta lifted up the fly swatter, and the *āman* instantly disappeared into Kōtarō's mouth. Furugen and Kinjō nervously put Kōtarō's head back on the pillow, and for a short while everyone was silent.

"All things considered, wouldn't it be best if we took him to a hospital and had the *āman* surgically removed?" Furugen suggested while trying to gauge Uta's feelings.

"But…" Shinzato stopped in mid-sentence, realizing that next to him Fumi was crying. Everyone was thoroughly exhausted. Genpachi had been gladly watching over Kōtarō during the day, as he was treated to meals and liquor. But finding two other people to keep watch all through the night was proving more and more difficult, especially because the others had their own work to attend to.

While Uta had been busy with the *mabuigumi*, the men had been trying ways to get the *āman* out of Kōtarō's mouth. Using dried squid and cheese as bait, they once had succeeded in hooking a pincer with wire; but the *āman* had snapped through it as if it were nothing. If this had been an ordinary *āman*, they could easily have forced it out by making an opening at the bottom of its shell and poking it with a nail or smoking it out with a lighter. But of course lighting a fire under Kōtarō's rear was out of the question.

Everyone was concerned about Kentarō and Tomoko, too. After getting married, it had taken more than ten years before Fumi and Kōtarō had any children. By the time Kentarō was born, Kōtarō was forty-two years old. This was one reason why Kōtarō was such a loving father and took his two kids down to the beach nearly every day at dusk to play with them. Over the last week, it had been unbearably painful to hear the children repeatedly ask, "When's Daddy gonna get better?" Everyone also felt guilty about making the children lie about their father being in Naha.

On top of that, there was another thing to worry about. A little past noon the day before, two young men with cameras were seen loitering around the village. Apparently one of them was a Yamato mainlander, while the other was supposedly from Naha. When the two visited Ward Chief Shinzato, they at first said they were taking photographs of each village's historical ruins and local events for a news story. By the end of the conversation, however, Shinzato could tell what they were really after—information about Kōtarō and his condition. "It seems that recently somebody has been confined to his bed with some peculiar ailment…," one of them had said.

After that, Shinzato made the two men stand out in the hot sun without inviting them in for tea, and he evaded their question by mentioning that not too long ago a man in the neighboring section of the village had been confined to his bed with a swollen leg. Soon afterwards, the two tried to get more information from senior citizens at the croquet field and children playing in front of the farmers' co-op. At dusk, they even approached Uta, who was busy with her prayers out on the beach. She ignored them, but inwardly she was not so calm. With forced smiles, they went away after she faced the camera and flashed them a fierce look that said "Stop!"

When the issue of who had leaked the story had come up the previous evening, the first person everyone suspected was Kinjō. During the ensuing argument, Kinjō became so upset he said he had had enough and threatened to withdraw from the undertaking. The group managed to calm him down and prevent things from going that far, but the tension had not completely dissipated. In the oppressive silence that enveloped the group, Uta felt an overwhelming helplessness. *If only I had more strength and was able to succeed with the* mabuigumi, *then Kōtarō and everyone who was helping would not have to go through this misery,* she thought. Having completely lost her confidence, she even began to wonder if Kōtarō should have been taken to the hospital from the beginning.

"Let's give it one more day, shall we?" Genpachi suggested, exhaling the smell of liquor with his breath. "In any case, this isn't the kind of thing that will be healed just by going to the hospital, and there's not much else we can do about it anymore. So I say we ask Uta to try the *mabuigumi* for one more day, all right?"

In appreciation of the encouragement, Uta bowed her head.

The following day, Uta didn't bother going to work in the fields. Instead, she spent the entire day on the *mabuigumi*. Usually, sitting in the broiling sun on the hot sand for more than an hour was too much for her, and she would have to return home frequently to recuperate. This day, however, she poured her heart and soul into her prayers, remaining at Kōtarō's side even though Shinzato and Fumi pleaded with her to stop because she was putting her health in danger. Yet, despite her efforts, Kōtarō's *mabui* remained the same, staring at the ocean and showing no sign of change. When the stars began to come out in the cloudless sky, Uta returned to the back room where Kōtarō's body lay. Fumi and Shinzato supported her on either side. Because the sliding shutters had been closed all day, the room smelled sour and was intensely hot. Inside were Tsuru, Furugen, and Kinjō, all sweating profusely. Sitting near the head of the unconscious Kōtarō was an unusually sober Genpachi. Seeing everyone there, Uta got down on her hands and knees and put her head to the floor in apology for the ineffectiveness of her prayers.

"Come now, Big Sister, please lift up your head."

"That's right, Grandma, you didn't do anything wrong."

In a fluster, Tsuru and Shinzato made Uta sit up.

"We know you gave it your all," Genpachi said, with Furugen and Kinjō nodding in agreement.

"Thank you so much," Fumi said, as she knelt down and put her head to the floor. Uta was moved to tears, with a mixed feeling of vexation and unbearable guilt. Kōtarō and Fumi were good, honest people who had actively participated in the village's religious events, always helping her with her duties as priestess. Why did this couple have to meet with such misfortune? For the first time in her life, Uta resented the gods of the *utaki,* who were supposed to protect the village. Meanwhile, Kōtarō's round bulging cheeks and throat stirred restlessly, and two shiny black feelers poked out from his nostrils, assessing the situation. After the feelers drew back in, periscope-like eyestalks about the size of pencils popped out from between his lips. By gently poking Kōtarō's cheek with the fly swatter, Genpachi made the *āman* pull its eyestalks back in. Having kept it company every day, he had become quite used to dealing with it. After confirming that they would contact Ōshiro at the medical clinic the next day, everyone moved into the main living room for dinner and *sake.*

Uta could hardly bring herself to touch the *nakami* soup. She went over to Kentarō and Tomoko, who had been watching TV in the next room, and patted them on the head. In her heart she begged for their forgiveness. Telling Fumi she was going home to bed, Uta left. Worrying about her, Tsuru accompanied her to her house. After Tsuru left, Uta turned and went straight to the beach.

The brightness of the moon was all but drowning out the light of the stars, and the seashore looked as if it were shrouded in a blue haze. Uta removed her rubber slippers, and carrying one in each hand she slowly made her way to the *hamasūki,* treading on sand as soft and warm as the body of a living creature. The flickering shadows of the leaves caused Kōtarō's form to fade in and out, so every now and then Uta could see right through it. Sitting down in the sand, she stared silently at the ocean along with Kōtarō's *mabui.* Sea fireflies glistened at the water's edge. Soon it would be June. Before long it would be the rainy season, and she was worried about what would happen to Kōtarō's *mabui* when the rain came. Even if the *āman* was surgically removed at a hospital, it didn't necessarily mean that his *mabui* would return to his body. Tomorrow and thereafter, she planned to continue as usual with the *mabuigumi.*

Before she knew it, Uta was stretched out in the sand sound asleep. She was awakened by sand pelting her face and what sounded like a deep sigh. She lifted her head to look and noticed that the *mabui* was no longer sitting in the shade of the *hamasūki.* In a panic, she rose to her feet. About five meters away, she saw Kōtarō standing with his back to her. At his feet, something flat and black was tossing sand into the air. Uta drew closer, peered around Kōtarō, and saw a sea turtle over a meter in length. Its shell was covered with sand and countless barnacles. As it dug its hole, the turtle breathed hoarsely, lifting its head every so often. With a solemn expression, Kōtarō watched.

"So this is what you were waiting for." The instant she uttered these words, Uta realized this was the exact spot where she had seen a sea turtle lay its eggs on the night Omito died. Knees trembling, she sat down on her heels, turned towards the turtle, and brought her hands together in prayer.

It had been close to a month after the attacks by American warplanes had burned down most of the houses in the area. The damage to Uta's village was especially heavy because it was close to a Japanese naval base. Those living in other villages had the luxury of being able to return from the safety of the mountains to their undamaged homes and retrieve things necessary for daily survival, such as food, tools, and other supplies. Uta's village, however, had been completely destroyed during the initial air raids. People from her village had to not only escape from the naval bombardment that followed, but also struggle to secure food. They had fled with only the clothes on their backs. In the evenings, Uta and others would leave their cave in the mountains and return to their village to dig up potatoes from the fields, or scavenge *miso* and salt from abandoned houses in neighboring villages. This was how they managed to stave off starvation.

On that fateful night, Uta and Omito went to a field by the ocean. Most of the fields had already been completely dug up, with only barren, infertile ones remaining. In a field sandwiched between an *adan* thicket and a sea cliff, Uta was digging up a small potato about the size of her thumb when Omito tugged at her sleeve. "Soldiers are coming."

The two drew back carefully and hid in the *adan* thicket. They could see the silhouettes of three men walking along in the cover of the cliff, crouched down, their rifles in hand. The women could clearly hear the soldiers breathing and their steel helmets brushing against the tree leaves. With their chins buried in the sand, Uta and Omito held their breath as they watched the Japanese soldiers silently pass by. Accounts had reached Uta's cave that Japanese soldiers had executed the chief of the civil defense unit and the principal of the elementary school in the neighboring settlement on suspicion of spying. Furthermore, people in the cave had also heard stories about a man named Kaneku, from a neighboring village, who, after visiting a house next to the ocean, was taken away by Japanese soldiers on false charges that he had sent signals to U.S. naval ships offshore. He was never seen again. The villagers no longer naively believed that they could rely on "friendly forces" to protect them. So even after the three soldiers were no longer in sight, Uta and Omito didn't dare move.

Unexpectedly from behind them came the sound of sand being scattered, and Uta almost cried out. Lying flat on the ground, with Omito clinging to her thigh, she again heard what sounded like the scattering of sand on patches of grass. Realizing it was not the footsteps of the Japanese soldiers, she quietly brushed off the sand from her sweat-drenched face, and, prompting Omito to follow suit, she shifted her body and looked towards the beach.

There in the moonlight was a sea turtle, digging a hole and tossing sand in the air. Offshore were hundreds of American warships that had been bombarding the island for days. Amazed that it had survived the crossing and come ashore just to lay its eggs, Uta had the feeling that the turtle was somehow not of this world. As she stared at the black mass on the beach and listened to the sound of sand being scattered on *hamahirugao* leaves, Uta had the strange sensation that she was back in the village before the war had started.

For close to an hour, she and Omito lay hiding in the *adan* thicket, flat on their stomachs, bodies overlapping. Uta listened warily as she looked back and forth between the beach and the precipice, searching for any movement by the Japanese soldiers. Omito carefully watched the sea turtle lay its eggs in the moonlit sand. Before long, the turtle had filled the hole and was crawling back to the ocean. After the turtle disappeared into the waves, Uta signaled to Omito that it was time to return to their cave. Omito hesitated, staring at the shore as if she were planning something. Then she looked back and said, "I'm going to gather the eggs." In the next instant, she dashed out of the *adan* thicket. Uta had no time to stop her. Crouching as she ran, Omito finally threw herself on the place where the turtle had been and started digging at the sand with both hands.

"Get back here!" Uta called out to her in a whisper. But Omito ignored her. She was reaching down into the hole, up to her shoulder, scooping the eggs into the bag with the potatoes.

Uta watched, surprised at Omito's boldness and ashamed of herself for not thinking of gathering the eggs. Everyone back in the cave was starving: being without food was particularly hard on the elderly and the children, who were growing weaker and weaker by the day. Even though Uta felt she ought to help Omito dig up the eggs, she couldn't muster up the courage to leave her hiding place. She fretted as she watched, when suddenly a dry noise—like the crackling of bamboo in fire—reverberated across the beach and Omito toppled over sideways. Instinctively, Uta pressed her body and face deeper into the sand. Anticipating machine-gun fire to begin at any moment, she silently uttered Seiei's name and prayed to the gods of the *utaki*. When the echoing sound of the single rifle shot faded, she could again hear the waves and rustling leaves. Uta raised her head and looked toward her friend. Omito remained completely still. She had fallen on her side, her hand at the opening of the bag; Uta could see the bottoms of her two tiny feet. Only her disheveled hair moved, blowing about in the wind.

When tinges of green began to lighten the eastern sky, Uta finally slipped out from the *adan* thicket. Before heading back to her cave, she called to

Omito in a whisper, but the roar of the waves drowned out her voice. She promised she'd come back for her with Seiei and Yūkichi after nightfall. Then Uta started back toward the cave.

It took over thirty minutes, running nonstop, for her to reach the shelter of the cave. It wasn't until she saw the entrance that she began thinking about how to tell Omito's parents and her husband, Yūkichi, what had happened. Uta dashed inside and crouched behind some rocks to catch her breath. The rumbling of waves and sand still echoed in her head, and she was unable to gather her thoughts or find the appropriate words to say. Gasping for breath, she climbed down the slippery rocks, deeper into the cave. Reaching the inner refuge where there were many families, Uta immediately sensed that something had changed. Although the interior was as dark as the depths of the ocean, with only the light of the moon filtering in through the cracks in the rock walls, Uta could tell that there were fewer people huddling together in each family.

"Uta, is that you?" It was the voice of Kamadā, Yūkichi's mother, speaking. A hand appeared from the middle of the darkness and grabbed Uta by the sleeve.

"What happened?" Uta asked, as she took hold of Kamadā's hand. At that moment, crying broke out from behind some rocks. Only the women and children were left in the cave. Japanese soldiers had come and taken all of the men away—Seiei, Yūkichi, and the others, including the elderly. They were never heard from again.

Finished with spawning, the sea turtle buried her eggs, refilled the hole, and packed down the sand with her abdomen. In her movements, the creature looked like a person down on all fours striking the sand with her stomach.

Kōtarō had been sleeping in the cave, unaware that his parents had died. He hadn't yet reached his first birthday. Later, when the war ended and the village was rebuilt, Kamadā raised the infant by herself. Uta—who had had no children with Seiei—helped Kamadā with the child, looking after him as if he were her own. While he was still an infant, whenever Uta held him in her arms she would see the fallen figure of Omito lying on the beach.

After Uta was released from the U.S. military internment camp, she had immediately gone back to the beach, but by then Omito's body was no longer there. Uta never found out where her friend had been laid to rest. Furthermore, she never learned where the men who had been taken away—under suspicion of spying—were buried. All that was left were stories that they had been executed, and the location of their bodies remained a mystery. In time, Uta came to regard the care and affection she gave Kōtarō as her small way of settling accounts with Omito and atoning for her sins. More than anything, for the widowed Uta, watching Kōtarō grow into a man had given meaning to her life.

Uta had the impression that the evening moonlight had not changed for decades, even centuries. She had the feeling that the sea turtle—the one that had just dug its hole and was now returning to the ocean—was either the same one she had seen during the war or one born from that turtle's eggs. The turtle glided into the ocean, and the waves washed away the sand from its shell. Then it bent its neck to look back at the shore. Kōtarō turned toward the ocean and slowly started walking.

"Don't go! Kōtarō, you must not go!" Uta shouted. He paused for a moment and looked at her, then looked back toward the sea turtle, afloat in the ocean, its head bobbing up and down on the rolling waves. As Kōtarō again began walking toward the sea, Uta suddenly had the sensation that this sea turtle was the reincarnation of Omito.

"Hey, Kōtarō! Wait! Wait!"

She tried to grab onto Kōtarō from behind, but his form suddenly flickered and faded, disappearing as if it had been sucked down into the sand. Falling to her hands and knees, Uta ran her hand in circles through the sand where Kōtarō had vanished. Two sea fireflies that had attached themselves to the turtle glowed in the sand. Seized by a premonition, Uta rose to her feet and ran to Fumi's house.

Before she even opened the front door, Uta could hear Fumi weeping. Hurrying inside, she found Genpachi sitting in front of the door to the back room with Kentarō and Tomoko in his lap, stroking their heads. He shook his head slightly. When Uta opened the door, Kinjō was standing by the entrance with a grim expression on his face. He saw her and moved out of the way to let her in. Fumi was crying and clinging to Kōtarō, her arms around his body, as Shinzato and Furugen looked on, their arms folded across their chests. In the back of the room, there were two sullen-faced men sitting by the sliding shutters with their hands tied behind their backs. A small pile of photographic film, pulled out and tangled, lay on the tatami next to a camera.

"These two guys—they suddenly opened the sliding shutters and started taking pictures, and, well, the *āman* was surprised by the camera flash, and in a panic it dove into Kōtarō's mouth and got stuck in his throat, and…," Kinjō explained, all worked up. Uta slowly sat down by Kōtarō's head.

"Big Sister," Fumi said, wrapping her arms around Uta.

Uta gently pushed Fumi away. She removed the white cloth that covered Kōtarō's face and saw that his nostrils were packed with cotton batting. *Perhaps people who lose their* mabui *do not feel any pain, even if choked to death*, she thought, as she looked at Kōtarō's peaceful face. At the sight of his grotesquely swollen throat, however, she found it difficult to breathe. Suppressing the trembling of her hand, she covered his throat and chin with the cloth and stroked his forehead. *Why did you have to die before me?* she thought, as the palms of her hands became cold.

From the time she had held Kōtarō's tiny body in the cave, when he could barely let out a feeble cry, she had never imagined that he might die before her. She knew that no matter how much love and affection she gave to Kōtarō, she could never replace Omito, and yet she did her best. When he was a young child and lost his *mabui*, it always seemed as if Omito was calling to him from the afterworld. Whenever Uta performed a *mabuigumi* for Kōtarō, in her prayers she would say, *I promise to do everything I can for Kōtarō, so please return his* mabui *to his body.* And, as soon as he regained his vigor, she would go right away to Omito's *ihē*, the family mortuary tablet on which Omito's name was inscribed, to offer incense and express her gratitude. As Kōtarō progressed from elementary school to junior high, he grew stronger, and the incidents of *mabui* detachment decreased. After finishing junior high, he went to the mainland to work. About three years later he returned to the village and began helping his grandmother with the farm. When she passed away, he gave himself up to gambling and liquor for a while. But even then, he never neglected his work; he expanded his fields, and even purchased a used boat for fishing at sea. Returning from a day of fishing, he was the spitting image of his father, Yūkichi. Kōtarō was quite pleased when Uta would tell him so. Kōtarō married Fumi and, after turning forty, was finally blessed with children, and he always remarked how at last he had something worth working for.

"Oh, Kōtarō." Fumi's tears fell on Kōtarō's thinly bearded cheek and parched lips. Then suddenly, without warning, the cotton batting stuffed in his nose fell out and two shiny black feelers extended from his nostrils. Kōtarō's lips moved, as if to say something, then contorted into a foolish grin as two purplish, pencil-shaped eyestalks jutted out, peering at Uta. Fumi stopped crying. Everyone stopped breathing and stared at Kōtarō's face. Before they knew it, two large pincers had pried open his mouth, revealing the front half of the *āman*'s body. At that instant, Uta grabbed the creature's left and right pincers with both her hands, braced her foot against Kōtarō's shoulder, and pulled with all her strength, yelling, "This rotten little *āman!*" The *āman* fought back, clinging to Kōtarō's jaw with its claws and snapping its pincers at Uta's fingers to cut them off.

"Hey, what are you all standing around for? Help me with this thing!" Uta shouted. Quickly, Kinjō responded by holding Kōtarō's jaw open, Shinzato and Fumi pressed themselves against Kōtarō's body, and Furugen took hold of Uta by the waist. *"Unehyā!"* he yelled as he pulled. The *āman*'s body creaked. Kinjō pressed down with his left elbow to keep Kōtarō's face from moving, and with his right hand pulled the *āman*'s claws off Kōtarō's jaw, one by one. The instant he removed the fourth leg from Kōtarō's left jaw, the claws grasping the right side tore through Kōtarō's cheek, and the *āman* popped out of Kōtarō's mouth. Uta and Furugen tumbled backwards. The *āman* immediately slashed Uta's hand, then ran towards the sliding doors, dragging its enormous, beetle-like abdomen glistening with slime.

"*Uwā!*" The cameramen, who had been watching in amazement, jumped out of the way of the approaching *āman*, and fell over Uta and Furugen. The *āman* scratched and clawed at the sliding doors. When it realized the doors wouldn't open, it ran along the wall. Shinzato and Fumi screamed, and the *āman* scuttled across Kōtarō's body, escaping to the other side of the room.

"Get out of the way and keep quiet," Uta ordered. She brushed aside the three men who had fallen on her, and chased the *āman* into a corner. Uta raised the empty half-gallon bottle of *awamori* over her head and swung it at the *āman*. The bottle came down with a fierce crash, but the *āman* deflected it with its pincers and escaped completely unscathed.

"Hiroshi, bring me a hoe!" At the sound of Uta's command, Kinjō leapt to his feet and ran out to the shed. Uta lifted the bottle back up to her shoulder and brought it crashing down again. This time the *āman* suffered only a bent feeler. Blood from the wound on her fingers inflicted earlier by the *āman* made her grip on the bottle slippery. The *āman* turned to face her in a defensive stance, holding up its large pincers as a shield; its eyes appeared to mock her.

Trembling with rage and indignation, Uta bellowed, "*Hiroshi, where are you?!*"

"Not ready yet," Shinzato replied in a silly voice as he and Fumi clung to each other. Uta gave him a fierce look, and Shinzato flashed an ingratiating smile. At that moment Kinjō burst through the door. "*Ari*, Big Sister, here!" Kinjō said as he tossed Uta a flat-bladed hoe.

With her right hand Uta threw the bottle at the *āman* and with her left she caught the hoe, spun it halfway around, raised it over her head, and brought it down with a yell: "Die, you scum!"

The blade of the hoe made a clanging *gash'tt* sound as it cut deeply into the tatami. Two or three of the *āman*'s legs were severed by the blow, but the creature managed to skitter towards the door. Fumi, Shinzato, and the cameramen, clinging tightly together in one mass, shrieked as they frantically tried to scramble out of its way.

"Hiroshi, don't let it get away!" Uta shouted.

"*Aaargh!*" Kinjō yelled, swinging a shovel from over his head down onto the *āman*.

"Whoah!" gasped an impressed Genpachi, who was behind the door, watching through a crack. The *āman* had skillfully blocked the first blow of the shovel with its two pincers. Uta didn't let her chance slip away, however. The blade of the hoe came whizzing down again, striking the *āman*'s soft, ham-sized abdomen. With a dull *squish*, liquid squirted out in all directions, and the smell of fish filled the air. The *āman*'s abdomen split in two. But the creature didn't release its hold on the shovel. Uta swung the hoe again, striking the *āman*'s joints and severing the pincers that held the shovel. As the pincers snapped off, Kinjō tumbled over. With its remaining legs, the *āman* dragged its wilting, oily body to the wall, turned around, and looked at Uta.

When she saw the fading gleam in the *āman*'s eyes, pangs of compassion suddenly welled up in her heart.

"Hiroshi, wait!" she yelled, but she was too late. Kinjō's shovel, already in mid-swing, struck the *āman*. The blow smashed the *amān*'s carapace, and a dark-green liquid gushed out. Even then, it was still alive. Uta realized that the creature's two eyes were still staring at her, and she was taken aback by a thought that suddenly flashed across her mind: *This* āman *might be the reincarnation of Omito…*

In a frenzy, Kinjō swung the shovel once more, delivering the finishing blow. For a short while, nobody moved or uttered a word. Then Uta went over to the dumbfounded, petrified cameramen and brandished the hoe.

"Big Sister Uta!" Fumi and Shinzato yelled at the same time.

The cameramen screamed in terror. The hoe blade whizzed past them and smashed their cameras to pieces.

"You are never to tell anybody what happened here tonight. If this old lady finds out otherwise, I swear I'll hunt you down all the way to Yamato and beat you to a pulp!"

The two men nodded their heads in submission over and over again. Then Uta asked Shinzato and the others to clear away the remains of the *āman* and bury them out on the beach. They shoveled up the pieces of the *āman* scattered around the room and placed them in an empty manure bag. Then Shinzato and Kinjō hauled the cameramen out of the house. Uta and Fumi carefully cleaned the room, wiped up the splashes of the *amān*'s body fluid that had landed on Kōtarō, and changed his clothes. In the living room, Genpachi was showing the children magic tricks as he gulped down glasses of *awamori*. After seeing Kentarō and Tomoko behaving so well as they watched Genpachi's tricks, Uta fought back tears. She then talked to Fumi about waiting until the next day to tell the children about their father.

The following day, the rest of the village was surprised to hear the news of Kōtarō's death. Rumors filled the air, but the funeral service was held without delay. What proved to be difficult was persuading Ōshiro, at the medical clinic, to let them proceed quickly. He insisted that an autopsy was necessary, and even though they confided in him, explaining everything that had happened, it was obvious he wasn't taking them seriously. In the end, Uta showed Ōshiro the wound on her hand and made her appeal. "Do you think I would lie about something like this?"

Seeing tears in Uta's eyes for the first time in his life, Ōshiro filled out the death certificate and made arrangements for the cremation to proceed as soon as possible.

Rumors about the *āman* continued to crop up. But with no way to verify them, they soon faded.

Forty-nine days. That's how long it takes for a person's spirit to make the journey to the afterworld and for baby turtles to hatch and enter the sea.

As she stood on the beach, Uta recalled her father repeating these words many times to her when she was a child. The rainy season was ending, and once again the light of the moon shone on the seashore.

That afternoon marked the end of the forty-nine-day period since Kōtarō's passing, so his photograph and the flowers, which had been placed before the Buddhist altar, were cleared away. Genpachi had purified the room by waving around a bamboo stick entwined with a potato vine. In a loud voice, he had encouraged Kōtarō's *mabui* to pass on to *gusō*, the afterworld, without any regrets or attachments to his home and village. While Uta was watching Genpachi, she had wondered if Kōtarō's *mabui* had been able to make it safely to the afterworld.

Uta left Fumi's house, where Shinzato, Genpachi, and the other men were drinking in the tatami room, under the watchful care of the members of the Women's Association. Before going to the beach, she returned home briefly to cut grass for the goat and have a quick meal. After Kōtarō's *mabui* disappeared in the sand, she never saw it again. For a time, she had gone out every night to sit under the *hamasūki* and gaze at the ocean. But after the rainy season began, she had visited the beach less and less frequently. The night before, she had started going to the beach again, because the time for the baby sea turtles to hatch was approaching.

Uta knew well enough that just past seven in the evening was too early, but she couldn't bear being at home any longer. She sat under the *hamasūki* and gazed at the ocean as she waited. The roar of the waves filled her ears. No longer able to distinguish between everyday reality and the memories that flooded her mind, she felt as if she herself had passed away and become a *mabui*.

Now Uta was a young child suffering from heat rash. Her mother was bathing her in the ocean, and her father laughed as he picked up the little naked Uta in his arms. She bashfully covered her newly budding breasts with her arms, and Seiei, who was standing under a *mokumaō*, came running up, moved her arms out of the way, and kissed her breasts. Letting out a giggle at the feeling of Seiei's tongue tickling her nipple, she wriggled loose and ran along the shore. When she reached the middle of the beach, she saw Omito, Yūkichi, and a crowd of young people from the village sitting in a circle in the moonlight, singing and dancing, the twang of the *sanshin* barely audible over the roar of the ocean and the howl of the wind.

Born in a village by the seaside, raised eating creatures from the ocean, Uta had been taught that when people were alive, they drew their sustenance from the waters, and when they passed away, they journeyed to the land on the far side of the sea. She saw, in her mind's eye, Omito's dark silhouette lying on the beach.

After Uta had been released from the U.S. internment camp, the first thing she had done was go straight to the seashore. With her back to the ocean, she had stood waiting, staring at the sandy beach, so bright in the sunlight that it hurt her eyes. The dry sand at her feet had stirred, and the black face of a little creature, like the nut of a tree, had peeped out. Pushing aside the sand with their fore-flippers and thrusting their brown bodies out onto the beach, the baby turtles had been temporarily immobilized by the scorching sand. Before long, however, they had lifted their heads and started crawling towards her. When she had looked closely at the sand around her feet, she had seen countless tiny tracks, traced in the sand by the baby turtles' brothers and sisters who had hatched the night before. The hatchlings hesitated when they reached her shadow, then turned their heads to look about. Without warning, they broke into a vigorous rush towards the ocean. Leaping into the breaking waves, they disappeared into a lucent, emerald world.

And this must be what it is like for everyone when returning to the land on the far side of the sea, Uta thought. The smooth surface of the sandy beach was streaked by many small tracks leading into the waves. Uta got to her feet and looked down the beach. She saw many baby turtles spilling over onto the sand. As she watched, the hatchlings fanned out in the moonlight, all heading for the ocean. Uta marveled at their speed and vigor. Land crabs came running from every direction, seizing hatchlings with their pincers, lifting them over their heads, and carrying them off. Nevertheless, without pause, the vigorous drive continued as one after another of the baby turtles entered the ocean. Gradually the stampede of turtles lessened. Uta looked out at the white waves breaking on the coral reef in the offing. Her father had paid special attention to the time when the sea turtles would hatch, because large fish that fed on them would come near the shore on those days. Hoping to capture the big fish, her father would go out to sea with a harpoon in hand. Only a few of the hatchlings ever survived the frenzy they created.

As Uta looked around, she noticed the leaves of the *hamasūki* swaying ever so slightly, and heard the sound of *āman* crawling through a nearby *adan* thicket. The *mokumaō* forest at the high-water line was like a barrier separating the ocean from the village. Uta was the sole person on the beach. Suddenly overcome by loneliness, she couldn't bear it any longer and went down to the water, letting the waves wash her ankles as she waded in the gentle surf. The light of sea fireflies faded in and out in the warm waves lapping the shore. Uta stopped, turned toward the horizon, and brought her hands together. But her prayer never reached its destination.

Translation by Kyle Ikeda

A Living Legacy: The Development of
Modern Okinawan Poetry

For a long time I've thought about what is meant by the term "the literature of Okinawa" or "Okinawan literature." Is this category the same as, for example, "the literature of Fukuoka" or "the literature of Tokyo"? That is, does it refer merely to writing that has emerged from a particular prefecture or geographical region of Japan?

Not everyone would agree that the best way to categorize what we call Japanese literature is by geographical divisions. For me, this kind of categorization is even more insupportable when we refer to "the literature of Okinawa." There is more to Okinawan writing than the fact that the prefecture is one of many where writing is produced.

The difficulty I have with Okinawan literature being regarded as merely a subcategory of Japanese literature arises from the tumultuous history of Okinawa vis-à-vis the rest of Japan—and the number of cultural, linguistic, and environmental differences that set Okinawa apart.

For almost five hundred years beginning around the fourteenth century, Okinawa was not part of Japan. It was the Kingdom of the Ryūkyūs. At the end of this period, during the Meiji Era, Okinawa went through a humiliating process known as *Ryūkyū shobun* (the annexation of the Ryūkyūs to Japan) and the kingdom lost its sovereign status. The people and government of mainland Japan regarded the Ryūkyūan language as an inferior dialect of Japanese and systematically set out to eradicate it. Nearly a century later, in the years leading up to and including World War II, Okinawa was still regarded by the Japanese as a remote frontier, an area to be cleansed of its old languages and ways. Okinawa was the only part of Japan where a ground battle was fought with the United States. Some people believe that Okinawa was sacrificed by the central Japanese government and regarded as a mere "throw-away stone" between the American invaders and the homeland: that is, the main islands to the north.

At the end of the war, Okinawa was separated from Japan, and for the next twenty-seven years it was under American military rule. Okinawa's reversion to the Japanese nation in 1972 did little to assure Okinawans that they were being put under the protection of Japan. Huge U.S. military bases remained on Okinawa, along with a justice system that gave special legal status to American military personnel.

From ancient times, the history and experiences of Okinawans have thus been distinct from the experiences of mainland Japanese. Authors who live and work in Okinawa have often written about their situation of repeatedly losing and regaining their sovereignty, language, and culture.

This is a major reason why "Okinawan literature" must be placed in a category neither within nor alongside "Japanese literature." If we take into account Okinawa's special characteristics and historical development, we might understand that Okinawan writing should be regarded as existing *in opposition to* the literature of Japan. It may sound a bit radical, but I believe this perspective will prove more valuable and meaningful than other approaches and will enrich our understanding not only of Okinawan literature but also of the literature of mainland Japan.

In this brief essay, I have space to speak only about the development of poetry and I will further limit my remarks to the modern period.

Early Modern Era (Meiji, Taisho, Early Shōwa)

The modern literature of Okinawa dates from about 1897. Around this time, Japan's central government rushed to modernize the nation and standardize the language. Okinawans were naturally preoccupied with such efforts to erase their native culture. While the Satsuma clan—a feudal barony empowered by the government in Edo—had ruled Okinawa since about 1609, it wished to maintain the appearance that the kingdom was independent. Thus, Okinawan language and cultural practices had remained largely intact. However, when Commodore Matthew C. Perry arrived in Okinawa in 1853, the central government felt compelled to review the tenuousness of its hold on Okinawa. Between 1872 and 1875, the Japanese emperor formally took control of the islands and began merging Okinawa into what would become the Meiji Empire. The process wasn't without conflicts, of course, and proceeded by trial and error. Okinawa lagged far behind the other prefectures in the process of assimilation. Because of its distance from the capital and the differences of Okinawan people, the seeds of discrimination and prejudice started to grow.

It was under these circumstances that Okinawan writers began to learn standard Japanese and adopt new ways to express themselves. Serei Kunio and Iha Fuyū were two of the first authors to write poems that were in many aspects "modern," yet incorporated the meters and passionate moods of traditional Okinawan verse forms, such as *ryūka*.

Yamanoguchi Baku (1903–1963) was one of the prominent experimental Okinawan poets of the early twentieth century. Having moved to Tokyo in 1922, where he lived for most of his life, he introduced elements of *uchinā-guchi* (the language of Okinawa) into his Japanese writings. His main themes concerned the discrimination and prejudices directed against Okinawans by the people of mainland Japan. Yamanoguchi employed a simple, unadorned style to create poetry of humor and pathos and wrote about subjects ranging from day-to-day living to global issues.

Iha Nantetsu was also active during this period. Born and raised on one of the islands of Yaeyama, he went to Tokyo at age twenty and became a member of the literary circle Shi-no-ie (House of Poetry), organized by the poet Satō Sōnosuke. Iha wrote numerous works based on the history and folklore of Okinawa. His most famous work depicted a legendary peasant on Ishigaki Island who led a rebel army to protest the heavy tax burden imposed by the Ryūkyūan court. The rebel hero, Oyake Akahachi, was captured and beheaded after a great battle. The narrative poem was adapted into a play that became widely known and that, in 1937, was made into a motion picture directed by Toyoda Shirō.

Post-war Era (1945–1972)

Okinawan poets who survived the unprecedented tragedies of the Battle of Okinawa were primarily concerned with rendering their experiences of the war. The difficulty of this task drove writers to seek a style of poetry that could accommodate descriptions of the atrocity and suffering. At the forefront of the task were such early post-war poets as Makiminato Tokuzō, Miyazato Seiko, Katsuyama Shigeru, and Funakoshi Gishō.

Makiminato Tokuzō was born in Naha City in 1912. Already a journalist and poet before the war, Makiminato renewed his resolve after the Battle of Okinawa to write a poetry of witness. Looking back on his experiences as a soldier, he questioned whether he himself had contributed to militarism, whether he was in any way a perpetrator. By closely examining his own ethical conflicts, Makiminato created poems of great moral intensity.

Miyazato Seiko spoke out for peace. Born on the island of Kumejima, he graduated from Okinawa Normal School and became a teacher. For a time, he left Okinawa for Tokyo, where he contributed to poetry magazines. During the war, he worked in Manchuria and was there when the war ended. He was taken prisoner by the Soviet army and sent to Siberia. In 1945 he was released and returned to Okinawa. Miyazato's carefully controlled depictions of what he experienced as a detainee in Siberia express the darkness inside the human heart and the absurdity of political ideologies.

Katsuyama Shigeru was one of the first Okinawan poets to use a surrealistic style to render the madness of war. He was born on Miyako Island in 1920, and in 1938 was admitted to the prestigious Waseda University in Tokyo. He dropped out of Waseda to study fine arts at Nihon University and began writing poetry in earnest. When the war came, he was drafted into military service; he fought in the South Pacific for six years. After the war, he returned to Okinawa, where he continued to write surrealistic works about his daily life and the American soldiers he had encountered. His first poetry book, *Shiroi tebukuro* (White gloves), was published on Miyako Island in 1948; four months after its publication, he was killed in a traffic accident.

As a young man during the war, Funakoshi Gishō allegedly shook his head in refusal when his mother asked him, "Should we just kill ourselves?" Though he barely survived the war, he was able to overcome the despair around him and became a man of tremendous gentleness and deep love for all living beings. He embraced life—past and present, the new and the traditional—and nurtured a love for Okinawa in his lyrical poems.

When Okinawa began to recover from the war, many people started to examine the country's new political and economic status under direct occupational authority of the United States. During the 1950s, Okinawans began to chafe at American military rule. They felt that the equal rights and democracy they deserved were denied to them as people in an occupied territory. A group of writers emerged that was determined to confront what it regarded as Okinawa's untenable political situation. The most representative of these young poets formed a literary circle at the University of the Ryukyus and published the journal *Ryūdai bungaku*. They severely criticized the older generation of writers for not speaking out against injustice in post-war Okinawa. Emphasizing the link between politics and literature, they regarded writing as a means to question government policies. The leading figures in this movement were Arakawa Akira and Kawamitsu Shinichi.

Arakawa was fourteen when the war ended. He had witnessed harrowing scenes of human cruelty and in the post-war years became disillusioned by the failure of the American government and its troops to live up to the democratic ideals they espoused. He felt that the Americans viewed themselves as emissaries of peace, but in fact governed Okinawans without regard for justice. Arakawa couldn't keep silent about this situation. Among his books are *Nihon ga mieru* (I Can See Japan), *Okinawa: Tōgō to hangyaku* (Okinawa: Integrations and Rebellion), and *Okinawa: Ikusa monogatari, Ryūko no shiroi hata* (Okinawa: Tale of War, Ryūko's White Flag). This last book portrays the war as continuing in the painful memories of the survivors and their descendants.

As in Arakawa's work, the poetry of Kawamitsu Shinichi contains no vague abstractions or lightheartedness. His collection *Kawamitsu Shinichi Shishū* looks back on the stark realities of Okinawa's history and people.

In the 1960s, however, writers emerged who felt that Okinawan poetry had become political to the exclusion of other styles and subjects. They believed in creating a place for quiet lyrics, for the personal, inner lives of individuals, while remaining aware of the issues of social justice emphasized by *Ryūdai bungaku*. At the movement's center was Kiyota Masanobu. His first collection, *Tōi asa, me no ayumi* (A Faraway Morning, The Eye's Steps), was published in 1963 and was followed by numerous other collections of poetry and critical writings. His work crossed the boundaries between politics and literature and dramatized the inner crises of being human, while avoiding conventional lyricism and sentiments. His fearless examination of the inner self spiraled deeper and deeper and eventually brought him perilously close to insanity.

Like Kiyota, Katsuren Sadatoshi also tried to look directly at humanity's inner darkness. Driven to poetry by the suicide of his friend K at age sixteen, Katsuren published his first collection, *Kisōsha no itami* (Homing Man's Pain), at age eighteen. He searched relentlessly for the reasons K killed himself and for the reasons other individuals were able to endure despair and suffering. Such questions preoccupied him for the rest of his life and were expressed in his poetry.

Contemporary Poetry (1972–Present)

Okinawa's reversion to Japan in May 1972 was a turning point in poetry, as in many other areas of life. Okinawa once again huddled under the political umbrella of Japan, but reversion raised its own set of questions. Artists and intellectuals asked, What kind of country is the Japan that we are now going back to? Pro-reversion and counter-reversion arguments were made.

The 1970s also brought a proliferation of alternative literary magazines and books, which provided greater opportunities for diversity of expression. The number of poetry titles printed during the seventies was triple that of the preceding decade, reaching more than sixty. Reversion had transformed the perspectives of many people, and poets were resolved to take advantage of the new freedom of thought and poetic styles. Of course, numerous conflicting points of view arose in this spirit of exploration, experimentation, and questioning.

Most of this generation of poets grew up in the late sixties and early seventies. Among the most active were Takara Ben, Mizuna Akira, Yamaguchi Kōji, Kamiya Kōki, Higa Katsuo, Shinjō Takekazu, Kōki Koyō, Miyagi Eitei, Kamiya Tsuyoshi, Miyagi Shūichi, Izumi Tōru, Kinjō Tetsuo, Katsuren Shigeo, Nishime Ikukazu, and myself. After reversion, some poets migrated from mainland Japan to Okinawa, including Hanada Eizō, Yaguchi Tetsuo, Takahashi Shōji, Sasaki Kaoru, Shiba Noriko, Ura Ichira, and Ose Takakazu; others moved in the opposite direction, such as Chinen Eiki, Ichihara Chikako, Akura Toshi, and Nakamine Shinbu.

Of special note is Yae Yoichirō, born on Ishigaki Island in 1942. Yae experimented with language in exciting ways and pushed the boundaries of literary possibilities. His first publication, *Sobyō* (Design), in 1972, mixed archaic Ryūkyūan language, words from ritualistic *omoro*, and words of his own invention. Yae received the 2001 Ono Tōzaburō award for his work *Yūgata mura* (Evening Village).

The poet Nakachi Yūko succeeded in capturing the deep sorrows of women who were compelled to work on the streets of Koza City, bordering the American military bases. Her poetry could also be bewitchingly playful or could evoke the sacred landscape of ancient times.

More than fifty years after Yamanoguchi Baku, the problem of language remains one of the main concerns for Okinawan poets: how to use native *uchinā-guchi* together with standard Japanese. Among those who show great interest in this endeavor are Nakazato Yūgō, Takara Ben, Yonaha Mikio, Matsubara Toshio, Uehara Kizen, and Yamanoha Toshiko.

Nakazato Yūgō and Takara Ben both treat *uchinā-guchi* not as a Japanese dialect but as the official mother tongue of the Ryūkyū Kingdom, as primary as modern Japanese. Yonaha Mikio, from Miyako Islands, also uses his native language as a mother tongue. His 1983 collection, *Sekido no koi* (Love of the Red Soil), is startling for its linkage of colors with the troubling local history and the spiritual crises of the islanders. Remarkably, the work presents an old woman narrating in a mix of dialects and languages. Matsubara Toshio, also from Miyako Islands, received the 1986 Yamanoguchi Baku Award for his collection *An'na gensō* (Maternal Visions). *An'na* means "the mother" in the Miyako dialect, and like Yonaha, Matsubara is exploring the possibilities of using dialect as the language of his poetry.

The list of Okinawan poets mentioned here is of course incomplete, as any list of this nature must be. Among others are Ashimine Eiichi, Iraha Morio, Makuda Tadashi, Hoshi Masahiko, Miyagi Matsutaka, Yamagawa Monta, Okamoto Sadakatsu, Kochinda Keiten, Nakamoto Akira, Ishikawa Tamemaru, and Akamine Seishō. The promising younger generation of poets includes Suzuki Jirō, Kirino Shigeru, Miyagi Takahiro, Matsunaga Tomoya, Tōma Hiroko, Yō Iroha, and Nakandakari Yoshie. With various styles and interests, each is expanding the boundaries of modern Okinawan poetry.

Over the centuries, Okinawa refined an ancient tradition of short syllabic verses. The *omoro*, the *ryūka*, the pre-ceremonial and thanksgiving verses for communal festivities, common expressions of the *ugan* (prayers) offered before the ancestral spirits—all contributed certain rhythms and tonal patterns to Okinawan culture and historical memory. This distinctive legacy continues to enrich the soil in which modern Okinawan poetry flourishes. It is in light of these rhythms and refinements, incorporated into our living literature, that I would like to call Okinawa "The Islands of Poets." I suggest that "literature of Okinawa" belongs in the category of world literature, taking its place alongside Japanese and other national literatures and adding its distinctive characteristics to the cultural wealth of all humanity.

Translation by Hamagawa Hitoshi

YONAHA MIKIO

The Love of the Red Soil

The following poems are part of a narrative sequence written by Yonaha Mikio while living on Miyako Island, about two hundred miles southwest of Okinawa's capital. The poems are written from the perspective of a seventy-year-old woman who has spent her entire life on Miyako. The largest island in the Miyako archipelago, it is nearly flat and encircled by wide, white-sand beaches and coral reefs. The island is exposed to typhoons that strike in early summer and late fall, and though they bring rain, the moisture quickly seeps underground because the soil is porous. The dry soil and intense heat make it difficult to grow crops on most of the island. Miyako people have an ancient culture and language distinct from those of the main islands in the Okinawan chain. Despite efforts to preserve sacred sites and spiritual practices, this ancient culture is quickly being overwhelmed by influences from the outside.

THE OCEAN OF THE DEAD

In the indigo sea
     new corals rise from the dead
          ancestors of the past, their chalky skeletons
of lime, the great heaps of the dead
     settling under them, bones upon bones,
          generations, fused one atop the next,
the enormous bone-pile and charnel house
     of long-dead children who reproduced
          over parents', grandparents',
great-grandparents' disembodied
     bones, tangled, extending skeletal heads,
          stony septa and gullets rising for millennia
over the uncountable fossilized kin,
     architects of brittle bodies, builders of the reef's
          infinite chambers, creators of feeding grounds
in the indigo timelessness, unfathomable,

nameless genealogies fused in death and life
　　　　　—this coral island of our ancestors.

Townspeople imagine coral islands
　　　　simply appear on the ocean's surface, can't imagine
　　　　　　unending spirit-time, or the limitless number
　　　　　　　　of ancestors' rocklike bones,
the calcified piling up of their corpses
　　　　until the last of them glimpse an indigo glitter,
　　　　　　small waves: making this island
　　　　　　　　　—my old mind unravels at the thought.

And who were the first
　　　　ancestors? Enthralled by their blue souls
　　　　　　to voyage to this place
and begin slowly turning to stone?
　　　　How is the spirit released as the body fossilizes
　　　　　　bit by bit, the metamorphosis
from soft polyp to chalky stone? Where are the souls
　　　　of the billions now? Did they melt like salt
　　　　　　into the sea, or descend into the blind abyss?
Without rest, do they drift homeless on the waves?

Blue ocean, blue sky, darker blue of night,
of the ocean's depths—generations of spirits
dyed the cloth of sky and ocean this pure blue.

Before they are spirits, are their souls scarlet
as the red hibiscus trembling in the wind
like living coral in the waves?—Yes, I think they are.

　　　　　　Whose were these bones
　　　　when their bodies were alive?
Those who turned slowly into skeletons
even before they died
from poverty
　　　　from hunger
　　　　　　from the greed
　　　　　　　of far-off rulers whose tax-stone
　　　　measured out their burden
and dried them into branches of lime
and heartache
　　　　　　hearing the typhoon winds?

Children, I'm singing you the story of Miyako
     the beautiful, the blue, the deepening indigo,
        and the red soil made from crushed bodies
     that lay down their genealogy of bones
—Their spirits are whispering to you: all of this is what is.

TIME DOES NOT MOVE

A cosmos, an island,
centered in a blue dome that arcs
high into the azure whose circumference
touches the horizon in all directions,
waves from far away break on the encircling reef
like white petals of blown flowers
and wash ashore at my feet
—Every day they do this, beautiful and sad.

Beyond the blue cosmos,
what others are there? Even dreams
leaping from the cape toward the horizon
cannot fly far enough, and they fall into the sea.
In this blue cosmos, time does not move.
—Only the white waves on the reef one by one
count the moments as they break.

SPRING AGAIN

Yes, Grandchildren, my song
sometimes strays here and there.
Remember, though, our island's story
under its blue spell is like that too.
Though the tax collectors no longer
come from the capital to decide
when you are grown up enough to pay
—fierce typhoon winds
shake the island and keep us poor.

I wonder if the billions of dead ancestors
who built the reefs, enchanted
by the deep indigo of the sea, wander

bitterly without rest, cursing the living.
The soil is red, not blue, and as infertile
as salt. Is the blue a curse on the soil?

I'm afraid my stories
are about the spirits who bring us misfortune.
You wonder then why we stay here,
one generation after the next, and cling so tightly
To our thin red soil? Well, remember,
I've not told you everything.
Even poor farmers of Miyako know life's joy.

Translation by Katsunori Yamazato and Frank Stewart

Higa Yasuo: Maternal Deities

Worshipping the Gods (Kami-agami)
Yonaguni Island, Hikawa, Winter Festival
1975

Higa Yasuo: Maternal Deities

Worshipping the Gods (Kami-agami)
Okinawa Island, Aha, Shinugu
1976

Images of the Sacred

Most of the images in *Living Spirit* are from *Hahatachi no kami: Ryūkyūko no saishi sekai* (Maternal Deities: The World of Sacred Ritual in the Ryūkyū Arc), a collection that photographer Higa Yasuo was preparing for publication at the time of his premature death in 2000, at age sixty-one. In 2010, the Okinawa Prefectural Museum & Art Museum, in Naha, honored Higa by exhibiting 162 of the images he had planned to include in this book. The images were then displayed at the Izu Photo Museum, in Shizuoka Prefecture, through May 2011.

With the generous cooperation of Higa's widow, Higa Nobuko, and that of the Okinawa Prefectural Museum's staff, we are able to feature a small selection of the images. This brief essay, compiled by the editors of *Living Spirit*, is based largely on notes and commentary produced by the curators of the exhibition, which was titled after Higa's proposed book, *Maternal Deities*.

For over three decades, Higa documented and studied ancient and sacred festivals and rituals that are held throughout the Ryūkyūan Archipelago. As other commentators have remarked, he did an extraordinary service to the field of ethnography. But he was above all a fine photographer and was passionate about honoring Ryūkyūan rituals. He believed them to be the *living continuum* of past and present time, the passageway connecting this world and the afterworld, and the fundamental means for understanding what it means to be human in Okinawa and in the world.

Higa planned to divide his volume into chapters, and we have retained his organization and sequence: each photograph is accompanied by a caption that indicates the section where he intended to place the image.

The majority of the photographs depict the most sacred festivals, which are held on Kudaka and Miyako Islands, and therefore provide extraordinary insights into the spirituality, temperament, and worldview that have made Okinawa such a culturally and artistically important place. These timeless photographs of timeless rituals also greatly enhance our understanding of even the most contemporary prose and poetry in *Living Spirit*.

In creating this groundbreaking work, Higa realized that at the heart of Ryūkyūan cosmology was a deep belief in maternal forces and principles. As Hirotaka Makino, Director of the Okinawan Prefectural Museum, wrote in his introduction to the exhibit catalogue, the maternal principle "constitutes the bedrock of the Okinawan spirit." And it was Higa's conviction "that culture stemming from the maternal principle provides clues to understanding the present age."

From ancient Ryūkyūan times, women occupied an extraordinary position in the spiritual affairs of their communities, and as a consequence, highly trained priestesses were the principal mediators between humans and the gods.

The writer Asato Eiko recounts a conversation she had with Higa in which he described the place of women in Okinawan society. While men and women both feel a love and attachment to deceased ancestors and to children, Higa said, it is mothers who

> during their lifetimes devote themselves absolutely to protecting their children. After they die, it follows that the mothers' protection continues into the other world, and this continuity is the origin of what we mean by the word "god." Maternal protectiveness brings gods into being.

According to traditional Okinawan religious beliefs, souls are transported after death to the spirit world of Nirai Kanai. There, the souls are reborn as protectors of the living. They may remain in Nirai Kanai or live in sacred places, such as groves of trees, streams, rocks, and shrines. By means of religious ceremonies, the spirits are invited to return to this world and are asked to bless the living and to pass on their protective powers to female children. Thus, the spiritual essence is kept alive through the female line.

Religious ceremonies vary by village and island. The following sections from Higa's proposed book roughly represent the stages in many of the sacred Ryūkyūan festivals.

Inviting and Greeting the Gods (Kami-nkē)
In the Ryūkyūs, a person's spirit (mabui) is believed to go to a realm that exists where the sun rises, over the eastern horizon, called Nirai Kanai (or, Nirā Harā). The maternal spirits—mothers, grandmothers, and so on—watch over the living from there, but may also remain in this world, dwelling in shrines (utaki) and other sacred places. During festivals, the spirits are asked to be present and bestow their blessing on the villages.

In preparation for the arrival of the gods, the priestesses (noro or kami-nchu) sequester and purify themselves for about a week in a shrine or sacred location.

The festival then begins with a ceremony inviting and greeting the gods (kami-nkē). Through this rite, the gods are summoned and powerful ancestral mabui inhabit the priestesses, possess them, and move among them.

Worshipping the Gods *(Kami-agami)*

After the gods arrive, the ritual worshipping *(kami-agami)* begins. Sometimes the priestesses sequester themselves again for several days in locations prohibited to outsiders. They sing divine songs of praise *(tirutu* and *otakabe)* or chant the creation story as they make offerings.

Later, the priestesses walk in procession, then form a circle and dance to express their joy at the arrival of the gods. They clap their hands and beat drums. As the rite proceeds, the presence of spiritual powers *(seji)* intensifies, and some of the women fall into trances or utter divine messages and divinations. At the height of this enthrallment, they may faint.

Divine Women *(Kami-nchu)*

In most places, divine rites are conducted solely by women priestesses *(kami-nchu):* men are forbidden to enter shrines and sacred sites, and all mediation with the gods is carried out by women. On some islands, all the females in the villages are expected to be initiated and take on their religious roles. They first serve as novice priestesses *(nanchu)*, and once they have reached a certain age, they may eventually become powerful *noro* and pass on their knowledge and powers to their daughters. The Izaihō ritual of Kudaka Island is representative of an initiation festival.

Women also play the central role in rituals because of the Okinawan belief that sisters *(unai)* and brothers *(ekeri)* are paired, and sisters have the power *(seji)* and responsibility to protect their brothers. The protective relationship can extend beyond kinship, and all females can be considered sister-deities *(unai-gami)* and all males their brothers.

Imploring the Gods *(Kami-nigai)*

In the Ryūkyūs, religious festivals are often held to pray for the gods' favor and ask for fertile harvests or bountiful fishing. Held throughout the seasons, they may occur at varying intervals: every three, seven, or twelve years. Examples include the Unjami and Shinugu festivals in the northern part of Okinawa, and Izaihō on Kudaka Island, which was traditionally held every twelve years. The Izaihō festival was discontinued in 1978.

Dancing with the Gods *(Kami-ashibi)*

Possessed by the divine spirits, the priestesses communicate the wishes of their village for prosperity and happiness and then join the gods in the butterfly and dragonfly dances. By this stage, the solemnity of the rituals is ending, and the mood becomes lighter and more relaxed.

Higa Yasuo wrote of witnessing the divine women dancing peacefully on the last day of the Izaihō on Kudaka Island:

> Probably because the dance in the courtyard was the last program of the ritual, it was very moving from beginning to end....The women became one with the song *(tiruru)* and their faces expressed both loneliness and sadness. The newly

initiated novices *(nanchu)* looked as if they were going to cry [yet] the *nanchu*'s faces were beaming with the joy of becoming young priestesses of Kudaka, after anxious years of anticipation.

The climax of the festival, dancing with the gods *(kami-ashibi)*, expresses a sense of satisfaction that the welcoming of the gods and transmitting of the village's supplications have been properly accomplished.

Seeing the Gods Off *(Kami-ukui)*

Having been worshipped and entertained by the people, the gods return to Nirai Kanai. The rite of sending off the gods takes place quietly, at the same site where they were welcomed, or on the outskirts of the village.

The people feel sad that the gods are departing, and they pray that the gods will return during the next divine festival. The priestesses' sacred songs express the reluctance of the people to say farewell to the gods. The spirits return to the sacred shrines, to the sacred hills and groves, or beyond the sea to Nirai Kanai.

Riding a Bus in a Castle Town

As quickly as the figure appeared outside the window of the bus, it was gone, left far behind. At first I wondered if I had seen anyone at all. A momentary vision among the houses that lined the street: "Agarie?"

He was gone before I had time to say his name. But then I was certain that it had been him, wearing a shabby shirt, with an open collar and no tie, an old man's alpine hat on his head. I recognized his face. He was waving, holding his right palm next to his ear.

The face was of Seishō Agarie: we used to call him by the nickname Small-Eyed Seishō because his eyes were so little and friendly. What I had glimpsed was the aged face of a second-year middle-school student I knew sixty-two years ago. It was bewildering for me to think that this had been the person waving at me.

Did he recognize me merely as Eisuke Kobashigawa, his classmate from the First Prefectural Middle School? It was forty years ago that I left Okinawa. It would have been next to impossible for him to recognize my face from where he stood as the bus passed him. I had recently sent him a letter asking for his help in recalling a sixty-two-year-old memory from the battlefield. No answer had arrived, so I decided to seek him out and meet face to face. When I called on the phone, his wife had picked up, responding to my request vaguely—neither encouraging me nor discouraging me. Even now, I'm not sure I should have come all this way. I think his wife must have already spoken to him about my call, but would he feel comfortable talking to me? Would he welcome me? Was it a good idea to come?

The Castle Town Bus Line was started three years ago, I'm told. It's just six kilometers long, and the trip takes only twenty minutes. The outbound bus leaves Shuri-Ishimine Town, passes by the monorail's Shuri Station, and circles about half of Shuri Castle. It then travels through Kinjō Town, in the southernmost corner of the old city of Shuri, runs along the ridge at Samukawa Town until it turns onto Prefectural Road 29, and arrives at Miyako Hotel & Resorts and Hotel Nikkō Naha Grand Castle, its final stop.

Having grown up in Okinawa before the war, I feel like calling these places by their old district names, Kanagushiku and Sungā, rather than by their modern names, Kinjō and Samukawa. One reason I feel this way is that these areas have always seemed set apart from the heart of old Shuri Town. As soon as I arrived in Okinawa after my forty-year absence and heard about the Castle Town Line, I jumped on the bus—not just because it was convenient for getting to my destinations, but out of curiosity and nostalgia.

I quickly learned about the bus stop called Entrance to Stone Path. I had lived in Okinawa for twenty years after the war and knew about this stone path, where the old part of the town remained intact, even after the battle had destroyed nearly everything. The narrow stone pavement descends steeply for about three hundred meters toward the south, so as the bus neared the stop, I was prepared to look straight down the path and see the hillside town of Hantagawa as we passed. But it can't be seen anymore, if only because the bus is rushing along as fast as a clicking camera. However, now that I caught a glimpse of the figure resembling Agarie, I'm convinced that his house is nearby and that the stone path is still there.

Halfway down the slope, as I recall, the path forks at a small spring shaded by a large banyan tree. People say that before the war, the residents of the area set up stands to sell their bean sprouts every morning. It was there, at a little open space facing the spring, where the 146 second-year students of the First Prefectural Middle School—none of us older than thirteen or fourteen—were assembled on 28 May 1945 and inducted as second-class privates into the army's communications corps. Two days prior to that, American troops had landed on the islands of Kerama, only thirty kilometers west of mainland Okinawa, and U.S. reconnaissance planes had begun appearing overhead. Looking up at those planes, we tried to picture the daily routines awaiting us as privates in the army.

It so happened that on that day an old gray-haired woman was offering prayers beside the spring. She said to us, "I mean, really, aren't you still too small to be soldiers?" Then she knelt toward the spring and said she would pray for us during the battle to come. Unperturbed by the roar of the reconnaissance plane overhead, she told us her son had already been sent to the southern front. I wonder now if she lived to see the end of the war.

Does the spring still have water? The question hovers in my mind as the bus stops in front of the memorial tower erected for the students of the First Prefectural Middle School. I get off, having planned to see the tower before visiting Agarie.

I now have a good view of the landscape stretching beyond the houses on the south side. I am standing at the point where the stone path begins its steep descent of three hundred meters. I have a mental image of boy soldiers tumbling from here to the bottom of the valley as they were hunted sixty-two years ago by Americans. But what appears before me are glittering urban houses, packed together all the way to the horizon. On my right is a view of the islands of Kerama, off the coast to the west, the site of so many suicides by civilians in March 1945, when American troops landed. They

Higa Yasuo: Maternal Deities

Worshipping the Gods (Kami-agami)
Miyako Island, Karimata, Mugi-pūzu
1974

look peaceful, as if nothing bad had ever happened there. The pleasure of these soft, moist breezes is the last sweet thing I can remember from the ordeal in the boiling-hot cave where our communications corps hunkered down. When we were driven out of the cave, it was the end of May, right in the middle of the rainy season. If I try, I can visualize Shimajiri field. Are people's remains still buried in the soil underneath the battlefield? Shaking off the thought for the moment, I watch the bus pull away, and then I turn north and come out to the steep slope that reminds me of old times. I walk up there, then turn right and follow a path flanked by grass-covered stone walls that seem to block out noises of the town. A turn around a huge shady banyan tree on the left brings me to Yōshū Hall, the grounds of the first middle school, and the war memorial tower.

The route to the spot remains the same, but the area has completely changed. The Yōshū dormitory was built beside a forest in 1940. Five years later, after I graduated from an elementary school in Nakagusuku Village, I became one of fifty students at the dormitory. A year later, I was suddenly a second-class private in the army communications corps. The dormitory building burned down during the war, and gone, too, is the concrete building that used to stand about three hundred meters to the northwest. Although the school's legacy was preserved, the newly built Shuri High School makes me feel as if every trace of the students of Yōshū dormitory has been wiped out.

To preserve the memory of what happened, a sculpture series known as *Statues of Young Men* was installed on the former site of the dormitory. The pieces formed the beginning of the current memorial tower and were donated by Mr. T, a student at the First Prefectural Middle School who went on to graduate from an art school in Tokyo. They depicted middle-school students sitting, relaxed and shirtless. The first statue was placed on the site six years after the end of the war, and the second was installed four years later, with the student in a slightly different pose. Together, these two figures were like pillars before a shrine. Though their poses were nothing like that of *The Thinker,* every time I saw or thought of them, they reminded me of Rodin's sculpture. During wartime, middle-school students were told not to think for themselves. You could say that these statues were created in order to restore the students' freedom to think.

I served as the model for the statues. I was nineteen years old on the first occasion, and twenty-three on the second. Mr. T resembled a huge, round rock, but in fact he was very tenderhearted. He had found a black, prewar school cap somewhere and put it on my head when I modeled for him.

The school cap, however, wasn't the same type that my peers and I used to wear. By the time we entered school, it had been replaced by a khaki field cap. The school uniform had also been changed and was made of a synthetic, khaki-colored textile called staple fiber. During the times I was posing for Mr. T, old memories would come back. For example, immediately before the battle, when we were in the third trimester, we began practicing to operate radios in preparation for our duties in the communications corps. An instructor by the name of Lieutenant Gotō had been sent from the military. Is he all right? I wondered. Did he manage to survive the war? These questions would preoccupy my mind as I sat.

One day, during the second modeling session, Small-Eyed Seishō came to visit the studio. Since he was working in an office of Shuri High School back then, he must have come with a message for Mr. T. In postwar Okinawa, bronze was still not available, so Mr. T was sculpting the statue by applying cement directly onto an armature, the way one makes a figure with clay. With the work nearly complete, Mr. T was making final adjustments, curving the muscles around the chest and shoulders. Looking at the work, Agarie made a simple yet perceptive comment: "He looks like a senior student now." Like me, Agarie had reentered Shuri High School after the war and had graduated. But I suspected Agarie wished he'd had the chance to become a senior in the First Prefectural Middle School. I'd like to ask him when I see him today if that's true, but I feel a little reluctant, given the way Small-Eyed looked as he waved at my bus.

Before asking a question like that, I have to get the facts about something else. The statues of the young men are gone now. About a dozen years after the war, someone methodically smashed them. The steel armature was nearly all that was left, indicating how totally the vandal had wished to destroy them. Ten years after the last modeling session, I had left Okinawa to be in charge of the Tokyo branch of the company I was working for, so I didn't actually see the damaged statues. I only learned about them later. While I was beset by mixed feelings of anger and sadness, in my imagination blaming the wanton act on a youth of the postwar generation, someone told me that Mr. T had died. I haven't been able to find out whether his death occurred before or after the destruction of the statues. I've been told that the wreckage is kept in Shuri High School, leading me to wonder if the statues should be considered yet another relic of the war's devastation. When I heard about it, I called Seishō Agarie for more information, but his response betrayed no particular emotion, apart from the fact he too didn't know who did it.

"I feel the same way...," he merely murmured, showing none of the thoughtfulness that characterized his observation that one of the statues resembled a middle-school senior. Perhaps such resignation was normal for someone who had continued to live in Okinawa after the war. I, on the other hand, had moved away and therefore remained sentimental. In any case, when I heard that Mr. T had passed away, I felt as though I had been given some new duty to perform.

I decided that, before meeting Seishō Agarie, I would pay a visit to the remains of the statues. I wished to see with my own eyes what had been done to them. Moreover, I felt that I might somehow have more insight once I actually stood in front of them. I also wanted to have the experience of seeing them with Agarie.

Looking up, I see the bold white letters THE FIRST PREFECTURAL MIDDLE SCHOOL YOUTHS carved horizontally in vivid strokes. The memorial is called a tower but is in fact a tall, wide concrete wall. The old middle school had a five-year curriculum. The third-year students and older were inducted into the Blood and Iron Scouts for the Emperor; younger students went into the communications corps. The names of all of those who died in the battle—305 students and teachers—are carved in white characters on a granite stone.

> SEVENTY-THREE OF THE SECOND-YEAR STUDENTS
> IN THE COMMUNICATIONS CORPS AND
> THIRTY-TWO OF THE FIRST-YEAR...

As I silently repeat the numbers, the May sunshine is falling on the monument, making the many colors in the granite glint. The names of the victims seem to overlap one another, reminding me of our days in the battlefields, when fleeting moments made all the difference between who lived and who died.

The tower, a full-scale war memorial, was erected in the northern corner of the new school grounds. It was completed in 1972, the centennial of the old middle school, and dedicated on 23 June, the date marking the end of the Battle of Okinawa. In February of that year, construction of the Yōshū alumni hall was completed. Reflecting the same design concept as the tower, a memorial exhibition room for the student soldiers was installed in the hall in 2005, also on 23 June.

Part of the exhibit consists of dozens of pictures of the war dead: the older students of the Blood and Iron Scouts and the younger students of the communications corps. Some pictures show the childish faces of the younger students, each grimly wearing a wartime cap. Also showcased are bravely worded letters, displaying the writers' eagerness to die proudly for their country. These are placed alongside some newspaper clippings and other wartime documents—but of course you won't find the real thoughts of the dead expressed there. All that's left is an eternal question. The question has something to do with the reason I came home this time. I feel a sudden urge to speak to the curator, but decide it would be impossible to explain my thoughts. As I study the artifacts dug out of caves, I come across a makeshift hand grenade among the personal effects. As soon as I see it, I have a flashback, then feel ashamed that I had completely forgotten about it for sixty years.

"I saw the makeshift hand grenade."

Sitting face-to-face with Seishō Agarie, I bring up the topic right away. I had found his house an hour after visiting the exhibit. When we were student soldiers on the island's southernmost coast of Mabuni, I had encountered him carrying a makeshift hand grenade. At the exhibit, I had felt as if I were seeing that same grenade—and now I'm speaking to Agarie about it.

The makeshift grenade was as large as an adult's fist, a crude, ridiculous-looking ceramic imitation of a real army grenade. It was hollow inside and had a hole about one centimeter in diameter on top. A firing pin was stuffed in the hole, and the grenade was supposed to explode when the detonator was pulled. Not all the student soldiers owned a hand grenade, but I happened to have one given to me by a higher-ranking soldier. Not knowing how to use it, I might as well have been tricked into possessing it. In any case, I had it with me, and that, as I recall now, got me into a situation that was shameful or, rather, humiliating.

"What the hell is this?" laughed Mitsuru Suzuki, a lance corporal who had been in the army six years. Sometimes kind and other times violent, Suzuki was an unpredictable soldier. He had an unforgettable face, which was frighteningly gaunt even before we started running out of food. I was only on my second day of assignment when I met him. Agarie and I had both been posted to the Fourth Company of the Thirty-sixth Telegraphic Communications Regiment. I was examining the grenade and wondering if I should take it with me when I went to fetch meals from the field kitchen, about five hundred meters away, on the other side of Kinjō Town. I was a little upset when the lance corporal caught me looking at it, and by the way he rebuked me, saying there was no sense in carrying such a thing just to get meals. I understood his point, but also felt that he could have been more considerate of me as a mere student soldier with no experience in such things. Little did I know that his fate and mine were going to stay entangled and that we would travel together to the southernmost coast three months later. At the time, I only felt angry at him for ridiculing me for being a mere kid.

When we managed to reach the southern coast of Mabuni alive, neither L.Cpl. Suzuki nor I had a hand grenade. Once in Haebaru, I fell into a crevice, and another time, in Kochinda, I fell into a huge pit blasted into the ground during naval bombardment. On either occasion, the grenade might have dropped out of my bag. As the troops withdrew from Hantagawa, L.Cpl. Suzuki was told that he could have a hand grenade, but they were in short supply. He declined to accept one. "I will just pick one up from a dead fellow," he said, then laughed. I later wondered if he had died by killing himself with the makeshift grenade that he took from Agarie at Mabuni.

Just now I tried to remind Agarie of the grenade, but he doesn't answer my questions and instead starts talking about something else.

"I fell into the latrine pit." He begins to chuckle. His smile seems more pronounced than when I saw him through the bus window.

"My husband talks about his falling into the latrine pit quite often," his wife says, interrupting him. "While he was his old self, he seemed rather embarrassed, but now he acts almost proud of it."

To my slight surprise, this makes her laugh so cheerfully that I also have to smile. Now that she seems more responsive to me, my expectations rise, and I dare hope that something might actually come of our conversations.

The incident concerning the latrine pit occurred about a week after we were assigned to the company at Hantagawa, when Agarie and three others went out on an assignment to fetch meals.

In the dawn light, as they were running down a hill while holding large bucket-shaped food carriers, Agarie tripped into a latrine pit that had been dug on the farm land. By chance, the cover of the pit had been removed. Luckily, the pit was only as deep as Agarie's chest. When he returned to the cave, the other soldiers howled. They told Agarie that if the stench went high enough, it would bring down an enemy plane.

But something else had also happened. After pulling Agarie out of the pit, Pfc. Shirai had gotten so mad that he had raised his fist to strike Agarie. But the sight of Agarie standing there defenseless, completely filthy from the chest down, his cheeks spattered with foul yellow waste, and the red second-class insignia on his collar covered in filth, caused Pfc. Shirai to only stamp his feet in frustration, yell at him to pay greater attention, and order him to leave immediately to bathe. As soon as Agarie had started running, an artillery round made a direct hit on Pfc. Shirai and the other men, blowing all of them to pieces.

Unharmed, Agarie had stared back to our position in a stupor. After a while, he pulled himself together and went to look for a place to wash off his feces-covered body. The well behind the company cave was reserved for drinking water, so he went to a civilian home in the village of Hantagawa, which he knew belonged to a local Okinawan like himself. When he got back to the cave after cleaning himself, L.Cpl. Suzuki started punching him. Suzuki blamed Agarie not only for being negligent but, worse, for abandoning the other men. He must have known it wasn't Agarie's fault. I suspected he was envious that Agarie, being Okinawan, could go into someone's house for help.

Suzuki treated the men in his team differently from the way Agarie's team was treated. I was observing his punishment at the hands of Suzuki when Agarie's team leader, Cpl. Takita, strode in. I expected the corporal would object to Suzuki's having taken the matter into his own hands. But Suzuki stared at Takita with such cold eyes that Takita turned around and left without a word.

Cpl. Takita was much younger than Suzuki and many of the other non-commissioned officers. He had probably volunteered before reaching conscription age so that he could become a cadet. As a result, he belonged to a category of men who were looked down on by the more experienced soldiers. The hierarchical system in the military appeared simple, but in practice was complex. There were times when a young noncommissioned officer could not discipline an older ordinary soldier. The incident with Takita and Suzuki was the first time I witnessed the deterioration in morale occuring among soldiers on the battlefield. Respect for military discipline and rank had already broken down inside the caves at Hantagawa. Agarie was probably more deeply confused than I was.

Agarie's house stands on a slope about fifty meters east of the stone path's halfway point. The guest room faces south and has a clear view of the hillside of Hantagawa, several hundred meters away. Since the war, Hantagawa has been transformed into a residential district. No latrine pits are to be seen, of course, but the memory of the incident seems to still be alive in Agarie. After the incident, soldiers were sent to fetch meals only at night. The fact that procedures were changed because of Agarie's experience may have given it even greater significance in his mind.

"There used to be a huge cave on the hillside…" I can now communicate only with his wife.

Back then, Hantagawa's lush vegetation had been stripped away to dig elaborate caves. The caves had three entrances, each four meters wide and about two meters high, which led to interconnected passageways and to other caves, each capable of sheltering a company of 350 soldiers, plus 35 middle-school students. By the time the army occupied these caves, the village of Hantagawa was deserted, the residents either having fled to safer areas or having found caves in which to hide.

Though we students had officially been assigned to the communications corps, we never had a chance to demonstrate our hastily learned knowledge of Morse code. Occasionally, we were ordered to crank up the makeshift power generator for the type 3 radio transmitter, but most of our days were spent standing sentry, fetching meals and water, and transporting fodder, ammunition, tools, and equipment. Other than that, we put up with being struck several times a day by our superiors.

As middle schoolers, we were too small to fit into regular military uniforms and boots. But that was just one of the numerous discomforts we had to learn to cope with. Students from the second middle school—or from the commercial, industrial, and agricultural schools—were apparently assigned to the wired communications corps. In practice this meant that every time a wire on the battlefield was damaged, the students were ordered to go out and fix it, fully exposing themselves to flying bullets. When I learned that later, I knew that our situation as middle-school conscripts could have been even more perilous.

Higa Yasuo: Maternal Deities

Worshipping the Gods (Kami-agami)
Kudaka Island, Fūbo Utaki, Fubawaku
1975

"Did he choose this site for the house?" I ask Agarie's wife, implying that he couldn't have enjoyed the memory of Hantagawa.

"As a matter of fact, my husband rather liked talking about it…"

I'm about to decide that his wife, who has fewer age spots and wrinkles than most women her age, is cheerful by nature, just like her husband, but then she adds, "I wonder, though, how he really felt."

For a fraction of a second, I see a hint of resignation pass over her face. Having built a house on the spot linked to her husband's wartime memories, the two have lived here with constant reminders of their suffering. How have they managed to cope with the memories? I try to imagine. Seemingly oblivious to his wife's words, his slender eyes even smaller than usual, Agarie is contemplating the transformed view of Hantagawa.

"Since when…" I stop myself as I am about to finish with "has he been senile?"

"It's been about a year."

Her bright voice puts me somewhat at ease. But if what she says is true, she has been resigned to her husband's condition a long time. Then why didn't she reply to my letter?

"My visit concerns what I wrote in my letter," I begin straightforwardly.

At the end of last year, a woman who identified herself as a niece of L.Cpl. Suzuki came up to speak to me when I attended a community get-together in Tokyo. The woman, whom I had never seen before, introduced herself. She had a broad forehead and shiny eyes and seemed to be an intelligent person. Her introduction, however, was not typical of someone you've just met. When I said I was from Okinawa, right away she began to talk about Suzuki.

It didn't take long before I realized that the Mitsuru Suzuki she was talking about was the same one I had shared life and death experiences with. While I was still wondering if I should try to deflect the conversation away from Suzuki, she expressed to me her wish to "find out the exact time and place of his death." Though Mitsuru's parents had long been deceased, his eldest sister was still living, unmarried and in good health, in Ehime Prefecture. The sister had been taking care of the ancestral grave and wanted to find out Mitsuru's date and place of death, the woman said. He had been the only son, and the youngest of five siblings. The woman said his death had also been of great concern to his mother. There was no way of knowing just how earnest the eldest sister's request was, but several days later, when I came across the woman on the street, she said she had already phoned her aunt and given assurance that someone she had just met would find out everything for her. Hearing that, I knew I couldn't refuse the request to at least try. Meanwhile, I couldn't bring myself to tell the niece that it's actually more difficult to determine the date and place of a soldier's death than most people realize.

Unable to resist the American forces bulldozing their way from the north, the headquarters of the Thirty-second Army—the central command for the defense of Okinawa—decided to withdraw south to Shimajiri. Accordingly, they left Shuri on 27 May, still early in the rainy season. Now under the direct command of headquarters, the Thirty-sixth Communications Regiment moved south as well. Most of the time, this meant we were drenched in rains and running and crawling across Shimajiri, wandering from cave to cave. After the rainy season ended on 22 June, it was decided that our regiment could no longer put up an effective defense and there was no way left for the army to protect us. We were told to destroy all communication devices and to disperse. The student soldiers were forced to find a way to survive on their own. Thus began the aimless battlefield wanderings of the de-commissioned student soldiers, who, individually or sometimes accompanied by their superiors, struggled to slip through gunfire and shelling.

After a while, I heard that the army commander and the chief of staff had committed suicide. That left tens of thousands of soldiers on the battlefields without leadership. Two days later, I learned that the abandoned military headquarters was nearby. This was where I was shot in my left thigh and received medical treatment from L.Cpl Suzuki. Because we had nothing to use for a bandage, Suzuki used his bayonet to cut off a piece of his shirt and tied it around my wound. Without medication to put on it, the wound was soon infested with maggots. I left the area hobbling on my infected leg, and arrived at the coast of Mabuni in the early afternoon of the next day.

I sat between two coral rocks, each almost ten meters high and joined in an arch at the top, feeling somewhat protected by the cavelike formation. This area of the coast is dotted with similar coral formations, behind which others like me were hiding. We were sometimes shot at by the American warships, which were increasing in number. Some soldiers were killed as they swam toward the ships, in apparent attempts to surrender. They were fired on not only by the Americans, but also by the Japanese soldiers on shore, who considered them to be traitors.

An announcement in poor Japanese with an unmistakable American accent was broadcast toward the coastline from the warships: "No more fighting is necessary, so please surrender immediately."

There were three options available to us: obey the announcement and surrender; kill ourselves with a hand grenade; try to sneak back north through the enemy line and come out on the other side. I heard grenades exploding, clearly the sounds of suicide, and sometimes felt as if each explosion was an invitation for me to detonate my own grenade. However, when I thought about the state of mind of those who couldn't take it anymore, I renewed my resolve to hold out as long as I could.

After dark, about half a day after I arrived in the area, I heard myself being hailed: "Kobashigawa!" I turned around, instantly on guard because the speaker's face and clothes were as obscured by dirt as mine. Finally I recognized the voice, and then those slender eyes we used to make fun of. Agarie was still alive! Just as I had been with L.Cpl. Suzuki, Agarie had been with Cpl. Takita.

It wasn't long before Agarie brought the makeshift hand grenade out of his bag. He held it in his right hand and then in his left, as though he were trying to measure something. At times, he seemed fully resolved to end his life, but in the next moment he seemed resigned to do nothing. Back and forth he pondered whether or not to use the makeshift grenade.

I was a little frightened when L.Cpl. Suzuki grabbed it from Agarie and said, "Give me that." I suspected he was going to invite us to join him in suicide. If he unplugged the grenade while we four held one another by the shoulders, the explosion would kill us all. "I will keep it," he said.

Seeing him carelessly toss the grenade into his bag, Agarie gave me a searching look. I could only stare blankly back at him, unsure how the grenade was going to be used. Once again, Suzuki ignored Cpl. Takita. It was another instance of insubordinate contempt; at the same time, perhaps Suzuki was acting out the subconscious awareness we all had that our situation was hopeless and defeat fast approaching.

"You got something to eat?" L.Cpl. Suzuki asked Agarie, suddenly switching to the familiar form of address. Out of his filthy, muddy bag, Agarie pulled out a pair of socks stuffed with rice and a miso ball the size of a chicken egg, wrapped in abaca leaves. The socks holding the rice were not dirty, probably because Agarie had taken care of them even while he was starving. As we had withdrawn from Shuri, each officer and soldier had received a ration of rice and a miso ball, but Suzuki and I had thrown ours away when we were no longer able to carry them.

"I sort of got it in exchange for falling into the latrine," Agarie said, surprising me. He screwed up his blackened face, his eyes nearly forming a straight line. It was bad luck—falling into the latrine pit—but he had survived because of it, and now, after all that had happened, he still had some rice in his socks. This seemed to console him.

Watching L.Cpl. Suzuki in profile, I wondered how he understood these words. But he didn't seem to take notice. He simply grabbed Agarie's rice without asking. It was impossible to tell whether he had forgotten about punching Agarie, who belonged to Takita's military team, or was just pretending to have forgotten.

I could never have anticipated or imagined that Agarie's fate—as if being switched with mine—would become entangled with Suzuki's soon after. I don't think Agarie could have imagined it either.

Was L.Cpl. Suzuki an enemy or a friend? All of us young boys in the communications corps had wondered about this for the first couple of weeks after enlisting. On and off duty, everyone probably came into contact with him in some way. He stood out from the noncommissioned officers and soldiers of higher rank.

My first memorable encounter with Suzuki occurred about five days after I had joined the corps. As he worked on sending a telegram, I sat next to him, covered in sweat and cranking a small generator. Usually we did this deep in the cave, but that day he took the liberty of bringing the equipment up near the entrance, where it was cooler. The change made the cranking a little more bearable, but it was still hard work.

"Just what do you think you are doing? The way you're cranking the handle, the signal will never reach…" L.Cpl. Suzuki stopped sending Morse code and yelled at me. "If the whole unit up in the north is wiped out, you're the one who'll take the blame!"

I was spurred on by the horrific image of the entire northern unit perishing due to a telegram arriving too late, but I could only keep cranking for several minutes at a time. My arm wasn't strong enough to keep up the necessary pace.

"You idiot!" I didn't know how hard L.Cpl. Suzuki's punches could be till he struck me. I fell down, letting go of the crank. My head slammed against a bed column, and for a moment I thought I'd breathed my last. Three beds were stacked on top of each other, and lying on the lowest was a superior private named Takeshita. He had been in the army for six years and was rumored to have been punished and not promoted because he had done something bad. We always found him lying on the bed when he was in the cave, even though it was poorly ventilated and so hot he kept his shirt unbuttoned at the front. He wouldn't go out on an errand and usually spent his free time picking lice off himself. All of us were troubled by lice, but student soldiers weren't given the leisure time to kill them one by one. The way Takeshita picked off lice gave him the appearance of a soldier who'd wandered in from a different cave. It was rumored that he had such nerve because even the company commander treated him with some respect.

"Stop that racket!" Takeshita got up and slapped me on the cheek.

"No, you shut up!" L.Cpl. Suzuki yelled. Leaping up from behind the transmitter, he grabbed Takeshita, who was about to get back into bed, and slapped him across the face. Rubbing his cheek, Takeshita again turned away to lie down on the bed, and as he did, I clearly heard him spit out ominously, "Watch your back, because a bullet may not always come from the front." He also mumbled, "Now that middle-school students are told to play soldier, it's no wonder there will be no victory for us." Suzuki made no response to these remarks, though he couldn't have missed hearing them.

Sometime later, there was an incident that made me believe Takeshita had meant what he said. About twelve hours after we withdrew from Hantagawa in the pouring rain, we crossed Yamagawa Bridge, in Haebaru Village. For some reason, Takeshita lagged behind the unit, and apparently losing his footing, he fell into a ditch. As soon as he got up, he pointed his gun directly at Suzuki. It so happened that a few moments earlier, the rain and bombardment had let up and the air had cleared. So I could clearly see

Takeshita. The next moment, however, aircraft started strafing our position, and Takeshita dropped his gun to take cover. I couldn't have proved what I saw, but I was convinced that some deadly form of infighting would soon occur.

L.Cpl. Suzuki must have known how dangerous S.Pvt. Takeshita could be. Why then did he stand up for me against Takeshita's bullying? I wondered about that every time I saw the two of them as we travelled through the muddy plains of Shimajiri, the air filled with gun smoke.

Sometime before the rainy season, a transmitter broke down at Hantagawa. A report came in saying that there had been casualties in the nearby Fifth Company, so I was ordered to get an extra transmitter from the area. The passage in the back of the cave was blocked, so I had to carry the transmitter out of the cave. When I returned safely, L.Cpl. Suzuki hailed me, standing at the entrance as if waiting to meet me there. He asked me where I was from and extended his right arm, pointing his hand toward the ridge line in the north and sweeping it from west to east. He pointed in the direction of the First Prefectural Middle School and Yoshu dormitory, whose memory brought me a small burst of pleasure. His finger moved to the right just before he lowered his arm, and he seemed to point in the direction of Nakagusuku.

"From Nakagusuku, sir." Although he said nothing in response, I felt happy.

Three days later, however, when my parents showed up with a gift of brown sugar for me, he raised his voice at them. "Do you realize how dangerous this is?!" The team leader, standing next to him, seemed very surprised by his tone.

While I knew the rebuke was made with good intentions, it could have been interpreted as blaming my parents for causing the troops trouble and endangering them. Since civilians were not supposed to know the exact location of a company, their visit indeed took us by surprise. Of course he couldn't be accusing my parents of spying, so I chose to regard his rebuke as a form of concern for everyone's safety. Or perhaps he was envious of me for being stationed near my hometown.

I learned later that around this time, the Nakagusuku area had been taken by the American troops, so my parents might have been on their way to Shimajiri to find refuge. In any case, that was the last time I ever saw them.

I came to share my own journey of escape with L.Cpl Suzuki as a result of a small accident. Before being conscripted, I had never realized that a fully equipped military backpack was so heavy. Containing a change of clothes, a blanket, a camping pot, and other daily items—a pickaxe and work shovel tied to the outside—a military backpack weighed as much as thirty kilos. Student soldiers were not considered grown up enough to carry a rifle; however, we often had to carry transmitters and small power generators in addition to our backpacks. I wonder now how thirteen- and fourteen-year-old middle-school boys were able to carry such loads.

Once, when I managed with great difficulty to carry a power generator out of a cave and was about to take my first step forward, I lost my footing in the mud. Inadvertently, I let go of the generator. In an instant, L.Cpl Suzuki yelled, "Idiot!" He didn't hit me, though; instead, he picked up the power generator himself. And so it was only by accident that when we began our retreat, L.Cpl. Suzuki undertook to be the one to carry the generator. I never volunteered to try to carry it again, perhaps because I secretly decided to take advantage of what had happened or perhaps, regrettably, because I simply wasn't up to the task. I don't remember anymore. In any case, from that time on, while the lance corporal carried the generator, I became responsible for carrying his rifle. No shot was fired with that rifle until the end of the war.

I first noticed that Suzuki was without the generator when one day, on our journey south, he suddenly slipped down a small mount, Yozadake. As he was about to fall, I reached out with both hands and stopped him.

"Lance Corporal, sir, what happened to the generator?"

"I wonder where…"

Either he had thrown it away somewhere or he had left it behind. "We have no use for it anyway," he said with a broad smile. He took his rifle back from me then. I think he was probably preparing for the worst, in the face of the impending defeat. Eventually, Japanese soldiers were driven to the coast of Mabuni and as far as the cape, Kyan-misaki. Even after we heard in late June that both the army commander and the chief of staff had committed suicide and that we no longer had any organized combat capability, we carried on day after day, unable to comprehend the momentousness of these events. Finally, the news of the unconditional surrender of Japan reached us. Even then, some of us didn't surrender, remaining in caves until as late as October or November and stubbornly refusing to believe in a "false rumor."

They say we all believed that Japan had been victorious, but I don't buy that. We felt ashamed of being taken prisoner. Or rather, we simply couldn't accept the reality that we had lost the war. Perhaps we felt ashamed for having believed victory was possible. Many of us couldn't bear to live with our feelings. Perhaps it was because L.Cpl Suzuki couldn't stand the loss of face that he killed himself using the makeshift hand grenade he had taken from Agarie…

The events began when a bomb exploded nearby, and Agarie and I immediately dropped to our stomachs out of fear of being caught in the blast. When we looked up, then at each other, we heard a voice.

"Suzuki, I'm going ahead," someone said as he passed by us.

"Ah, Kurihara…," Suzuki said, then fell silent. In my daze, the memory of something flickered. I remembered that when I had gone over to the neighboring Fifth Company to borrow a transmitter, it had been handed to me by a L.Cpl Kurihara. I had reported to the baby-faced man the name of my superior, L.Cpl Suzuki. Later, L.Cpl Suzuki told me that he and Kurihara had been classmates in elementary school in Ehime Prefecture. "So, Kurihara has been doing well," said Suzuki with a pleased expression, seemingly satisfied with my report.

It was the voice of the same L.Cpl Kurihara, calling Suzuki's name, that I had heard. A soldier from the Fifth Company, Kurihara might have strayed into our Fourth Company—or maybe it was the other way around.

The woman I met in Tokyo at the community gathering told me that L.Cpl Kurihara had gotten home safely and had mentioned Suzuki to her.

Kurihara had said to Suzuki's niece, "There were young student soldiers in the communications troop, and I met one of them, someone by the name of Kobashigawa,"adding that she could perhaps ask me to find out the details of Suzuki's death. Being a Christian, she said she considered it no less than God's will that she had found me right in the middle of Tokyo.

I have come down from Tokyo to meet Seishō Agarie in part to see just whether "God's will" is in fact a certainty. Agarie is the only one I can depend on in this matter. Out of all of the many people whose destinies I shared in Hantagawa and Mabuni, I had no one else to ask, and this in itself seemed to me a strange twist of fate.

"Those lemon powders." Agarie takes a drink of orange juice and looks at me, then holds the glass in front of him as if to ask for my agreement.

"He says that quite often," his wife observes. She looks at me as if to apologize. According to her, those were the first words he had uttered after a long time of being unable to maintain a normal conversation.

I see that Agarie remembers something, so maybe to revive his memories in full, he needs just one more little push…

I had entirely forgotten about the lemon powder. After the war, the Americans started distributing all kinds of food, some of it totally unfamiliar to us, such as lemon powder. Cubes of dried apples came in cans, and there were yellow powders, resembling wheat flour, called ice cream *gū*, which seemed to have a bit of the Okinawan language in its name. Much of the food was very strange, surprising us with unimaginable flavors. Although it was tasty, as I recall, it could not fill our stomachs. The food had probably been part of field rations. Lemon powder was the only thing we called by its English name. It dissolved instantly in water, creating a real lemon drink. Now, seeing that Agarie's mind retains the memory of it, I'm deeply moved, and encouraged to try to revive more memories.

Though Agarie seems unable to recognize me as Eisuke Kobashigawa, he can still recall things about lemon powder. Perhaps he may be nudged into remembering something about L.Cpl. Suzuki.

"We should undertake a sword attack," L.Cpl. Suzuki had suggested soon after the American bombardment had ceased that evening. One of the things we had learned back in Hantagawa, while we were exposed daily to naval bombardment and machine-gun fire, was that the assault would stop for about an hour during the evening. We guessed that it was probably mealtime for the American soldiers. When I reached the coast of Mabuni, I felt relieved for a short while during one of the lulls between bombardments. The beams from the setting sun in the west were casting shades of colors on the clouds above the east coast. Watching the clouds gradually shifting from bright red to purple, and from purple to the darkness of black ink, I wondered how many more times I would be able to enjoy this view. When the color of the ocean in front of us began to shift from deep purple to pitch black, every one of us dispersed soldiers must have been entertaining the same thought: the hour of the sword attack is approaching.

"Sword attack" originally referred to a desperate, disorganized charge by a small band of dispersed soldiers against the Americans. But for some time now, we had been using the same phrase to refer to our forays for food. The Japanese military had left caches of wartime supplies hidden in Shimajiri, in preparation for a drawn-out battle. With no other choices, the dispersed soldiers learned to raid these caches under cover of darkness in order to get such supplies as rice, miso, and canned food. Even young soldiers like me, with no weapons to fight with, would call this a sword attack.

"Perhaps, Team Leader Takita," Suzuki said, as if to suggest that this was a big favor to us all, "or perhaps Agarie can tell me…Do you know where those caches are located?"

"I can," Takita replied, resigned to Suzuki's presumptuous tone. Suzuki responded with his proposal for a sword attack.

"Yes, but the moon…" The sun had gone down. Takita gazed hesitantly at the eastern sea, where we could see the familiar, dark array of warships. High overhead, directly above the ships, was a large moon, perhaps marking the sixteenth or seventeenth day of the lunar calendar. It reminded me that the expression "the night of the full moon" was usually linked with festivity. But our immediate concern was that the bright moon would increase our risk of being seen and shot by the enemy. After the war, I studied an old calendar and saw that 16 May of the lunar calendar for that year, or 25 June of the new calendar, came just two days after the army commander committed suicide. The ships of the American fleet kept broadcasting the announcement "No more fighting is necessary, so please surrender immediately." I don't know whether the Americans knew about the army commander's suicide, but the announcement was effective in driving the dispersed soldiers into abject despair. It did not necessarily help us embrace defeat; rather, it sometimes had the effect of focusing our minds on death and encouraging us to mount a real, suicidal sword attack.

In this situation, Suzuki stopped using honorifics for Takita, and so, as four equals, we came to agree on attempting a raid on a supply cache.

"I see the moonlight presents a risk, but…" While he acknowledged Takita's concern about the moonlight, Suzuki proceeded to insist that we procure food supplies without delay. Takita's facial expression told us that he no longer cared about preserving his dignity. Suzuki seemed to get the message. He pointed to me and said, "Kobashigawa will be of no use with that wounded leg of his."

To me, Suzuki's words conveyed no sympathy, but rather his intention to leave me behind as useless. I was excused. I decided to spend the time by picking maggots out of my wound, using the moonlight to see by.

Moonlight reminds you of sweet dreams only when your world is not consumed by war. On the battlefield, the moonlight will show you miserable ruins of buildings and trees, piles of dead bodies in which you can't tell soldiers from civilians, mounds of feces smothering plants and grasses. A profoundly horrible stench envelopes everything. It's in the midst of such chaos that one makes a final attack.

Earlier in our journey south, after leaving Shuri, we passed through the villages of Haebaru and Kochinda, then arrived at the village of Mabuni. I had been enchanted by the rich greenery in every direction. Set in the landscape were the villagers' moist, dusky houses, with roofs made of dark-brown thatch or red tiles. The same orderly enchantment permeated our home villages, the town of Shuri, and the villages to the north. Now, they had all been burnt down. For a while longer, the southern village was still intact. When I saw it, I was as surprised as if I'd discovered something of great beauty. By that time, however, no one had been living in the village for a week, and very quickly it would become a wasteland of wretched, stinking ruins. In the village, you could desperately try to reach a cache of things to eat. But could you find one before a bullet found you? In a mixture of hope and fear, I waited for the three others to come back.

At about the time the moon reached its highest point, or perhaps had even dipped down toward the west, I woke up with a start and realized that I had fallen asleep. If you are so tired that you fall asleep in the midst of picking maggots out of your flesh, then you will have no problem falling asleep on coral rocks, but you will not sleep for very long. I woke up dizzy from lack of food. At around two in the morning, wracked by hunger, I worried if the others would come back safely. The soldiers who until just a short while ago had been hiding behind the nearby rocks were gone. I wondered if they had departed to mount their own raids or to attempt to break through the enemy line to escape to the north.

Around three, Takita came back alone. He carried a cardboard box containing a dozen combat food supplies we would learn after the war to call K-rations.

I had thought that all supply caches belonged to the Japanese, but it appeared the Americans had been creating their own. I later learned that the American military had a large supply cache near the coast of Gushichan. They apparently also created smaller caches for the inland units, and it was one of these that Takita must have come across.

"This is incredible!" I cried out in surprise. Each container of K-rations had biscuits as the main staple, small cans of cheese and ham as side dishes, and four cigarettes to complete the meal. After the war, when Japanese survivors first received these rations from the American military, some would smile wryly and say, "No wonder Japan lost the war."

I was on the point of asking Takita what had happened to Agarie.

"It's war bounty." Takita stuck out his chest in a rare demonstration of pride. Pillaged from the American supplies, this was certainly a bounty beyond all expectations. I laughed out loud for the first time in a long time. Shortly after that, however, Takita fell to the ground. He lay there without moving until daybreak, and even after the sun rose high. From time to time I thought he was dead.

Two full days later, Agarie returned. It was night, and the moon was about to rise. In almost total silence, he too came carrying a cardboard box, but it contained only twelve dozen small packs of powder, which I could not identify. I guessed what it was when I made out the words LEMON POWDER. I felt a little sorry to see his embarrassed smile as he opened up one of the packets. I refrained from pointing out how little he had gained after risking his life. Agarie might have been the first Okinawan to see lemon powder, but that was something he would have to wait quite a while to learn and feel proud about. I was about to say that I had almost given him up for dead. But I refrained, fearing that my words might sound mocking. And after all, we could still use the powder to alleviate hunger. We somehow figured out that by adding water, we could make lemon water. But where were we to get water? We ended up eating the powder dry. Not only did that not help fill our empty stomachs, but it also made us terribly thirsty. We walked around in desperation, searching for the canteen of a dead soldier. I suffered so greatly that I almost clawed at my throat. The moment I found a canteen next to a corpse, I sensed keenly that, though I was suffering terribly, I was indeed alive. When Agarie says "lemon powder" now, does he recall this incident?

Several days later, the three of us surrendered and became prisoners of war. Suzuki, however, never showed up.

I was reminded of S.Pvt. Takeshita. I had seen a man leaning against a nearby rock. He was alone, holding his rifle between his knees and pointing its muzzle at his throat. I held my breath, expecting to see him die the next second. Instead I saw that he was merely practicing. He was still wearing his shoes and so couldn't possibly pull the trigger with his foot. I felt odd witnessing this. The way he took the rifle from his throat reminded me of the way Takeshita had aimed at Suzuki and then lowered his rifle.

Could Takeshita have killed Suzuki?

When did I last see Takeshita? Was it before or after the regiment was disbanded? He might have encountered Suzuki at some point. And who knows? He might have had another opportunity to kill him. After Suzuki was separated from Agarie during the raid on the supply cache, he must have wandered around alone for several days. Perhaps he had been killed during that time.

"No way." I abandoned that obsessive thought. If Takeshita had chanced to meet Suzuki somewhere, they would have just looked at each other in a stupor, making eye contact in silence and merely noting the fact that neither had yet died. Takeshita must now be dead, and Suzuki must have met the same fate. Before long, I had accepted as fact the idea that they had died.

"I am to blame, right?" Weeping, Agarie mumbled quietly in front of the wire mesh surrounding our POW camp, somewhere far to the north. I remember that I had already received treatment at the American army hospital, and there were signs of autumn on the devastated landscape.

Agarie had gotten separated from Takita early in their hunt for a supply cache, and they had ended up at different places. Agarie had lost his way to the Japanese cache that Takita had been talking about, and while wandering around, he came across the American cache. He was in a difficult predicament because every time he caught sight of an enemy soldier, he had to dive to the ground or hide behind something. Suddenly he realized that Suzuki was by his side and that the lance corporal had perhaps been with him all the time. "Suzuki seemed to be trying to protect me," said Agarie.

They sneaked up to the American cache together, but were spotted by a guard. Agarie heard a gunshot that he was sure was aimed at them.

"It's dangerous here. We should pass on this one," Suzuki advised.

But Agarie wouldn't give up with a massive stack of white cardboard boxes right in front of him. "It's going to be a glorious bounty," he thought. There was no time to figure out the English words stamped on the boxes. He was elated the moment he grabbed one of them. He figured he had gotten away with it when he managed to evade the guard, ran for about a hundred meters, and hid himself in a half-burned sugarcane field. At that point, Agarie realized Suzuki wasn't with him anymore. He put the box on the ground and returned to the supply cache, but he finally had to give up looking for Suzuki.

When he first sneaked up to the American supply cache, Agarie had seen the moon still in the eastern sky, so he thought it must have been before twelve. He had no memory of the location of the moon when he left with the cardboard box. In any case, he had already lost sight of Suzuki. Recalling that he had heard a gunshot the moment he picked up the box, he wondered if Suzuki had been hit.

"What about the hand grenade?" I asked. As far as I could tell, after Suzuki had taken Agarie's hand grenade, he never returned it. Suzuki hadn't liked the awkward way Agarie had been handling it. Perhaps Suzuki used it for his own purposes at some point. Ironically, Suzuki's having taken it from Agarie may have enabled Agarie to survive the war.

Agarie gave me a sidelong look and did not respond to my question.

After becoming separated from Suzuki, he hadn't been able to find his way back and had wandered around for three days, carrying the war bounty that turned out to be nearly inedible. The way he looked at me may have indicated a sense of shame about the experience.

I remember how he looked then, standing in front of the wire mesh of the POW camp. Or rather, I'm reminded of it now as Agarie picks up the glass of orange juice and looks at me out of the corners of his eyes.

"He died between 25 and 28 June," I told Suzuki's niece, meaning I believed the death occured during the two or three days I had been anxiously waiting for him to return from the raid on the supply cache.

However, when it comes to knowing exactly when and where he died, and whether he managed to reach a POW camp, I honestly have no clue. Although the war came to an end for Japan on 15 August, some of the first middle-school students in the communications corps weren't taken prisoner until October. There is no way now to determine if Suzuki had been among them.

Things get even fuzzier.

"The war is over, so please surrender immediately." I have a memory of listening to this announcement as I was opening up Agarie's cardboard box. If my memory serves me correctly, the moon was illuminating the side of the white, American-made box, and that means Agarie returned with it soon after the moon rose, on about the twentieth day of the lunar calendar. The day Japan surrendered was the eighth day of the seventh month according to the lunar calendar, so that would have made it towards the end of August. I can further recall coming across an American supply cache myself, sometime around the end of June, and I may be confusing those two incidents. But what a huge difference between the end of June and the end of August.

I am now plagued by a thought that hadn't occurred to me before, not even back in the POW camp. I now regret having told Suzuki's niece that he died between 25 and 28 June. I cannot bring myself to tell her that August is also a possibility. We who survived may adjust the dates casually, but for her—or rather for the eldest sister of Suzuki, who is said to be close to one hundred years old—such dates are considerably more important.

How significant is it for the average Japanese person to know the exact day of someone's death? You never know. It all depends on how closely each person is linked to the deceased. To be more exact, I've come to be haunted by the feeling that it is terribly negligent and disrespectful for a person who didn't experience losing someone in the war to underestimate the pain of uncertainty.

I hesitated to ask Suzuki's niece about his remains. Upon being conscripted into the military, all of us student soldiers were told to submit a strand of hair and chips of fingernails—and to prepare a will—in the event that we died in battle. Actually, though, this was required of us merely to make us feel better. Thinking about it now, it seems obvious that we will never find any remains of Suzuki.

When I first became fully aware that no one would ever be able to give an account of Suzuki's death, it struck me that not only were the details unknowable, but the memory of my own wartime wandering was lost as well. In fact, the memories of my whole life evaporated into the sky over Shimajiri. "I was injured on the left thigh, and then received kind and careful treatment from L.Cpl. Suzuki, and it was with his support that I managed to reach as far south as the coast of Mabuni…" I wished to communicate these thoughts and express my gratitude to Suzuki's niece, but the words were stuck in my throat and never came out, partly because I was afraid that they might sound false or insincere. Not remembering my experiences on the battlefield may be merely a selfish way to protect myself from pain.

Was it June or August? I felt compelled to ask Agarie and wished that he were there in front of me. But if he had been there, would I have been excused from my own responsibility to remember?

"I will ask a man named Seishō Agarie," I had told the woman. I was being evasive, but I also wished to demonstrate my sincere desire to explore one last avenue for finding out the truth. Agarie, after all, was the only person who might be able to provide information about the death of the Mitsuru Suzuki. The lance corporal might have committed suicide with a hand grenade that Agarie had turned over to him. I decided that I would ask Agarie once again.

While holding a glass of orange juice in his hand, Agarie remembers things about the lemon powder from the end of the war. Perhaps I still have some hope. The words "supply cache" may help him remember the rest. I'm ready to ask another question, but then I swallow it before speaking. Squinting the slender eyes we used to make fun of, Agarie just now raised his right hand to wave at me. That is the same hand I saw waving from the road. All memories are perhaps lost in him.

"He often goes out to the street where the bus runs," his wife says. "He waves at everyone on the bus," she adds. She feels a little better than before because he at least doesn't go prowling around or urinate in his pants.

The fact remains, however, that Agarie chose to build his house here, near the stone streets of Kinjō Town, where he has a good view of the cave in which the former communications corps took cover. And this convinces me that he is still trying to deal with his wartime memories. Did he choose this site because of simple, innocent nostalgia for the old times, the kind of sentiment that causes some people to sing old military songs? Or was he determined to face a past that was full of profound regret? His condition makes me believe he was moved by deeper concerns. There is no longer any way to know, but I console myself with the thought that contacting him and sharing these moments have been meaningful for both of us.

I tell his wife I will give up trying to find out more about L.Cpl. Suzuki. Nevertheless, I say, I feel happy that I came to see him.

She replies, "I thought I would feel sorry to see you come all this way to meet my husband in his present state, but I couldn't bring myself to tell you about him over the phone or in a letter."

"That's all right now," I'm about to say, but stop myself because I realize that the wartime memories are forever impressed in Agarie's mind.

"But of course I'm glad to have you here..." Her words almost sound like an attempt to excuse herself. "I hear you were the model for the statues of the young men." Then she starts to talk about something that seems unrelated.

Agarie's son is now a police officer working for Naha Police Station. One day, an elderly man, apparently a laborer, reported to the station. It was last year, shortly after New Year's Day. Assistant Police Inspector Agarie came out to speak to him. The man identified himself as Yasuo Mihara and confessed that he was the one who had vandalized the statues of the young men. Having been born in 1971, the year of Okinawa's "reversion" to Japan, the assistant inspector had never heard about the vandalism. In fact, he was learning just then that the tower of youths had originally been statues of students; and he had never once heard anyone mention the name of the architect, Mr. T. Now, as Yasuo Mihara turned himself in, it was possible to retrieve a missing piece of history. From the viewpoint of the police, however, the incident was just an ordinary case of minor vandalism. The statute of limitations had run out, so the police deemed the case no longer fit for prosecution. In the end, they could do nothing but courteously ask the man to leave.

When Assistant Police Inspector Agarie casually mentioned this incident to his father, Seishō Agarie, something unexpected happened.

Agarie forced his son to reveal the man's name and address—he had a hunch about who had vandalized the statues—and paid a visit to the man's house. Located in the southern corner of the settlement of Makabi, it was a two-story house of modest size and about as cheerful looking as other ordinary houses. From its southward garden, one could overlook the basin of Matsugawa. Agarie experienced a moment of déjà vu when he saw the landscape before him, perhaps because it resembled the distant view of Hantagawa from the town of Kinjō.

Agarie asked the man, with a hint of reproach, why he had destroyed the statues. The man began his story by identifying himself as the younger brother of Kōmei Mihara, a middle-school student who had died while in the communications corps. "So, it's about Kōmei Mihara," Agarie thought. His hunch proven right, he kept asking questions, meanwhile visualizing the caves in Hantagawa and Sakiyama.

As I recall, Kōmei Mihara was enlisted in a stationary company located on the slope of Sakiyama Town, next to the town of Kinjō, which faced

Higa Yasuo: Maternal Deities

Worshipping the Gods (Kami-agami)
Kudaka Island, Kudaka-udun-myā Hatigwati
1978

Hantagawa. The word "stationary" didn't mean much to us, and I didn't think that his company differed from ours with respect to everyday routines and duties. Once, however, while I was on an errand to fetch provisions and fodder, I saw a large naval bomb land and explode right in front of the cave that housed the stationary company. Even though I witnessed the explosion from about two hundred meters away, my whole body stiffened, and I wondered if any of my fellow middle-school student soldiers had been injured. I wanted to set down the two-wheeled cart that I was pushing and wait for the smoke to clear, but the soldier with me urged me to move on. Agarie might have seen the same explosion.

"Did he die at Sakiyama?" asked Agarie, thinking that Kōmei Mihara might have been killed in that explosion. "No, some people say he died at Komesu," the brother replied calmly, "and others say at Kakazu." Komesu and Kakazu are quite far apart, however. Such conflicting information seemed to indicate that no one saw him die, and it was all second hand. One has to conclude that though nobody was able to confirm Kōmei Mihara's place of death, Shimajiri could not be eliminated as a possibility. The same goes for the date of his death. I'm told that, on hearing this news, Agarie seemed more agitated than Yasuo Mihara did.

How had the small-bodied Kōmei Mihara—who was much shorter than average— managed to duck the bombs and bullets all the way down to Shimajiri and end up dying there? Was he perhaps with someone severe but also caring, like L.Cpl. Suzuki, who was with me? I can only sigh.

"When they built these statues of young men, I was terribly upset," Yasuo Mihara said, facing the direction of the tower of youths, "but I guess I was more jealous than resentful. These statues of young men were to live forever. The peaceful figures, though not even human, would live better than we humans had, and it felt unbearably wrong." This was the reasoning of the man who had lost his loving brother on the battlefield, where, though still a boy, the brother had been hastily turned into a fledgling soldier. The man wanted to let people know how he truly felt, and to explain that he hadn't done it for fun. But the police officer had been merely dismissive. Mihara smiled at Agarie—a lonely sort of smile.

According to his wife, Agarie had started acting strangely immediately after this meeting. Listening to her story, I suspected that the meeting intensified Agarie's deep regrets about Suzuki. While the memories of the war seem to be lost in his mind, I believe that the meeting triggered in Agarie an even stronger mental fixation on the war. His memories will never perish now. It's just that they will remain unexpressed. It's a matter of little importance whether or not other people can understand him, isn't it?

I'm certain that my visit has been worthwhile. I will now be able to give an account that Suzuki's niece can understand.

"I wonder: what does it mean when you say, 'remembering the war'?" Agarie's wife asks. Undecided if she should let the memories fade away, she will nevertheless keep on talking to her husband about them. At the same time, she will continue to express her indecisiveness. I can imagine her inner struggle.

"So, the date of death can be any day." When I say this, I see an ambiguous smile around the eyes of his wife. Does she feel relieved that she is no longer responsible for his memories?

Instead of catching the inbound bus, I get on the outbound bus I had taken earlier. At the end of the line, I board an inbound bus to return. As I pass the tower of youths for the second time, I try to imagine that the statues of young men are still standing. But when I recall how unforgivable that thought may be for Yasuo Mihara, for a brief moment the landscape in front of the bus dissolves into an illusion.

I realize that soon my bus will once again pass by the spot where Agarie had waved at me.

Translation by Hamagawa Hitoshi

Three Poems

THE WELL

Crossing a battlefield in single file,
A woman leads a child and an old farmer.
In the lead-gray light before dawn,
The weedy grasses are silvered by dew.

Empty tin buckets swing on the ends
Of the pole the old man carries across
His shoulders. This quiet May morning!

Around them, defeated soldiers squat
On the beach, under the poor shade of palms,
Under rock ledges. Their eyes are glazed,
Their canteens dangle from their shoulder clips.

On a hardscrabble trail toward a palm grove,
In the lead-gray mist before dawn,
The three—this quiet May morning!

—begin running in desperation,
Exposed to enemy gunfire,
For the grove beyond the open field.
This quiet May morning.

At the grove's edge is a well
In the limestone, and a cave so dark,
Sunlight reaches it bent and broken.

Inside the cave the terrified people
Huddle together, dip their cups in the well,
Whispering to one another
Like the sounds of water dripping.

Higa Yasuo: Maternal Deities

Divine Women (Kami-nchu)
Miyako Island, Karimata
1995

If a bomb kills everyone here, the water
Will continue seeping into the well,
As if you had never existed. So drink up.

Slake your thirst. And listen
As enough sweet water touches your lips
For you to survive another day.
Outside the grove, a legless soldier begs.

His phantom limbs extend
Into the nothingness, his pleading mouth
A hole of emptiness to be filled.

Oh, give him water!
Give him his last water
And don't leave him to die thirsty,
This quiet May morning!

Where the dawn breaks soundlessly
As if silence were a shelter against the rain
Of fire that each day starts falling.

A CORAL ISLAND

Inside, the cave's walls and ceiling
The steady seeping of rain.
Outside, the May rain falling,
Falling.

This shining rain
On the concrete, on the naval ship
Floating invisibly,
Inside the season's rain,
The steady May rain.

The rain in Saigon,
The rain in Naha,
The rain in the naval harbor,
A nuclear submarine in the mist.

Agitating the heavy water,
Drunk on the goblets of black crude,
A shark thrashes out to sea.

The sweet May rain
Runs down my cheeks.
In a rice paddy an artillery shell
Wallows in the mud.

Sweet waters of the stream
Moisten my dry mouth.
I am burdened like a pack animal.
Several men accompany me,

Walking single file through the field,
In the open, exposed,
We leave our fate to the gods.

The horn blaring,
The bus halts in the neon rain.
The red fins of her raincoat fluttering,
A woman swims off the bus, in rain,

In the rain seeping in the cave,
The rain on the cave's walls and ceiling,
On the black trees where
The bus stops in the neon rain.

And I plunge into the town
Where the people like embryonic
Fish, all safe in their bubble-sac,
Watch the rain falling.

The rain in Saigon,
The rain in Tokyo falling.
On the bus for the airport,
The pounding rain, the rain

Falling in the town's listless boredom,
In the insufferable boredom of peacetime.

UMANORI: RIDING HORSES

What kind of "riding horses" is this?
It's simple: you bore a hole down
Through the ceiling of a cave,
Pour something flammable in,
Then toss a match, or a grenade.

Umanori is what Americans learned
On the battlefields of the Pacific war,
Perfected it on Okinawa Island.
Regarded it as permissible during war.
Above the caves: American soldiers.

Underground: the ones who will wear
Flaming hoods of sorrow.
Needless to say there are infants
In the arms of mothers, old women
Old men, amidst the Japanese soldiers

All wearing hoods of sorrow, cooked alive
Inside the ovens. Can you restore the bodies
Of pregnant mothers, whose bodies were tombs
Inside a flaming tomb? Foolish dreams.
To ride such horses is to ride them forever.

Translation by Katsunori Yamazato and Frank Stewart

Higa Yasuo: *Maternal Deities*

Divine Women (Kami-nchu)
Kudaka Island, Hokama noro
1976

Two Poems

Cape Kyan is the southernmost tip of Okinawa Island, where some of the most desperate fighting occurred in the last days of the Battle of Okinawa. Fearing capture by American troops, many civilians jumped to their deaths from the cliffs. A monument to peace and to the souls of those who perished now stands on the cape.

CAPE KYAN

By car I reach Cape Kyan,
A place of red earth,
Of infertile soil,
Where the farmers
With their hoes nevertheless
Chop beautifully shaped furrows.

The sea below
Is transparent blue.
The waves pound the cliff,
Wearing away rock already weary
And crumbling. And bones
Of a fossilized mammoth

Bake in the relentless sun.
On the rocky cliff the yellow
Tsuwabuki flowers wave
At the year's first sunrise.
They hurt my eyes. The grasses
Spread a green shroud

Over the blood-soaked earth.
In the intense light the sculpture
To Peace—through its hollow circle,
Across the small stone sphere,

You gaze intently southward,
Through an eternal absence.

We dedicate a *tsuwabuki* flower
And its evergreen leaves
And pray, as if murmuring
To a lover, our palms together,
Rubbing away at the resentment,
At the sadness, and anger

Until they sink one after the next
Deep inside us
At Cape Kyan,
Like the sea
Like the waves that growl
From the ocean's abyss, we pray

As if pulling the last trigger
At Cape Kyan.

AN ANCIENT BANYAN

Today through a breach in the encircling reef
the son who departs dreaming
of joining a revolution in a northern city
someday will return on the tide—
the son who renounced a village
that still believes in the spirit world
and the gods. In the same village,
the mother never gives up waiting.

In rainy May and June,
harvesting sweet potato leaves
she told him as a child of the *kijimunā*,
mischievous tree spirits. But not of
her own dreams, folded in the deep
lines of her brow. They will not be fulfilled
by a revolution, even the one her wayward
son thinks is worth dying for—

But the ancient mother
has pleaded for the son
to call or write from time to time.

She has no telephone in her house.
If a call comes to the village store
she rushes from home.

Whenever he would call, she saw
the image of her son beyond
the black receiver. But calls
are less frequent. Her feet are weak.
This evening,
a shout from a neighbor comes.

     A call is for her.
On shaking legs, she stumbles
along the stone path, head throbbing,
the banyans creaking louder
in the wind, a coming storm
—an ominous sign.

Out of breath, she imagines him
on the other side of the receiver, hears
his voice: *Mother, this year,*
like last, I cannot come home.
The dreams of the woman in the storm
blow away, her white hair undone.

Translation by Katsunori Yamazato and Frank Stewart

Higa Yasuo: Maternal Deities

Divine Women (Kami-nchu)
Kohama Island, Tsukasa and attendant
1976

The Wild Boar That George Gunned Down

Two days till payday. John and the others had long since run out of money, and George had no more to lend them. Hostesses at the bar no longer sat with and entertained them as they usually did. George noticed that the hostesses kept looking toward the entranceway, waiting for other customers to arrive. George wanted to leave but couldn't say this to his companions. They seemed now to be feeling awkward themselves, after the berserk frenzy of a few moments before. Their bottle of whiskey had been emptied long ago. Requests for more were met with demands for "cash, cash" from the hostesses, who no longer let them touch their breasts and thighs. John, Wilde, and Washington, smoldering just below the surface, seemed on the verge of something. The faces of all three were red and puffed up from the alcohol. Each face, in fact, was getting redder and redder, and each of their muscled bodies was getting more and more tensed. Soon something was bound to set them off. George remained calm and in control of himself, but he felt his heart pounding a bit harder as he observed the mood of his companions. Their vacillation, he thought, was making things worse. *If you're not going to drink, then don't take a drop of the stuff and don't say a word to the hostesses; but if you are going to drink, then you should drink yourself silly, feel up the hostesses, and go on and have sex with them. It has to be one or the other.*

Two of the hostesses casually got to their feet and turned toward the door. Three Caucasians with faces darkly tanned from long exposure to the sun had entered the bar. Each scanned the place with his large eyes. George could tell immediately that they were back from Vietnam on R&R leave. Military on R&R are very free with their money. Hostesses in the A-sign bars—the ones U.S. military personnel were authorized to frequent—called them *yama-otoko* ("men back from the wilds") and went out of their way to offer them every imaginable service. They were the best source of money. George and his group recognized their own less favorable status. George's group was still stationed in Okinawa, having just arrived from the States, while the *yama-otoko* were old-timers, hardened by combat in numerous battles. Even in their sleep, George imagined, these men were never free from thoughts of war. However much they drank, however much they partied, however much they amused themselves with women and sex, still their minds were always in a state of battle readiness. They kept pistols and knives hidden in their pockets, and while this made no difference as long as they were on base, once they went off base they were capable of incalculable violence. In some ways, George looked down on these men.

The last of the hostesses finally got up from their table. With his thick, hairy hand, John grabbed hold of one of them by her arm. "You meaning to leave us?" he hollered. "You turning your nose up at us, you barbarian bitch?" As she struggled to free her arm, the woman pushed with her free hand at John's head, but he forced her to sit down on his lap. Wilde and Washington, on either side of her, pinned her arms and legs. She struggle, screaming hysterically. Wilde pulled down her sheer, black panties and howled with laughter as he tossed them into George's face. Wilde then wedged his knee between her legs, adroitly spread them as he lit a match and then, laughing loudly, shone the light on her crotch. John and Washington bent over to get a clearer view. They also laughed loudly and stared intently at her crotch. George watched the situation with increasing apprehension. The woman struggled frantically to free herself, yelling words that none of them understood. John jammed a handkerchief into her mouth as Wilde placed his match close to her pubic hairs, which frizzled, shriveled up, and in an instant burned out. George glanced at the *yama-otoko*. They were smiling scornfully. The other hostesses were frantically urging them to get George's group to stop, but the *yama-otoko* just stared and did nothing. The trapped woman wore a skin-tight, thick-fabric white dress. John and the other two struggled to pull it off, but were having no luck. Washington took out a jackknife, inserted the blade at the opening at the neck, and cut the front of the dress down to the belly. The woman struggled even harder. She seemed convinced they intended to kill her.

The knife had grazed her skin, and blood oozed out into her dress. George could see the woman was gnashing at the handkerchief in despair. Her eyes were wide with panic. George got up and moved off to the edge of the seat. Washington stroked the woman's neck and cheeks with his knife. There may have been a smile on George's face, but he knew this was no laughing matter. His heart was racing. It was different from when he was drunk. Washington might gouge out one of her eyes, slice off her nose, or poke open an artery in her neck.

The other hostesses were crowded in a circle around them, yelling incomprehensibly. They seemed to be pleading with the men. They also seemed enraged. And sad. George didn't know which it was. One of them grabbed John's jaw from behind with both hands and tugged at him with all her might. Clearly in pain from this, John raised his chin and glared into the woman's face. He clenched his right fist and hit her in the jaw. The blow landed with a loud, cracking sound. She sank to the floor without a word. Screaming and hollering even louder now, the other women bent over the fallen woman. Still hollering and yelling, they carried her to the counter, laid her down, and applied ice wrapped in a towel to her chin. They then came back and again crowded around George's group, each of them gesturing toward the woman on the counter and shouting incomprehensibly. The *yama-otoko* were standing now, casually taking in the scene. They were talking among themselves, with hands on hips or in their pockets, or with their arms folded across their chests. Washington's knife was moving slowly across the trapped woman's small, flattened breasts. The large, dark nipples were prominent in the room's slowly rotating blue light. George estimated she had had five or six children and was nearing her forties. Except for the heavy makeup, her face would have lacked any youthful color, he imagined, and her skin would be flabby and dried out. This was the sort of woman left for the American soldiers to find their pleasure in.

George felt sick. He hoped the others would rape her and get it over with. When they were done, Washington would shoot her dead with his pistol. Trying to grab the knife from Washington, two of the women got into a skirmish with him. Both received cuts on their arms and were bleeding. One of the women, bleeding profusely, retreated behind the counter and pressed moist hand cloths to her cuts. Washington was now incensed. He glanced at the two women who jumped him, released the shoulder of the woman he was holding down, and rose to his feet. The released woman wriggled herself free and stood up. Her feet became entangled in Wilde's legs, and as she furiously shook herself from John's grip she landed on the floor. She began to crawl away on all fours. Washington, shouting something, jumped on her from behind and slashed at her back and buttocks, splitting open her dress. Blood oozed out and soaked her white dress. She hadn't freed the handkerchief from her mouth, yet you could tell she was crying and screaming. Her false eyelashes had been knocked crooked, her eye makeup was running, the white facial cream was smeared, and her heavily painted lips were twisted. George thought her ugly.

Finally, she freed herself from Washington and ran into the women's restroom. He ran after her and inserted the handle of his jackknife between the door and its frame, preventing her from closing the door and locking it. Washington then began yanking on the door knob with both hands. The knife clattered to the floor as the door flew open and Washington fell back onto the seat of his pants. A somewhat heavyset hostess had retrieved the jackknife from the floor, and was pointing it at him. Washington scrambled to his feet and shouted threateningly at the women, who were gathered near the door. In the instant they recoiled from his shouts, he dashed into the restroom and closed the door. The lock clicked shut. In a rush, the women pounded on the door. They could hear wailing, screaming, and moaning from inside, along with high-pitched, ear-splitting laughter, angry shouts, and what sounded like cursing. The handkerchief had come out, it seemed. The women on the outside took turns working the doorknob, tugging on it with all their might, and pounding on the door. They yelled back and forth at each other, terrified at what might be going on inside.

John and Wilde had calmed down quite a bit. Every so often, though, they broke out in loud laughter and angry shouts. George, on the other hand, was getting edgy. He felt like throwing liquor into the women's faces, or smashing glasses or bottles into the shelves behind the counter, or shattering them on the floor. If he didn't do something, he felt, he'd be called a weakling and incapable by the other guys. But he saw no way to involve himself. It was all too chaotic. *How come I held back and couldn't join in with the others? Must be letting myself think too much. And there's no way I'd get any thanks from them screaming women. They'd just accuse me of being a wimp. This is like the rampage John and the guys went on a month ago. Not surprising that they did that. But I did nothing then, either. Also not surprising. A few days later the women in the bar were hanging all over John and the others. I sat there remembering every detail of what had happened, but not those stupid women. They're hopeless. Even Washington, now holed up in that restroom, won't be turned away next time he shows up at this bar. Tomorrow night will roll around and they'll pour his drinks for him and let him fondle their breasts as if nothing ever happened. I'd like to take his jackknife to that moustache he's so proud of, hack the damned thing off, skin and all. And shoot every last one of the hostesses. They're all dis- gusting. Too bad I don't have my pistol with me. I should always carry it. Hearing the bullets shattering the whiskey bottles, the lights, the neon signs, the jukebox. Hearing everything getting busted, that'd be sweet. Firing slugs into the throats of all these repulsive people, laughing with their mouths wide open. That'd be good, huh?*

The front door swung open and the bar owner rushed in. His yellow shirt and black bow tie were a strangely appropriate match to his oily, round face and short, thick-set frame. The middle-aged man went right up to John and began saying something to him. He seemed to know what was going on. George moved over behind John. The owner's English was quite good. But he was speaking in a quiet voice and George couldn't catch all he was saying. The owner seemed to be making a great effort to appear calm. George picked up the general drift. The owner apparently was trying to settle the matter with money. John got to his feet and hollered at him: "I can get them to revoke your A-sign license. Is that what you want?"

A number of local establishments that had lost favor with the American authorities had had their A-sign licenses revoked; their business suffered bitterly as a result. George knew how intimidating this threat was. The owner abruptly turned all smiles, pleaded with John to calm down, and showed himself ready to make a deal. He tried to sound John out, and as he talked he kept lowering the settlement figure. The soldiers, actually, could not care less what he said. "How about we stroke you with this here jackknife," they threatened. To this the owner smiled broadly, looked at each of their faces, and announced his final price. "Twenty dollars," he said. "Last offer. Can't take anything less." George could not believe what he was hearing. *Payment for assaulting the woman, her physical injuries, and the damage to the bar—all this for a measly twenty bucks? Hell, if he is willing to take that,* George told himself, *we should beat down his price even more. Why in the world is this pathetic guy so obsessed with getting so piddling a sum? I can't even look at this guy any longer, he's so disgusting.*

John and the others glared at the man and yelled, "It's all her fault. We're not giving you one damned cent."

The women were now all abuzz over by the restroom. Washington had emerged from it, fastening his belt buckle as he did. The owner immediately approached him and began proposing a negotiated settlement with him. The bleary-eyed Washington barely glanced at the man, and with a hand that seemed as big as a boxing glove pushed him aside as if removing a repulsive eyesore. The owner staggered, tripped over the seats, and fell backwards onto the floor. Moving like a sleepwalker, Washington made his way to the front door, opened it, and went outside. "What's all the fuss about anyway?" John said as he also went through the door. "We were just having a little fun, you inferior bunch of war-losers." George shifted his gaze to the restroom, where the woman, apparently having been raped, was curled up on the floor, surrounded by the other women. Seeing her so still and quiet, George thought she might be dead. The *yama-otoko* repeatedly called out to the women: "What're you all waiting for? Get over here and sit with us!"

George hurried after the others and left the bar. The air outside was suffocating. He could hear a loud voice, apparently the owner's, behind him. George did not turn to look. It sounded like the owner was giving them a tongue-lashing. In Okinawan, most likely. In any case, from the tone, George could tell they were being cussed out. *I imagine he's waving his fists and baring his teeth at us, and all the while inching backwards ready to run,* George thought. *And those hostesses, they must be fawning all over the* yama-otoko *by now.* For some time the abusive language lingered in George's ear. *Why should they be mad at me? I did nothing to harm them.*

George walked two or three steps behind the others. They were talking loudly about wanting to kill Okinawans. Hard to tell if they were serious. They were trying to decide if it would be a cabbie or a clerk in some food store. George realized that their real desire was to rob someone. Whatever it was, they were determined to commit an even crazier act of violence than what they had just done. *But why take things that far?* George thought. *All they want is some money to buy their drinks and some money to buy their women.* The men walked along bantering back and forth. "Hey, they flip up their skirts at you." "Yeah, and none of them are wearing any panties. At the

Green, that is. They squeal with delight when they do it, they love it." "At the Oriental they let you stick your finger in their panties. You can touch anything you want. My fingers get worn out doing it. Do they let you, too?" "Yeah, but that Emiko there, she climbs right up on your lap and wraps her arms around your neck. Won't let go for anything. She's more than I can handle." "Come on, man, what are you saying? That grin shows you don't seem to mind." "Yeah, it's really wild there. People spraying beer around on each other, raising hell." "Hey, George, what bar do you like to go to?" "Anywhere's OK," George replied without thinking. "Aren't we heading back to the base soon?" George wasn't in the mood for drinking. He felt sweaty under his arms and had a feeling something bad was about to happen. There was nothing unusual in the way Washington was behaving now, but seeing him pull out his jackknife was still vivid in George's mind.

"I've had women drink beer through there, many's the time," Washington was saying proudly. "You force the bottle up in there. They get drunk, too, even when they drink it through there. It's true. Most of 'em end up drop-dead drunk."

As they walked down the street, women from the bars grabbed at their arms trying to get them to come in. John and the others walked by each group, responding only with obscenities and teasing. They were all familiar with this scene.

After a while the men came to a halt. "Hey, George," Washington turned around to address him. "What about that watch of yours."

"Watch?" But George knew immediately what Washington meant. They wanted to pawn it. "This watch won't fetch much," George said. "The pawn shops are all so tight-fisted."

"What, then, are you proposing we do, George?" John was looking at him expectantly. "You can get money some other way?"

"George would be the one to have money," Wilde chimed in. "You've got some stashed away, quite a pile, I bet."

"Oh, that's right," John smiled thinly. "Just like George says, you can't expect much from pawning a watch, or a cigarette lighter, a pendant—or a jackknife? Isn't that right, Washington?"

"OK, I'll go back and get some," George said. George didn't like the way they were looking at him, as if to say, "What in the world are you hoarding all your money for?"

"Yeah, you do that, George. We'll chip in and pay you back on payday. Promise." John patted George on the shoulder. *Of course, they never do pay me back,* George thought. *But, what the hell. It doesn't matter.*

"Washington, you go back with him," Wilde said.

"I'll go by myself," George responded, glancing at Washington, who wrapped a thick arm over George's shoulder, as if about to escort him away.

"No, let me," Washington said. "We can be back in half an hour if we take a cab."

"Good. We'll be at the Mississippi," John replied, tapping George lightly on the cheek and then striding off down the street.

George and Washington found a cab right away. "Let's do this up big and have some fun, George. We'll be in Vietnam soon and won't be able to do this for awhile." Washington kept patting George on the shoulder.

George kept thinking he wanted to hand over the money to Washington, then stretch out on his barracks bed and write a letter to Emily. It was not yet ten o'clock. He knew that if he stayed behind, John would surely come and get him. *I'll have to go in any case. John comes almost every night to get me. What does he think I am?*

They were young Caucasian women. Each of them had longish curly hair, some blond, some chestnut-brown. Their breasts were large and firm, and the pale orange nipples seemed small. They must be virgins and surely younger than he was, George thought. He couldn't tell which tits belonged to which woman. They all looked alike, and the women were wrapped snake-like around each other. *These Okinawan bar hostesses are so cheap. The way they wriggle their bodies, sitting right up against me, rubbing their gnarled hands over my chest and down my pants trying to turn me on. And their collection of smells—sweat, semen, smoke, whiskey, cosmetics—that jumble of strong smells is always there.*

He spotted one woman who looked like Emily. He studied the screen intently. The woman shook her brown hair that hung down from her upside-down head, which George could see between the white fleshy thighs spread wide apart. She moved her tongue sensuously. The red of her lips and the size of her large eyes made her look childlike. *No*, George corrected himself, *it's not Emily. Emily smiles all the time, showing her white teeth. And she ties her hair up in back.*

Over and over the private parts of the young women were shown in close-up, filling the screen. The women were on a yacht that bobbed on the ocean. The five white, wriggling nude bodies on deck in the midday sun were highlighted against the blue setting. Directly behind George, the 16-mm projector hummed, but he didn't notice. The women fondled and caressed each other, moving in and out of one unusual position after another, and in and out of smaller and larger groupings—now three of them, now five, and so on. It seemed even stranger because there was no sound. The twisting of their bodies, with the intent of getting into position so they could spread their legs in front of the camera, was completely unnatural and obviously an act. But George didn't notice this. *It's a fake*, he concluded, nevertheless. *They aren't American women. It's not possible—those faces, those arms and legs. Not one wrinkle, not one blemish, no flab anywhere. Not one thing that could turn someone off. Shiny, soft, white. Not one of the five looks to be over twenty.*

A bar hostess pulled down George's zipper and thrusts her small, rough hand inside. George grabbed the hand instantly. Apparently his grip was stronger than he thought, causing the hostess to shriek hoarsely, jump up, and storm off. John, Washington, and Wilde were each silently making out with their own women, climbing all over them and moving ceaselessly in the dark. Elsewhere here and there in the bar, hostesses without customers sat smoking cigarettes. The smoke drifted up through the blue light from the movie projector. George again fixed his attention on the screen. *Still at it,* he thought. *They really throw themselves into it, like there's no life without it. But all of them,* George had the vague sense, *must feel so embarrassed they could just about die.* There was some consolation for him in that idea.

The film ended. The dark red lights in the bar came on. A fixture hanging from the ceiling revolved silently, shining red, blue, and yellow light on wall-posters of nude Western women. George decided to get smashed. He knew he wouldn't be getting any sleep that night. He had a feeling he'd be having bad dreams about Emily. He forced himself to drink the beer that had been poured in his glass, now warm and foamless. He filled his glass from the bottle again and drained it in one gulp. Two or three cupfuls and the small bottle was emptied. George snapped his fingers to get the attention of a hostess standing at the bar and gestured for her to bring him another. She quickly brought it over, sat down at George's side, and filled his glass. Her face was thin and the lipstick and white power she wore seemed unsuited to her pale-brown complexion. The squeals of the hostesses, combined with the grating sound of the recorded jazz in the bar irritated George. The woman sat through it silently and without expression. She topped off his glass after each mouthful George drank. George didn't think beer ought to be topped off that way. She left and, without being asked, went to fetch a new bottle as soon as he emptied the old.

If she were to proposition me, I wouldn't mind going off with her to a hotel. But I'm the American, he told himself, *so I can't be asking her. Okinawans never deal straight with us. I always see that when I go off base.* George glanced at her out of the corner of his eye and noticed she was staring at him, full in the face. He felt confused. And then he felt he might throw up. Drinking any more was out of the question, but she kept putting the glass to his mouth. George sipped just enough to wet his lips, and recalled John telling him to distract a hostess by fondling their breasts or something. That way you don't have to drink too much. George hesitated to touch her body. Of course, there was no chance she would start screaming and run off just because he touched her.

George got to his feet, walked over to jukebox, shoved in a quarter and selected five of the loudest songs. *Screw it,* he told himself. *What do I care if everyone gets blasted out by the music.* And then, *How does John do it? How can he go out with a small, dark-skinned woman like that? Walking around*

with her in broad daylight, shopping and going to the movies and stuff. Any-
one seeing that has to think it's weird. She doesn't even come up to his chest.

The woman was still at the table, smoking. George wanted to leave. He wanted to go back to the base and write a letter to Emily. He could never have told this to John and the others; they would have made fun of him. He sat down. The woman filled his glass, lifted it to his mouth, and whispered in his ear, "Let's go sleep together." George gulped down the beer. "Ten dollar, all night. Whatever you want," she said. She wrapped an arm around his neck and moistened his ear with her tongue. She entwined her dark, rough-skinned arms in his, inviting him again and again to go with her. Grinning, she mimicked the sex act with her fingers and made other sexual gestures. George looked over at John and the others sitting nearby. *They are watching me,* he thought. *And grinning, because they think I'm not up to it. It looks like they are all about to leave for a hotel.* George turned to the woman and nodded his head in assent. She lifted her glass and toasted him over and over. *I can't keep up, although I do want to get drunker. I'll end up puking if I drink any more.* The woman got her handbag from the counter and went to the restroom. *Maybe I'll feel better about these Okinawan people if I sleep with that woman.*

The woman emerged from the restroom, took George by the hand and said in English, "Let's go." John and the others were still fooling around with their hostesses. George wanted to stay with them, but the woman pushed him on. Aware that John, the other men, and the women they were with were all watching him, George made for the door with confident strides and went out.

Red, blue, green. Neon signs were flashing everywhere. The lettering scampered every which way. Some top to bottom, some right to left, others at every conceivable angle. The lights cast flickering colors on the sidewalk. Barely noticeable amidst the reflected light were the black, fan-shaped shadows of the Chusan palms planted at regular intervals along the street, lined with parked taxis and expensive American cars. Cabbies stood outside their cars in small groups, moodily awaiting fares. Women with a worn-out air about them gathered in the dimly lit alleys. They stood perfectly still and silent. They stared at George and the woman as the two passed by them. Empty beer cans, whiskey bottles, and other junk littered the sides of the alley. George wanted to send some of it flying with a good kick, but hesitated, knowing what a racket it would make as it clattered against the walls of the alley. The woman held George by the arm, but said nothing to him. Her face, too, was without expression. She seemed different now that they weren't in the bar. "Let's take a cab," George said, glancing at her. "We're almost there," she answered sharply, without looking at him.

It was a three-story hotel, furnished in American style. The woman did the talking at the front desk. A short, plump, middle-aged woman led them to a room on the top floor. George looked down at the woman's head as she led the way. She wore her naturally straight, black, Okinawan hair permed into a mass of tangled curls. It annoyed him. *No doubt,* he thought, *it is this woman who cleans the toilets and throws out the soiled sex things people leave behind.* She turned on the light and they entered the room. She handed the key to George. As Mrs. Tangled Mop was about to leave, the bar hostess said something to her in Okinawan and flashed a quick grin. George noticed that the room seemed decorated to appeal to a woman's tastes. The curtains, bedspread, dressing table, and carpet were all garish reds and pinks. Still holding her handbag, the bar hostess went into the bathroom. George could hear the sound of water from the faucet. She eventually came out and told George it was his turn. George soaped himself down carefully. He wrapped a towel around his waist and returned to the room. He had once been laughed at by a woman for coming out in his shirt and underpants.

"Took you long enough," the woman said in English as she blew smoke from her cigarette. Now in her underthings, she went back into the bathroom, the cigarette held in her lips. George's head felt heavy, perhaps because he had showered after drinking so much. He stretched out on the double bed. He smelled a jumble of odors—skin lotion, sweat, semen. *Perhaps it is just my imagination, since the sheets are newly laundered. But, the sweat of sex must have penetrated hundreds of times to the bed mat under them.*

The woman was experienced and skilled at sex. Her nude body was that of a middle-aged woman. It was as if Emily's face had been superimposed on a pornographic film. Once they had finished, George was immediately overcome with disgust. *They're all drunk. None of 'em in their right minds. Me neither, I'm not in my right mind, either.* George felt trapped. *What in the world is going on? Who did this to me? Why am I here, in this town, on this island?* He sat down on the toilet. *Is it that woman out there, stretched out on the bed still naked and smoking her cigarette?* He felt fatigued, listless, his mind drifting in and out of focus. It occurred to him that Lt. James, the officer in charge of his unit, might be the culprit. George had asked him any number of times when they'd be shipping out to Vietnam, but each time, Lt. James avoided giving a definite answer, claiming the orders had not yet come in. "In that case," George would ask him, "when can we go back to the States?" Always the same answer, no orders. But George was convinced it was a lie. *Lt. James knows very well. He is just pretending that he doesn't know. It's a lie. Lt. James knows everything about it. He's just putting on that he doesn't know, keeping me in total suspense. All he does is force me to train to kill people. But we never actually do any real killing. The Okinawan midday sun beats down on me, makes me feel like my skull is going to crack open. I get dizzy. No enemy anywhere but there I am, shooting off live ammunition for no good reason. It's nuts. Whenever I lose focus out there, Lt. James yells and curses at me, like his hatred has been building up for a hundred years or something. No enemy is shooting at us, so he's the one acting nuts by taking it so seriously. I guess he just has it in for me. The training goes on and on and I'm about to pass out any moment. I gotta get out of this. Either I get into the real war in Vietnam, or I go back to Emily. One way or the other. I don't get what it is we're doing now. There's no way to train for "killing for real." I wonder if I could, actually. Kill a human being. What is that, anyway, killing another person?*

Late almost every night, after the alcohol had worn off and George still could not fall asleep, he stared at the ceiling and followed his thoughts. Sometimes he thought he wanted to kill right away and see what it was like, but the orders never came. Just training, training, day after day. *I'm trained! I'm trained already! I know exactly what to do. Know it so well I'm about to explode with it…If I do something great in Vietnam and write Emily and tell her about it, she'll write back, I'm sure of it. She doesn't write me because we haven't shipped out yet. How else to explain it? It's been sixty-seven days already since I wrote her. Racked my brains two whole weeks over that letter …I know why Lt. James hates me. I'm short and skinny. He says that about me all the time, just loud enough so I'm sure to hear him. Soldiers should be big and strong, he says. Why did they drag me into the military, if that's the case? I haven't the slightest desire to be here.*

George decided to go back to the barracks. He left the bathroom. The woman was still stretched out on the bed, smoking. She sat up, crushed out her cigarette in the ashtray, and turned to George. "Once more?" she asked in English as she extended an inviting hand toward him. "Please." George was suspicious. "Only ten dollars," she said. "But I already paid you," said George shaking his head. "No, that was for before. The ten dollars is for doing it again," she said, gesturing with her hand for him to come to her. *This isn't what we agreed on. I'm sure she said that it was ten dollars for all night. No doubt about it, in fact. John and the guys always said that's the rate—ten dollars for all night, five for a single trick.*

George levelled his eyes on her. "It's ten dollars for one time," she said again.

No, George thought, *I can't let this woman make a fool of me.* He began speaking to her with a slight stutter. "Look, at the beginning we agreed it'd be ten dollars for all night." The woman repeated herself in English that was smoother than his. George tensed up. "I'm sure you agreed it was ten dollars for all night."

"No, I said ten for short time. Regular price. Ask any of the women. You're the one who's wrong." She spoke quickly.

"John can prove it," George responded.

"Ok, tell John to come here," she said, moving over closer to him.

John and the guys will certainly back me up. But they'll also get to won-
dering how I can expect to enjoy a woman if I squabble so much over the
money. I'll become a laughingstock, and it'll take forever to live it down.
They're having fun with their own women right now, so asking them to come
here would only piss 'em off.

George was at a loss how to get her to agree. His insistence was starting
to look ridiculous. "Why make such a big deal over ten dollars?" she said.
"All the girls say you're a cheapskate greenhorn. Why in the world are you
worrying about your money so much, when you could die in Vietnam anytime?"

George started to feel sick. "I have my Emily back home," he now said.
"What would any of you know about what I'm going through?"

"Oh, you're all the same," the woman replied, throwing up her hands.
"It never changes. Okinawan women are just playthings for you. That's the
way it is, and I can understand that. But, what about the guys who marry
one of us, take the vows in a church before your priests and your God, but
then when any of you go back to the States, you just abandon the woman
like she's some filthy piece of trash. What's that? Ah…there's women like
that who've returned to my village…my little sister is one of them. Left her
own red-headed child in the States. You American soldiers are all the
same. All of you have an Emily back home and all of us are fools to be
taken in by you. Your Emily's are wrecking us Okinawan women."

George shouted back at her. "Don't you dare say anything about my
Emily. She's not like any of you. She's not the shameless kind of woman
who gets naked for any man that comes along." George eyed the woman's
meager breasts.

She placed her hands on her hips and seemed to be thrusting her breasts
toward George. "If that's what you think, then why pay for sex in the first
place, someone like you so stingy over a lousy ten dollars. Don't you know
that the new recruits are generous with their money, lots of them paying a
hundred or two hundred for a night?"

George folded his arms across his chest and turned to face the woman
directly. "What are you talking about? I can't stand being in a filthy hole
like this!"

"Then why come?"

"What else is there to do on this island? No woods to walk in, no open
spaces to ride a horse in. Nothing. Just this tiny little island with its disease-
filled nights, its disease-filled bars. There's not one single thing, not a single
person here for me. You being one example. Isn't that right?" The alcohol
seemed to have lubricated his throat, and as his words flowed out he felt an
inexplicable pleasure in saying them.

"You're a chicken. You're afraid of war," she said. "Emily, horses—that's
the talk of a child. I've had men who cry out in their sleep, *yama-otoko* back

from the war, half asleep and suddenly they cry out: "Hold up! Stay back! There're gooks out there!" Dripping wet in their sweat. Whenever I'm with these guys I never get any sleep, the crybabies cling to me all night, shaking, waiting for the morning light to come." She began putting her clothes on. George was at a loss. Impulsively he grabbed her shoulders. The bath towel around his waist loosened. She quickly pushed his hands away. "I'll get the manager to change it to a quick time," she said as she stepped into her skirt. "Which means we can't be wasting any more time here."

George sensed he was being tricked. None of it added up. She opened the door and held out her hand to him. "Give me the money for the woman's tip. It's fifty cents." She stood there, her hand held out, the door wide open. George handed her a dollar. "Come back right away," he told her. "I mean it. Don't forget." She nodded ambiguously and closed the door.

Strange if she's coming right back that she'd take her handbag with her, George thought. Actually, he didn't know what to think. He got dressed. It occurred to him that maybe she wasn't coming back. Maybe he should follow her. He wasn't sure. He felt confused. After fifteen minutes of waiting, he decided to leave. He bounded down the stairs, the sound of his leather shoes reverberating through the stairwell. He had no idea what awaited him, but he rushed down the stairs nonetheless. The manager was standing at the desk. When he approached, she smiled and asked for the room fee. He knew from John that the room fee is always paid in advance. *Hadn't the woman paid already? And tomorrow at the bar, she'll be holding her hand out for me to pay again.* George paid the manager the amount she asked for. *I know what Jack was feeling. That guy unloaded every last round he had into the bathroom at that bar. Didn't matter that he spent all the money he had just to please that bar hostess. When closing time came, she sneaked away from him anyway.*

George didn't know what street he was on. It seemed to be an alley. He wanted to quickly find a cab. A scrawny dog rooted around in the trash can overflowing nearby. Empty cans and bottles were piled up in untidy heaps. The walls stunk of urine. George quickened his pace. His foot struck a bottle in his path and it skipped across the alley, setting off a shrill echo between the walls of concrete. Complete quiet returned. It was dark, with only the occasional street light or neon sign. *John brags lots about the sixteen times he's pulled a razor on cabbies and beat them out of a fare and took all the money they had. If it ever comes to a tussle, a big guy like John isn't about to lose to some cabbie. I wonder if I could beat them. There are Okinawans a whole lot bigger than me. Beating them out of a fare—it's only twenty-five cents. And, really, how much money could they be carrying?*

George realized he would never find a cab until he got out on a main street. Neon signs were becoming more frequent. There were more hostesses and doormen on the street trying to entice passersby, too. It was long past two in the morning, but these people were still clapping their hands and calling out loudly. "Hey, hey. Floorshow, floorshow!" "Hey, strip show!" "Hey, hey. Movies!" "Hey, special service!" George kept walking, avoiding them. He pretended that he didn't notice, but if one of them grabbed him by the arm, he was afraid he'd have no way to refuse. *If only that woman were still with me. Then I could just walk on by...Okinawan women and their like should be taken by force. What could there be to fear from them? Can't I even handle that, either? All the guys boast about doing it. Wilde raped some woman working at the PX, Washington took a house-maid, and John some high-school student...But I don't think I could rape a woman. For sure they'd resist like crazy. Even if I could overpower one, I wouldn't want to do it with a woman who fought back...Besides, isn't the child of a woman you rape your own child? I wonder what John would say about that? How about it, John, have you no feelings at all? But then, George, I hear a voice saying to me, you're still only twenty-one. What makes you think you know so much? Well, for sure I'm not completely help-less. How good a marksman I am is something the women just don't know about. The guys, though, they know. Why does she show no fear? Why does she feel nothing but contempt? Does she think I don't have the nerve to do it? Women with brown hair are better. I hate her black hair. Am I following her now? No, that's not it...or, maybe it's...I don't know...Lt. James's wife looks a little bit like Emily. I'd really like to get to talk with her, even just once. But Lt. James is ranked so high above me. Well, no, maybe he's not. At the least, I'd probably have to get promoted to sergeant. Emily won't be happy if I remain a private. I'll have to do something great...Lt. James has it made, what with an American wife and all.*

"Hey, hey." George turned in the direction of the voice. A plump, dark-skinned Okinawan man wearing a Hawaiian shirt was speaking to him in broken English, apparently offering him a Caucasian prostitute. George looked intently into the man's face. *How many nights,* he wondered, *have I wished I held an American woman in my arms? It's an impossible dream. No American woman would be a prostitute here, not in this filthy place.*

"They're different from you Okinawans," George yelled at the man as he began running from him. "You can't fool me, you sons of bitches." George heard the pimp yelling back at him as he increased the distance between them.

Red, blue, yellow, pink tight-fitting pants held up by suspenders. Sure are a lot of Blacks around here, George noticed. With their ferociously large, gleaming eyes. Their black faces sickly looking in the reflected neon colors. Thick lips spread wide in laughter. Big white teeth. Seems I might've wan-dered into the wrong place, George thought. His earlier tipsiness had worn off. The Blacks were gathered in groups of fours and fives, standing around American cars, leaning against walls, huddled at entrances to the bars, some in the shadows, some in the lights, some with arms on the shoulders of host-esses and girlfriends, some with arms around the women's waists, some holding hands, and all following George with their eyes. Just as he neared the end of this row of eyes, George was hit with spit and someone's chewing gum. Obscenities come flying. George set his eyes directly ahead. And made no change in his gait. Were he to quicken his pace, he thought, they would jump him. And as he walked on, more and more of the eyes had the appearance of wild beasts about to pounce on prey. George began to understand that his primary concern was no longer with the women. I should be carrying my pistol, he thought. He not infrequently carried it when he went out, but luck was not with him this time. Even so, with these guys, he thought, I could plug them with a dozen rounds and they'd still be coming at me with teeth bared and eyes bulging. I'd have to shoot 'em right in both eyes and blind 'em. Wonder if I'm a good enough shot to do that? Unknowingly, he quickened his pace. Insults and challenges escalated. Then a clear, sharp sound. George looked down at his feet. A bottle smashed to pieces near him. Foaming beer streamed darkly over the pavement. Open-mouthed laughter erupted and grew louder and louder. More shouted insults came amid the laughter, greeted by even louder bursts of laughter. Caught between concrete walls on both sides of the street, the sounds refused to fade.

George instinctively came to an abrupt halt. A fist has been thrust toward his face. A short black man, muscles rippling all over, was imitating a boxer as he danced around George, poking jabs in the air with his fists. The arms protruding from his sleeveless green T-shirt were glossy black in the flickering neon lights and twice the thickness of George's. George started walking again, pretending not to notice. The boxer lightly tapped and poked at George's face, his jaw, his sides, his back, the back of his head. Some of the punches landed with a bit of a sting, perhaps intentionally. George continued to walk on as if he hadn't noticed. The boxer commenced butting his rock-hard head into George's back. When George glanced back to see what was happening, the boxer had circled to his front and flicked punches at George's face. He glared into George's eyes and laughed derisively at him, all the while continuing his pedaling footwork. The crowd of black men moved along with them, laughing and hollering. Some in the crowd raised clenched fists, others shook their arms at George. Some danced about like boxers. A short, youthful black man kicked an empty beer can toward George, as accurately as a soccer player. A thin, long-limbed black man broke from those clustered at the entrance to Club Niagara and began wrapping his arms around George. Instinctively, George stepped aside, but his head got caught in the man's long arms. He walked along beside George for a few paces with his arms curled around George's neck and then whispered softly in George's ear, "Let's have a drink, my good friend." George shuddered. The man had stopped walking, but George continued, so it looked as if the man's long arms had George firmly in a neck-hold. The man had enormous strength. George offered no resistance. Several other black men, apparently

companions of the long-armed man, surrounded George and amidst bois-
terous laughter and shouting, led him into the Niagara. To an onlooker, it
might have seemed George was in the company of good friends.

George was set down—or, rather, pinned down—on a hard, black seat.
People all around him began asking him, "Whiskey? Beer?" George responded barely audibly, "What?" When the Blacks shouted their questions again, George said, "Beer. Beer is fine." One of the Okinawan hostesses brought over several bottles. Each of the black men filled a glass to
overflowing, raised it to George, and urged him to drink up, too. George
took up the challenge and chugged his glass dry. Someone immediately
refilled his glass and urged him to do it again. Others followed, taking
turns refilling George's glass. More beer was brought. Shouts of praise
went up after each drained glass, followed by urgings for him to have
another. Eventually, George had an uncomfortably bloated feeling. His
belly could take no more. The others kept urging him on, firing one question after another at him. George was now almost totally silent. They
forced the glass to his mouth, claiming his silence must mean he hadn't
had enough to drink. "Go ahead, drink up!" George seemed to hear them
saying above the jukebox. "After all, you're the one paying for all this."

George realized he had to get up. If he stayed where he was there could
only be big trouble for him. *Is there any way I can get out of here,* he wondered, *without having my ass handed to me?* He continued not saying a
word. He made no acknowledgement of anything said to him or of their
laughter. The Black men kept pushing beer on him. George didn't touch it.
He knew his innards would erupt. One of the men jammed a bottle into
George's mouth. George reacted furiously, but his shoulders and arms were
pinned down by others and his jaw pried open. The beer violently thrust
down his throat overwhelmed his windpipe and threw his gut into turmoil.
He couldn't breathe. Tears filled his eyes. Another bottle was jammed into
his mouth, this time whiskey was poured down his throat. George's mouth,
throat, chest, and gut were all on fire. His coughing further inflamed him.
Even his swallowed saliva pained his throat. He felt he was about to vomit,
but frantically tried to hold it back. If he threw up, he feared, his insides
would likely burst. When he coughed, the Black men around him rubbed
his back sympathetically, but then just as quickly thrust another bottle of
beer down his throat. At one point in these repetitions, the hand holding
George's right arm let up and George, mustering his strength, broke the arm
free and flung the bottle from his mouth. It shattered against the floor, making a crisp, clear sound. The men raised a great howl and started pouring
beer all over George's head and back. Pushing against the men closest to
him, George struggled to his feet. His knee struck a table, lifting it by one
end. Bottles, glasses, and an ice holder clattered to the floor. Then, mar-
shalling all his energy in one great burst, George ripped himself away from

the hands that clung to him, headed for the door, but tripped over someone's foot and tumbled to the ground. Someone shouted something and grabbed George by the hair, yanking with both hands. George's face rose from the floor. All he saw was a forest of long, sinewy black legs. Two men took hold of George's arms and twisted them into a painful angle. George quickly sat up. The man who had earlier grabbed George's hair now pulled his head upright with one hand and slapped him hard across the face, one cheek and then the other, with the other. The stinging sound of the slaps lingered in the room. George felt deep inside that his ears had gone numb. The sound of the men screaming at him emerged only in fits and starts from somewhere deep down. He felt no pain from his hair being pulled.

Then the hold on his arms loosened. George collapsed into a ball. *Best to pretend I've passed out from the drink,* he thought. His hair was yanked again and his mouth pulled open, but George kept his eyes shut. He was kicked in the chest and gut. It seemed to be those gigantic pointy leather shoes he had noticed earlier. He grimaced despite himself, and squeezed his eyes shut more tightly. He was kicked again and again. The dull pain of each blow stayed with him. "You sons of bitches," George muttered to himself. "You'll pay for this." Bitter anger consumed him. But, his body was going numb, just as if he really had passed out from the drink. *I'll remember the faces of each one of you bastards,* he thought, *and I'll get back at every last one of you.* His eyes remained shut, however, so he had hardly any recollection of the faces. *How come all Blacks look alike, anyway?*

George had been clenching his teeth, but now he let his mouth fall open, relaxed his body, and pretended he had passed out. There was hardly any letup in the kicking and hair pulling and they didn't seem about to let him get up. Several of the men grabbed George's arms and legs, while one or two others removed his belt and began pulling off his trousers. George's eyes flew open, he yelled and cursed and struggled furiously, but he was pinned tight. His underpants were pulled off. He felt something strange going on in his pubic region. The Black men were hollering for someone to come over. George then saw three Black women peering down at him. He wondered where they could have come from. They were springing up and down like thin-legged antelopes caught in a trap. George's eyes were wide open now. And he was gritting his teeth. The women smiled broadly through mouthfuls of big, white teeth. *They all look alike,* he thought. *No individuality, just like animals.*

"Oh, so pretty, pretty," they said as they jiggled and rubbed at him with the tips of their shoes and poured beer over his groin. There seemed to be no end to the interest the women took in doing this. One, having fetched a small kitchen knife from the counter, smiled knowingly at him. She flicked the knife in front of his face. It shone dully in the light. As she wriggled and twisted, dancing around his prone and immobile body, the woman brought the knife close to his privates and slowly moved it around in the air. George ground his teeth.

I'm going to have to kill these Black women, he thought. *One way or another.* He was about out of his mind from having that knife worming around his private parts. Suddenly all went dark. Another Black woman was standing over him. She squatted straight down, her tight buttocks planted squarely over his face.

"Go ahead, piss on him," George could hear the men saying. Instead, the woman raised and lowered her buttocks and made gyrating movements over and over, as if having sex with George, and then laughed loudly and dismounted.

The women eventually went off somewhere, apparently having lost interest in the fun. Another woman appeared, jabbering loudly about something or other. She spit twice in rapid succession onto George's privates. He felt a tingling pain down there, like you might get from shaving. He imagined that what cuts were there were no more than fine threads, but the Black men were back now, spraying him with whiskey and beer they had first swished around in their mouths. They stripped all the money they could find from his trousers. George kept his eyes shut. Two of the men, jeering and laughing loudly at George, lifted up his legs, dragged him to the entranceway, and flung him out onto the sidewalk. As a final insult, one of them, still laughing, urinated onto George's face. To George, it had alcohol, semen, and animal smells all mixed together. It was a steady, powerful stream of urine and felt slimy and disagreeably warm. George had a violent urge to throw up, but he suppressed it. And kept his eyes shut.

George thought about it every night. Jefferson had raped a young girl, Parker had broken into a household of females and raped a middle-school girl, Washington had raped a bar hostess. Every day, sleeplessness plagued him deep into the night. *I guess it's true that I really can't do it to some weak woman or girl who wouldn't have a chance in a million of stopping me. But, if I pull the trigger, then all of them will respect me: John, the officers, Black men, women…Pull the heavy cock back, then pull back on the tightly sprung trigger. The ear-splitting thunderclap, my right arm snapping back from the recoil, my body tensing up. That indescribable fraction of a second. If only I do pull the trigger…*

During one of those sleepless nights, a target began to take shape in George's mind. *For the old man, it really will be completely unforeseen. Just like what has happened to me. I never could have dreamed I would be dragged into the military and then brought over to a place like this. Completely out of the blue. The old man seems to be gathering scrap metal. Maybe he does that every night to earn a living. He carries some kind of coarse, fiber sack. He's not in a no-trespass zone. There are shell fragments and casings strewn about there from the no-trespass live-ammunition practice area nearby. I've seen Okinawans picking up stuff there any number of times. Usually just one person. Always the same guy? Makes no difference, really. Night after next the collector of those shell casings will die by my hand. His luck is up. But I'm not doing it because I have some reason to kill that particular person.*

The ear-splitting sound that seemed to scream from the deepest part of his ears—the sound of jet fighters revving up—went on and on, night after night, endlessly. George's barracks was equipped with extra-strength sound-proofing, but the sound created an interminable ringing in the ears that made sleep impossible. The metallic roar of the engines maintained the same pitch, never rising, never falling, and seemed to go on for all eternity. Day after day the number of sleeping pills George took increased. The insomnia was agonizing. Until two or three months ago, he had been able to immerse himself in pleasant recollections of Emily, and so the long nights had caused him no trouble. Once he stepped outside the barracks, though, the sound assailed him from all sides. He knew the sleeping pills were harmful. He had earlier tried to find relief in alcohol, but he didn't have the constitution for drinking great amounts, could never drink enough to get good and drunk, and so drinking never had the desired effect. To gaze at the stars or listen to the insects sing were no more than fantasies now that he was here. The Rockies had been quiet and still. And the time George spent dreaming of such things increased. *There were so many stars there. We often looked at them from our window. The forests and the lakes were quiet and still. Sometimes we'd hear wild animals howling in the distance. The howls hung in the air for a long time...*

His dreams of the mountains were always fragmentary and incoherent.

George checked his watch. It was 7:40. Some daylight remained to him. Outside the chain-link fence on the base perimeter, mole crickets chirped in the swaying grasses. The breeze was cool. *Damned pleasant evening. This is about the time we usually go out to the bars. But this spot is about as unlike a bar as you can get. I envy the guys on sentry duty. They don't have to bother making up excuses for not going out with the guys. Not that I turned down any invitations from John tonight. I left the barracks before he could come around to see me.*

The old man was there. The smell of his body carried over to George on the soft breeze. No doubt he had heard George's leather shoes striking the asphalt walkway. He was hunched over in a dark ball. *We always see him beyond the fence just when we're heading out for the night. Bent over, fearful of who might be watching him. He uses the weeds and bushes in the rocky field to hide himself from us, just like that bug that hides in those cases patched together with dried-out pieces of leaf and twig. John and the others never notice him, they're so absorbed in the talk about the pleasures awaiting them at the Mississippi. The old guy remains still as a rock as we pass on by.*

But he kept an unblinking, vigilant eye on George. *There he is,* George told himself. *Never fails.* The man had his straw, lampshade hat pulled down low on his brow, but George clearly saw his wrinkled, monkey face, saw his monkey eyes: those unmoving, dark, monkey eyes. For a long time George could not fathom the expression in those wide-open eyes. *Fear? Hatred?* Now it finally came to him. *Those are the eyes of the enemy. Those greedy eyes, open wide with terror and malevolence. They're the eyes of the Vietnamese. The color of his skin, his physique, they're the same. My enemy is just such a person.* George shuddered at the thought.

He's in the way. I can't see, a voice inside George shouted. *Get away from me. Any hunted animal when it hears me coming runs off. But the old guy doesn't. He just keeps his eyes fixed on me. Those eyes that are so aloof from me and show such contempt for me.*

George stopped, turned the side of his face toward the old man and lit a cigarette. "Go on, beat it," he said to himself as he realized something else. *I've seen those eyes before. John's eyes... and Washington's... and the lieutenant's. They all have eyes like that. But not Emily. Hers are different. Their eyes scorn me, make me feel depressed and small.*

George started walking again, leaving the old man behind. *Okinawans never do look you in the eye. When you pass by them they always look down. But just as you pass them, they're sneaking a look out of the corner of their eye. I can tell that's what they do. And after they've gone past you, they turn around and stare. I of course never turn and stare at them. They're the ones left over after their country lost the war. Who do they think they are anyway, looking at me that way? Acting so big. And what's that old guy thinking? That if he just stays absolutely still he won't get killed? You lost, old man, so put up your hands, raise your flag of surrender, admit you're defeated. The Blacks are not like you people. If I threatened them with death, they'd fight back against me. Eyes bulging, white teeth bared, yelling wildly. They'd be shameless about it. Wouldn't care a bit what others thought of them. They'd shriek and wail, try every which way to stay alive. Beg for their lives. But you Okinawans, what would you do? Nothing. No resistance, the look on your faces barely changing, saying not a word. Well, this once, I'll give you a stay of execution.*

George didn't look back at the old man, nor did he change his pace. *I'll come back in a little while. If you haven't run away by then, I'll gun you down. I'm not kidding. You'll be gunned down. For you, it will be totally unexpected. For me, it's not something I can't comprehend. It's the same for everybody. It's just what happens to you.*

George kept on walking. *It's not that I ever took any special interest in what's going on outside the fence. Then why, I wonder, did my eyes land on him? His old, drab clothes are all but lost in the colors of twilight. But, he was found by me, the one who will be his murderer. There's nothing you can call that but fate. Vietnam's the same. Squirming to set yourself free doesn't help. Even so, old man, why didn't you hide yourself? You must have heard me coming. Were you so involved in your work, were the sounds the insects make so loud you couldn't hear?*

It occurred to George that he should just keep walking straight and not turn back. *No, not possible. I can't do it. The insomnia would just get worse. I'd be a wreck. I'm not incapable of taking matters into my own hands. None of you has the right to feel superior to me, not you Okinawans, not you, John, not Lt. James, not anybody. I won't let you, you or anybody who thinks I'm incapable. I have the power of life and death over another person. The fate of that other, and all the many others involved with that other, rests with this finger of mine. Nothing more certain. Some thoughtless decision by me and one of God's creatures gets sent off into the eternity of space. Beautiful, don't you think? Isn't that right, George?*

George made a complete turn and began retracing his steps. "It's his fault, for not running away from me," George muttered under his breath. *When was it, I wonder. I think it was on a day off, around midday sometime. I was walking along beside this fence when all of a sudden rocks come sailing over towards me from the other side. All of them hit the fence and fell to the ground without reaching me. A dark-skinned Okinawan kid in a dirty sleeveless T-shirt was over there, with his teeth clenched and a face filled with earnest determination. When I moved toward him, he began running. He held a straw hat to his head with one hand and continued to throw rocks at me with the other. He ran all around the rock-strewn field in his bare feet. He's afraid I'm going to shoot him, I thought. He did escape and so I didn't kill him. The old man's eyes are just like that child's. Why doesn't he escape, too? I remember another day. It was raining, not very late in the day but already dusky. I was sopping wet, walking along beside this fence looking at nothing in particular. I let myself get wet on purpose. What harm could it do? From the other side of the fence, large black eyes were staring at me, unmoving eyes. It was a she-dog. It had sopping-wet fur clinging to its emaciated body. Dried-out teats hung down from her. It seemed to me that the dog was struggling just to stay alive. There's nothing here for you to eat, I thought. The dog must have misread what I was thinking and limped away. I have no intention of taking life just for the hell of it.*

George set his foot down firmly and brought himself to a halt. His shoe made a sharp sound against the asphalt, breaking the silence enveloping him. *It's been fifteen minutes by now.* He didn't bother looking at his watch. *Won't I be spotted by someone standing guard or out on patrol?* This idea popped into his mind. *No,* he shook his head. *It makes no difference if they see me now or not. My mind's made up.*

He became aware of a buzzing in his ears. It was one of those rare times when there was no noise from jet engines revving up. *So what is this constant ringing deep in my ears? Insects? How could that be? There are no rocks, no weeds, no dirt here, just this flat expanse of asphalt. Maybe it's insects on the other side of the fence. The sound seems too close to be from there, though. Where are they, the damned summer bugs making all this noise? That thing I saw back there a couple of minutes ago, that thing hidden in the shadows by the fence. That thing wasn't a person. It was wild game. A wild boar come looking for food. Those animals that look like pigs but have coarse hair on their bodies and sharp, pointy tusks. I've seen 'em before. That must've been what it was, I'm sure. That thing's a night animal, five feet long give or take, and it roots around with its snout in the dirt. I wonder if it'll put up a fight against me, squealing like crazy. Or beat it out of there so fast you'll wonder what you're looking at. But I'm not confident I can bring down a wild boar. It'll be hard at my level of marksmanship…I'll do the best I can.*

George noticed it had become much darker. Then it struck him: *Is that all I can kill, a decrepit old man incapable of either putting up a fight or making his escape? That's not the way it is in Vietnam…No, but that thing out there is a wild boar, not a person.*

The darkness was thickest near the ground. There was no identifying the black mass crouching in the grass. George stood still, planted his feet firmly, and calmed himself. Eight or ten yards separated him from the unmoving black mass, which seemed to keep its eyes fixed on George's every move. *I can't let this thing stare me down,* he thought. He strained to get a better look. His face grew rigid. *Looking at me like I'm some damned foreigner! I know that's what you're thinking. But there's no need to bother looking at me like that. I myself don't want to be here in this crummy place. What can I do? Nothing, there's nothing I can do about it.*

George suppressed an urge to break into a tirade. *What qualifies you to look at me like that anyway? You're probably the parent of a hostess at some filthy bar yourself. Women at those places talk freely enough and laugh. Not like you. You don't say anything, but your eyes are the same as theirs.*

George reached around behind and pulled out the Magnum pistol he had concealed under his loose-fitting Hawaiian shirt. He released the safety, which made a clear, satisfying sound. The dark shadow seemed to move slightly. George leveled the gun. *Put all my strength in the index finger of my right hand—that's all I have to do. Then everything'll be taken care of. The old man gets his peek at eternity. The sun sets, the sun rises, it sets again. The daily round of life's repetitions is coming to an end. The old man will be eternal. It's so easy. Life is so simple. The moment the black mass moves again, I'll pull the trigger.*

George had resolved the matter. But there was no movement. His finger's grip on the trigger tightened. His arm felt heavy. He began to lose feeling in it. *Go ahead and move, make a break for it, try and stop me,* George was screaming inside. He lowered one knee to the ground, and firmly grasping his right wrist in his left hand, set himself at the ready. At that instant the black mass straightened itself up. George pulled hard on the trigger. As an ear-splitting roar reverberated through the air and the spent cartridge popped out, the shadowy figure slowly sank to the ground. For a moment, George's arms felt paralyzed from the recoil. He staggered over toward the black thing. The strength drained from his legs, they got tangled in each other, and he tripped forward onto the fence. Since the straw hat was still on, the neck on the body was bent unnaturally and the face was even more horribly contorted. The body was on its stomach, but the misshapen face was turned toward George. *Kept his eyes on me right up to the end,* George thought. In his right hand, the old man still held his cloth sack, nearly empty, it seemed, of any scavenged findings.

George returned the pistol to his back pocket with the safety still off and moved away from the fence on his unsteady legs. Without him noticing, the outdoor lamps high up on poles that were spaced at regular intervals had come on, illuminating the military base in a strong, white light. George began walking again, just walking, with no particular destination in mind. *Maybe he's still alive. I only plugged him once. Could very well not have been fatal. I bet he's just lying there, still as can be, and holding his breath until I clear out. I didn't see any blood. And no blood splashed back onto me…Am I a wanted man now? Did I leave fingerprints on the fence? Are they going to execute me for murder? But that's not possible. The Ryūkyūan police have no authority to arrest me. Proclamation No. 817 doesn't allow it. A court-martial? A court-martial would never sentence me to death. In fact, if I'm lucky, it could just mean I won't be sent to the front lines in Vietnam. Maybe they'll ship me back to the States. I'll be able to see Emily…*

George smiled broadly as he walked. But his heart was still thumping wildly. *I don't care if the guy is dead,* he assured himself. *Tomorrow morning I'll invite the lieutenant's wife out for a drive and show her the body. That means Lt. James, too, will probably change his opinion of me a little… Or, I could douse it with gasoline and burn it at the outdoor garbage incinerator. No, that guy doesn't deserve a proper cremation or a proper burial. Besides, I could never climb over this fence. It's too high and it has layers of barbed wire on top. The nearest gate's two miles away. I'll just leave it to the flies and maggots until it rots, sweats black sweat, and is absorbed back into the earth…Then again, they'd probably know from the bullet they get out of him that it was me that did it. There'll be an investigation. What story will I tell them? That I mistook him for a wild boar? Shall I tell them it was a little later when it got darker and the visibility was poor? Or, did I see him making a getaway back over the fence, shot two warning shots into the air and when he didn't stop I had no choice but to shoot him? That would work. Anytime an Okinawan makes unauthorized entry onto the base, for whatever reason, it's OK to shoot and kill the guy on the spot…But, could that old man even have climbed over the fence? Or…*

George's mind was strangely clear now…*or, maybe I should drag the body fifty or so yards from there and leave it in a no-trespass zone…Do I really even have to think about making up some story that'll work? The military court officers will never do a thorough investigation…But I would like to tell John and the lieutenant what actually happened…*

No matter how far George walked, he felt not the least bit tired. He was now a considerable distance from the grasses, but something like the buzzing of those insects was rising to peculiar levels in his ears.

Translation by David Fahy

Higa Yasuo: Maternal Deities

Imploring the Gods (Kami-nigai)
Iheya Island, Gakiya, Unjami
1975

The Cocktail Party

Setting

Acts one and four are set in summer 1995 in Washington, D.C. Acts two and three are set in summer 1971 in Okinawa. The plot involves two families: the Okinawans Mr. and Mrs. Uehara and their daughter, Yōko; and the Americans Mr. Miller, his wife, Helen, and their son, Ben. The parents first meet in Okinawa in 1971.

Cast of Characters (in order of appearance)

Yōko, Uehara's daughter and wife of Ben Miller, age 17 in 1971
Mr. Uehara, Okinawan, age 48 in 1971
Ben Miller, lawyer in Washington D.C., age 40 in 1995
Helen, Mr. Miller's wife, English teacher, age 45 in 1971
Mr. Morgan, American civilian, age 45 in 1971
Mr. Lincoln, American civilian, age 35 in 1971
Mr. Ogawa, Japanese newspaper reporter, age 43 in 1971
Mr. Yang, Chinese lawyer, occasionally working in Okinawa, age 57 in 1971
Mr. Miller, American, working for Counter-Intelligence Corps, age 47 in 1971
Robert Harris, American soldier, age 23 in 1971
Okinawan police officer

Act One

Washington, D.C., 1995. Tidy living room of middle-class home. One window looks out on the street. A framed image of an Okinawan landscape hangs on the wall facing the audience.

YŌKO	[*Preparing a beverage.*] Otōsan! Your iced coffee is ready.
UEHARA	[*Entering.*] Ah, taking a shower is so refreshing. How do people survive the humidity here in Washington? Your mother would have really suffered.
YŌKO	Is her heart condition getting worse?

UEHARA	She's fine as long as she stays indoors and takes it easy.
YŌKO	It's really too bad. Ben and I so hoped she would join you— she's never met Ben or seen America. I guess it may not ever happen now. [*Beat.*] Otōsan, isn't D.C. huge? What did you see today?
UEHARA	Of course…I was especially impressed by the statue of Lincoln.
YŌKO	I can see why. He's called The Great Emancipator.
UEHARA	Yes, in 1945—when the war with Japan ended—Okinawans welcomed the American military. We thought of them as emancipators. And then, some people think that the 1972 movement to return Okinawa to Japan was a different kind of emancipation…That was the year after you came here for college, wasn't it? Twenty-four years ago this month. I still remember how surprised your mother and I were when you left home. But you made a good decision.
YŌKO	I think I surprised myself, too—especially after what happened…I was lucky I found Ben when I came here—he changed my feelings about American men. He's been wonderful to me.
UEHARA	Still, the shock your mother and I felt when you told us he was Mr. Miller's son…you really can't imagine.
YŌKO	After I read your letter, I wandered around in a daze. Finally, I just decided it was fate, our meeting. [*Beat.*] Maybe it was selfish of me to ignore your objections…
UEHARA	Before meeting Ben's father, we had a peaceful life, despite the American occupation. I'd almost forgotten the war and my time as a soldier in China—and then after what happened to you, and the incident with Mr. Miller…
YŌKO	It's so ironic. Everything started because of a cocktail party that was supposed to create international friendships.
UEHARA	Did you ever tell Ben about it?
YŌKO	Never. I can imagine what he'd say—that he would have protected me, and that he became a lawyer just because such injustice happens. Lawyers can make a lot of money in D.C., but Ben works pro bono on cases that are about justice. His sense of justice is what attracted me to him.
UEHARA	He seems awfully busy, no? He's hardly had time to see me.

YŌKO	But tonight's party is for you—he wants his friends to meet you.
UEHARA	Well, I appreciate the gesture. Are these friends from his law school days?
YŌKO	Some. They're still amazed that the son of an American and daughter of an Okinawan who met in Okinawa should meet by chance in America and get married.
UEHARA	At first, your mother and I thought you had somehow planned the whole thing—a kind of revenge.
YŌKO	Otōsan! By the time I got your letter about you and Ben's father…well, by then, we were already in love…Anyway, let's make the most of the party tonight, shall we?
UEHARA	Will Ben be back in time?
YŌKO	I'm sure he will be. He's not in court today. He's helping a veterans' group with some issues about international law.
UEHARA	American veterans?
BEN	[*Entering.*] Hi, Mr. Uehara…Yōko. [*Beat.*] Sorry I couldn't take you around today.
UEHARA	You must be busy…
BEN	I apologize. But your English is great—I bet you got along fine…and you have Yōko.
YŌKO	We've just been talking about languages bringing people together. How back in Okinawa in the seventies, your dad and mine used to meet to practice conversational Chinese. [*To Uehara.*] Ben was very impressed.
BEN	It amazes me that you can speak Chinese and English as well as Japanese.
UEHARA	Remember, your father also spoke Japanese, Chinese, and English. [*The following exchange between Uehara and Yōko is spoken in Japanese.*] You told me his father passed away.
YŌKO	When we told him that Ben and I were going to be married, he was moved to tears. He said he was thinking of you… well, Ben and I also hoped our engagement might help bury some sad memories.
UEHARA	We do our best.
BEN	Hey…do you realize you're speaking in Japanese again?
UEHARA	Oh, sorry. We were talking about the old days.

BEN	That reminds me. I have something to ask you. [*Beat.*] What are your views on Pearl Harbor?
UEHARA	Pearl Harbor?
YŌKO	The Smithsonian Institute has been planning an exhibition to mark the fiftieth anniversary of the end of World War II. Some veterans' groups are very critical. They feel the exhibit emphasizes the horrible effects of the atomic bombs, but not why they had to be used—or Pearl Harbor...
UEHARA	Oh, yes. I was reading about it in the newspaper.
YŌKO	American resentment over Pearl Harbor is much stronger than people in Japan realize.
BEN	I've read that many Japanese think dropping the A-bombs on Hiroshima and Nagasaki was inhumane. But many Americans say, "Hey, what about Pearl Harbor?"
	Uehara begins to speak, but is distracted by sounds from outside. He goes to the window and looks out.
UEHARA	"Stars and Stripes Forever"...Isn't that the title of this march?
YŌKO	Americans are the proudest people in the world when it comes to their country.
	The march outside the window gets louder, then softer as it passes by.
BEN	[*Goes to the window and looks down.*] It looks like a protest against the Smithsonian's A-bomb exhibition.
UEHARA	Ben, tell me: are you also critical of the exhibition?
BEN	My personal opinion is irrelevant. As a lawyer advising a veterans' association, I'm being asked to consider the legality in international law of using atomic weapons. That's the position I'm in.
UEHARA	Do people put the Pearl Harbor attack in the same category as dropping the A-bombs?
BEN	Both incidents are discussed in international law. The point is, for the average American, Pearl Harbor is simply unforgivable, a deceitful sneak attack...something terribly unethical, especially since Japan and the U.S. were not at war.
UEHARA	Well, aren't the A-bombs dropped on Hiroshima and Nagasaki an even more unforgivable outrage?

BEN	Many Americans believe that the Japanese brought it on themselves—their refusal to surrender forced America to drop the bombs. Otherwise, many more soldiers and civilians would have been killed in an invasion of Japan. If you think of it like that, dropping the atomic bombs can be seen as a humane act because it saved lives.
UEHARA	I see. You are your father's son after all.
BEN	Wait. As a lawyer, I'm trying to explain the two sides…and what do you mean about my father? Did he do anything wrong in Okinawa?
UEHARA	Well… [Gropes for words.]
YŌKO	[Speaking in Japanese.] Now, let's not start arguing, Otōsan. [In English.] It's not easy for Ben to understand what happened in Okinawa. [Turns to leave.] I better start preparing for the party.
BEN	Wait a minute, Yōko. I'm a lawyer. I have been trained to look rationally at all sides of a conflict—
YŌKO	Well, it has nothing to do with… [Exits without finishing her sentence.]
BEN	Whatever your father has to say that concerns my father, I want to hear it. [To Uehara.] OK, please. Tell me what happened in Okinawa. What's this about my father?
UEHARA	[Smirking.] Defending justice by looking at both sides… American democracy, the bastion of equality. But when Okinawa was a possession of the U.S., there were no individual freedoms for us. Instead, countless violations of human rights unimaginable in the United States. Your American justice—
BEN	What are you talking about?
UEHARA	And then the pleasant cocktail party to cover it up.
BEN	A cocktail party?
UEHARA	For a long time I could not figure out why your father spoke fluent Chinese. We were even invited to your father's home for cocktails.
BEN	I don't know anything about this. I lived with my grandparents here in D.C. in those days…So, what happened?
UEHARA	We met regularly to practice conversational Chinese. In addition to your father and me, there were two others: Mr. Ogawa, a Japanese reporter; and Mr. Yang, a Chinese

lawyer. On one particular evening, two other Americans,
Mr. Morgan and Mr. Lincoln—your parents' neighbors—
were also invited…

Lights fade.

Act Two   *Okinawa, 1971.*

Scene One

*Living room in American home. Morgan, Lincoln, Ogawa, and Yang are listening to
an Okinawan song such as "Hamachidori" (A Plover), each holding a glass of
liquor.*

HELEN
[*Entering with a plate of snacks.*] How do you like this song,
Mr. Morgan? It's very popular.

MORGAN
[*Feigning interest.*] Well, I don't know, it's hard to say.

LINCOLN
[*With an expression of total cluelessness.*] I was born in Ala-
bama, and, you know, I'm just helpless when it comes to
appreciating Asian music.

MORGAN
How about you, Mr. Ogawa?

OGAWA
[*Uncommitted, but feigning sympathy with Morgan.*] Well, as
a Japanese, I may have a better feeling for this than you do.

MORGAN
You're a Japanese, but I understand Okinawa was not part
of Japan before the war. Different language, different
music—

OGAWA
No, Okinawa has always been part of Japan; that's why it
will be returned to Japanese control next May.

MORGAN
You mean that the American administration of Okinawa
will be replaced by a Japanese administration, another
occupier. Wasn't Okinawa forcibly annexed by Japan in the
nineteenth century—and prior to that, it was the independent Ryūkyū Kingdom?

OGAWA
The way you put it is an historical simplification that leaves
out a great deal. Okinawans have been Japanese nationals
for a very long time. Legally, by the international peace
treaty of 1951, Okinawa is currently a possession of the U.S.
As a result, Okinawans live in a foreign country. Regardless
of your interpretation of history, Okinawans were Japanese
before the war and are Japanese now.

*Morgan nods, though not completely satisfied with the argu-
ment. The music stops.*

LINCOLN	[*To Yang.*] What's your position on that, Mr. Yang? I hear Okinawa was a Chinese colony before it was Japanese.
YANG	I don't think it was ever a Chinese colony. Certainly, Chinese envoys visited the Ryūkyūs whenever they had a new king.
OGAWA	Well, let's just say the Ryūkyū Kingdom paid tribute to Japan and China equally.
MORGAN	Doesn't that mean that, rationally speaking, Okinawa—or, rather, the former Ryūkyū Kingdom—is now simply paying tribute to a new power, the U.S., which is just as legitimate as the occupations that came before? I'm just a civilian worker on the base, but I must say I'm very interested in Okinawan history.
OGAWA	[*Slightly sarcastically.*] If you're so interested, Mr. Morgan, you might begin by listening to this music a bit more attentively.
MORGAN	[*Offended.*] I *am* listening to this music. But, you know, listening to it and learning to like it are two separate things, aren't they? [*To no one in particular.*] Newspaper reporters are the same everywhere; they never get the facts right.
OGAWA	I didn't mean to offend you. I just wanted to say that if you dislike foreign things, your life will be uncomfortable whenever you leave home.
MORGAN	Excuse me, but it's this gentleman [*indicating Lincoln*], not me, sir, who said the music made him uncomfortable.
LINCOLN	[*Scratching his head.*] He's right. I'm sorry, Mrs. Miller. I didn't mean to offend anyone.
HELEN	It's perfectly OK. Candid conversations are always welcome at an American cocktail party.
LINCOLN	That's absolutely right. Coming all the way from home to this isolated island in the middle of nowhere…
MORGAN	There you go again, Lincoln.
LINCOLN	Oh, no. Excuse me! [*Everyone laughs.*] What I meant was, recognizing the fact that even such a small island in the Western Pacific contributes to the defense of freedom in the Free World…and the military exercises carried out in the northern hills of the island are necessary for…and we civilians are civilians and, well, uh…

Everyone laughs.

	[*Amid laughter.*] Well, cheers!
	They all toast each other, laughing.
MILLER	[*Entering.*] I'm so sorry for being late. I had an emergency call.
LINCOLN	What a host! But we've had a great conversation without you.
MILLER	Well, help me catch up with you. What's the hot topic?
MORGAN	We've been discussing our feelings about Ryūkyūan folk songs.
LINCOLN	Mr. Miller, I understand there are four people in your Chinese club: you, Mr. Yang, Mr. Ogawa…and who's the fourth one?
MILLER	Mr. Uehara. He is late, isn't he? He called in the afternoon and said he would definitely be here. Hmm…
LINCOLN	I hear that you four gentlemen get together regularly to speak Chinese to each other. It's very nice of you to have Mr. Morgan and me over tonight, seeing that we limit the conversation to English.
MILLER	Thanks for joining us. I thought it would be fun to have a multiethnic get-together here, just like ones we have in America.
MORGAN	"American-Ryūkyūan friendship" is now a household phrase, and here we are doing our part.
HELEN	I played a recording of Okinawan music and asked for everyone's opinion, which then led to—
MILLER	[*Interrupting.*] I see. The music is the cause of tonight's hot discussion!
LINCOLN	I'm to blame.
MORGAN	No, I'm responsible.
MILLER	Wonderful! Graciousness and humility! This is exactly the attitude needed to make an international party successful in a foreign country.
OGAWA	Maybe you shouldn't emphasize the fact that you are in a foreign country when Mr. Uehara gets here. Being Okinawan, he may be sensitive…
MILLER	You're very right. But why is he so late? [*To his wife.*] Helen, did his daughter say anything about his not coming tonight? Or that he might be late?

HELEN	Actually, she's been absent from my class recently.
MORGAN	Your class?
MILLER	Helen teaches English conversation to Okinawan students after their regular school day ends. Yōko is one of her students. She's almost out of high school, and wants to go to America for college.
MORGAN	It seems the whole family is interested in foreign languages.
MILLER	Yōko's just about our son Ben's age. He's living with my parents in Washington. They'd be great friends if they ever met.
UEHARA	[*Enters.*] Good evening. I'm sorry I'm late. I had a little quarrel with my wife as I was leaving.
OGAWA	He means he hates to leave his charming wife home alone.
	Laughter.
	Please excuse my bad joke. In fact, I was beginning to worry you got lost coming here.
UEHARA	That's one of the reasons I'm late. I wandered around the housing area for almost ten minutes.
MILLER	You were lost?
OGAWA	Your house is hard to find. All the houses in the American compound look the same. And many of the streets end in circles…
MORGAN	That's true. For Okinawans, this area must look like a foreign place.
MILLER	Will I have to apologize for this too?
YANG	[*Calmly.*] You might as well…
MILLER	I see. OK, I'll follow the wise advice from Mr. Lawyer. On behalf of the president of the United States, I would like to apologize for the inconvenience caused by our streets.
	Laughter.
	Since I apologized, I claim the right to ask that Mr. Uehara immediately drink three cups of *sake*.
	Uehara forces a smile and is ready to agree with the proposal.
LINCOLN	Why three cups?
MILLER	It's a Japanese custom. A latecomer to a party must chug three cups to catch up.

Ōshiro . *The Cocktail Party*   221

LINCOLN	That sounds fun. I'd like to see him do it.
MORGAN	What if someone doesn't drink?
MILLER	Well, uh…I don't think they have words for "doesn't drink" in Japanese. [*Laughs.*]
MORGAN	[*To Yang.*] Do you have the same custom in China?
OGAWA	I think there's something similar.
YANG	*Hou lai chui shang?*
UEHARA	That's not quite equivalent to the Japanese expression. "*Hou lai chui shang*" means that a latecomer takes a seat of honor. That's different from making someone drink as a penalty.
MORGAN	I'm afraid I can't follow you gentlemen. Can you explain that in English?
YANG	There's no "seat of honor" at American parties…[*Laughs.*]
MILLER	Anyway…Cheers, everybody!
HELEN	Mr. Uehara, how is your daughter doing? I haven't seen her in our English class lately.
UEHARA	She is fine. Thank you. She's just busy with extracurricular activities.
HELEN	Yōko's a serious student. She studies hard all day at her school, and then she comes to my class.
UEHARA	I'm beginning to wonder how serious she is. The quarrel with my wife was about Yōko.
HELEN	Oh, may I ask what happened?
UEHARA	I approve of her wanting to learn English, but she went out for a ride with an American soldier. This young man has an Okinawan girlfriend in our neighborhood. He pays her rent. I scolded my wife for allowing Yōko to go with him.
HELEN	Please don't be concerned. American freedoms won't harm a good Okinawan like Yōko.
	Telephone rings.
UEHARA	[*Standing up reflexively.*] Maybe that's for me.
MILLER	[*Answering the phone.*] It's for Mr. Morgan.
MORGAN	[*Speaks into phone, then suddenly looks alarmed.*] Excuse me. Something urgent. I must go home. [*Exits quickly.*]

OGAWA	What happened?
	Miller follows Morgan.
LINCOLN	[*Unconcerned.*] Mr. Uehara, your Chinese sounds perfect. Where did you study it?
UEHARA	Shanghai.
LINCOLN	Shanghai? Was it before or after the war?
	Uehara hesitates.
OGAWA	There has always been a strong tradition of Chinese studies in the Ryūkyū Kingdom. [*To Uehara, speaking in Japanese.*] Is this explanation sufficient?
	Uehara nods slowly.
MILLER	[*Entering.*] Everyone, I need your help. Mr. Morgan's three-year-old son is missing.
OGAWA	Missing? Inside the housing area?
MILLER	He and their live-in Okinawan maid weren't there when Mrs. Morgan came home at dinnertime, and they still haven't turned up. We don't know where the maid's family lives or their phone number.
LINCOLN	Have the Morgans called all the neighbors?
MILLER	Naturally.
UEHARA	Is it possible he could have been taken off the base?
YANG	[*Calmly.*] We had better start looking for him.
LINCOLN	What a twist this cocktail party's taken. Let's go! [*Exits.*]
	Everyone rushes out but Uehara and Yang.
YANG	It's hard to believe that a boy could go missing in such a well-planned American housing area, especially inside a military base.
UEHARA	Let's join the others. I hope *we* don't get lost.
	Exit with awkward smiles.

Scene Two

The stage is dark. A spotlight downstage indicates a streetlamp. Carrying flashlights, actors ask about Morgan's son, speaking to others in the dark or in the wings.

MILLER	Yes, it's Mr. Morgan's son. He's three years old. Have you seen him?
MORGAN	We're looking for my son. If you hear or see anything, please call this number. [*Hands out a slip of paper.*]
LINCOLN	Well, this housing area certainly is big, isn't it? The whole base is huge! A kid could hide anywhere here. Or maybe somebody's hiding him. [*Beat.*] No way an American would do that. This is some mystery.
MILLER	[*Encounters Lincoln under the streetlamp.*] Oh, Mr. Lincoln. You must have come from the other direction…
LINCOLN	Right. I started from house number 200 and knocked on every door. How many houses are in this area? And most of them are dark, like everyone's gone to bed. I haven't even seen a dog on the street. Maybe the kid is home by now…
MILLER	I hope so. Let's split up and keep looking.
	Miller and Lincoln go in opposite directions. Uehara and Yang enter, walking leisurely, then pause under the lamp.
UEHARA	We've been searching a long time. [*Beat.*] Ah, a beautiful night sky.
YANG	Yes. It's been a long time since I've seen so many stars.
UEHARA	People say Okinawa's night sky is especially beautiful. What about your hometown in China?
YANG	You lived in China; you've seen what it's like.
UEHARA	Yes, I went to a university in Shanghai. But all the city lights obscured the stars. It must be different in the countryside.
YANG	I don't remember China's night sky anymore. The blue sky and the night sky south of the Yangtze River have faded from my mind. What I remember most vividly is being driven out of Shanghai during the war, and the devastated landscape. I remember the ruins of Nanking, Wuhan, and Chungking.
UEHARA	I'm sorry to hear that.
YANG	Please excuse my imagination, but looking at the stars, I almost feel Mr. Morgan's son has flown up there.
UEHARA	[*Shocked by Yang's bold words.*] What?!
YANG	I suppose I've shocked you.
UEHARA	Of all things…Mr. Morgan would be horrified if he heard you.

YANG	Of course, but it's not unreasonable to wonder if he may have been kidnapped.
UEHARA	How is that even thinkable?
YANG	[*Pauses.*] Mr. Uehara, didn't you say you were worried about your daughter?
UEHARA	What?

Scene Three

Near dusk, on a cliff overlooking the sea. Distant sounds of military activity, such as cannons and trucks, are heard, then fade out. Robert and Yōko enter, cheerful. They face the audience as if it were the sea.

HARRIS	Wow, this is Maeda Point. What a cliff. And look how big the military base is. We're lucky there're no exercises going on today.
YŌKO	Robert, wouldn't Michiko's feelings be hurt if she knew we came alone here?
HARRIS	Michiko's at her parents' place today. And your mom said it's OK to go for a ride with me.
YŌKO	She thought I was going with you to English class.
HARRIS	Well, consider me your teacher, for speaking English with you.
YŌKO	That's true…we are speaking English. [*Beat.*] What a beautiful ocean. And so quiet…
HARRIS	The world's most beautiful sunsets are in Okinawa.
YŌKO	[*Serious.*] You have seen the sunsets all over the world?
HARRIS	[*Laughing.*] No, my captain told me that.
YŌKO	I think we should go back now.
HARRIS	What do you mean? We just got here. Look, the sun is sinking into the ocean. I have never imagined that a sunset could be so beautiful.
YŌKO	You just said Okinawan sunsets are always beautiful.
HARRIS	Maybe it's particularly beautiful because I'm with you. [*Moves closer.*]
YŌKO	[*Alarmed.*] People might see us.

HARRIS	There's nothing wrong about us being together. Americans and Okinawans are on friendly terms. People will think we're neighbors. [*Tries to embrace her.*]
YŌKO	[*Pushing him* off.] No!

The stage darkens. Yōko and Robert struggle. "Stars and Stripes Forever" plays in the distance.

I'm not like Michiko!

HARRIS	Don't worry, nobody's watching us. Yōko, I love you.

Stage is nearly black. Lights above suggest stars. Sounds of rough surf. Yōko and Robert continue to struggle. Robert overpowers and rapes Yōko. She pushes him off her. He stumbles and falls over the cliff. Sounds of surf grow louder.

YŌKO	Oh, no! Did I push him off the cliff? Robert? [*Listens.*]
HARRIS	[*From below.*] Yōko! Help me! I'm losing my grip on the rocks!
YŌKO	[*Extending her hand.*] Robert, reach for my hand!

Scene Four

Living room of Millers' home. Uehara and Yang enter.

UEHARA	Looks like we're the first ones to return. The others might think we just walked around.
YANG	The boy will be all right. He will turn up shortly.
UEHARA	Well, I hope so.
YANG	Mr. Uehara, if you think otherwise, why don't you go out and look for the child again?
UEHARA	[*Addressing Yang stiffly.*] But you suggested that we should come back. You said we had tried hard enough.
YANG	Being out there reminded me of a day in Chungking thirty years ago.
UEHARA	Chungking? That must have been when you were fleeing from the Japanese army?
YANG	Yes, one of those days. My four-year-old son got lost.
UEHARA	What happened?
YANG	He went out to play with his friends. They all came home except him. It was getting dark, so I went looking for him.

The Japanese army had occupied one section of the city, and I feared that they might have picked him up. The streets were nearly dark, and walking there, I felt surrounded on all sides by an invisible enemy.

UEHARA   Had he been kidnapped? Or…

YANG   He had been taken into custody by the Japanese military police.

UEHARA   Perhaps Mr. Morgan's son has also been found by the military police.

YANG   The Japanese returned my son. But only after endless hours of interrogating me. They suspected me of plotting against them. We Chinese had to obey the Japanese. They were very strict about everything. China was no longer my own country…I felt great despair.

UEHARA   Are you telling me this because you're optimistic about Mr. Morgan's son being found safe, or are you recalling the despair of an occupied China?

YANG   Both. What makes the current matter complicated is that the boy who was kidnapped—excuse me, who is missing— is an American, a child of the occupying forces. That makes the case clearly different from mine.

UEHARA   [*Irritated.*] What are you getting at?

YANG   [*As if being roused from a daydream.*] Yes, what am I trying to say?

UEHARA   I sympathize with your confusion. You left China after the Communist Party replaced Japanese rule, came to Okinawa, and now you work as a lawyer, sometimes for the American military. But even though you work for Americans, you still have the perspective of an outsider. In that sense, you feel uneasy about the child, even while you are hopeful that he might be safe. Do you recognize how your judgment could be confused in a moment like this?

YANG   You may be right, Mr. Uehara. Do you remember that I asked you a while ago if you were worried about your daughter?

UEHARA   I do.

YANG   I was concerned about your daughter's safety at that moment, and now I may appear unconcerned. Do you think my attitude is contradictory?

UEHARA	Yes, it appears contradictory. But somehow I understand this contradiction.
YANG	Do you see my contradictory attitudes simply as two sides of the same coin? That is, I feel both the fear and the resignation of a people who have lost their country?
UEHARA	That's going too far!
YANG	You know, Mr. Uehara, I fear I am simply superimposing my own experiences on the situation in Okinawa.
UEHARA	All the more reason your thoughts are confused…
YANG	Ah, of course… [*Laughs weakly.*]
MILLER	[*Entering.*] Enjoying yourselves?
YANG	Oh, Mr. Miller…
UEHARA	What has happened to the child?
HELEN	[*Entering.*] Hi, honey. So…?
LINCOLN	[*Enters cheerfully. Interrupting.*] What a kidnapping!
UEHARA	A kidnap?
LINCOLN	[*Laughs loudly.*] Yes, a kidnapping, but a harmless one. Mrs. Morgan didn't realize it, but the maid had the afternoon off, and so when Mrs. Morgan didn't show up by noon, the maid took the boy home with her rather than leave him alone.
YANG	How did Mr. Morgan react? Was he angry?
LINCOLN	Anybody would get mad. He got the phone number of the maid's family through her friend and was yelling into the phone. I don't know if he was speaking to the maid or someone in her family.
MILLER	But I would imagine they understood why Mr. Morgan was so upset.
LINCOLN	I don't know. [*As if unable to suppress a laugh.*] Okinawans may not understand why they would be scolded for committing a crime when there was no criminal intention. Such peace-loving people are rare in the world.
YANG	I hope this doesn't lead to complications.
MILLER	What do you mean?
YANG	[*Feigning lightheartedness.*] Oh, nothing serious.

UEHARA	For example, you mean the maid and her family are feeling the sting of Mr. Morgan's accusations and resent him for being angry at them for no reason?
MILLER	Their resentment would be unjustified. The maid should have known better.
LINCOLN	Well, we had a happy ending. Okinawans are incapable of kidnapping. Morgan would understand that if he got to know these people better. Hey, this is supposed to be a cocktail party. Let's have another drink.
HELEN	Okinawa is such a peaceful place. What's important is international friendship. Harmony is what we need.
YANG	I hope nothing will happen to the maid. [*To Uehara.*] Don't you agree?

Fade to black.

Act Three

Okinawa, 1971.

Scene One

Living room of Millers' home.

HELEN	[*Frowning.*] I never would have imagined! I thought that Yōko had caught a cold or something, and that's why she was missing class. Is she still in custody at the police station?
UEHARA	Not at the Okinawan police station. At the C.I.D.—the Criminal Investigation Division of the U.S. military.
HELEN	Ah, yes. Crimes against Americans are handled by the C.I.D.
MILLER	[*To Helen.*] Mr. Uehara would like to have a cup of coffee. Can I have the same?
HELEN	Sorry. I was so upset. I'll prepare coffee for us right away.
UEHARA	I'm sorry to trouble you.
MILLER	No need to apologize. So, what would you like me to do?
UEHARA	As I said, it would be a great help if you could meet with this American soldier, Robert Harris, and persuade him to…
MILLER	Persuade him to what?

UEHARA	[*Irritated.*] Harris has filed a criminal complaint against Yōko! But she is the victim here.
MILLER	You've told me already that Harris raped your daughter. Then, after the rape, Yōko pushed him over a cliff. Now, Harris has filed a criminal complaint against her for injuring him. There is a kind of logic to it all, is there not?
UEHARA	Do you honestly think so?
MILLER	Now, please don't misunderstand me. I'm not saying your daughter wasn't injured. But, whatever happened, Harris was also injured by Yōko. So, his response is neither surprising nor unreasonable. His complaint is legal, don't you think?
UEHARA	So you believe what he is doing is right?
MILLER	Let me repeat my point to avoid any misunderstanding. I am saying that, under the law, Yōko can also file a criminal complaint, or you can file one for her.
UEHARA	You must realize how very difficult that is to do. I've explained to you what happened at the Okinawan police station.
	At a corner downstage, under a spotlight, an Okinawan police officer sits at a desk. Uehara walks across the stage and sits down across from him.
POLICE OFFICER	[*Agonized.*] Mr. Uehara, I deeply sympathize with you. As an Okinawan police officer, I would like to arrest this guy—what was his name?—Harris—but we have no authority when it comes to American soldiers. Legally we simply have no jurisdiction…Besides—
UEHARA	I know all about it! Even if you arrested Harris, his case would be moved to the U.S. military court.
POLICE OFFICER	And the court-martial by the military—supposing there is one—will be held in English, on the base. In addition, even if your daughter files a complaint, it is extremely difficult to prove rape. In fact, that's the most difficult crime to prove. You'd end up making your daughter suffer tremendously during cross-examination.
UEHARA	OK. I will forget about trying to win the case in the military court. But his complaint against my daughter—that will at least be heard in the Okinawan district court.
POLICE OFFICER	Yes, his complaint against her will eventually be transferred from the C.I.D. to the Okinawan police, and she will be tried in the Okinawan civilian system.

UEHARA	And so I'm asking you to summon Harris as a witness to the civilian court. Then, we can prove my daughter's claim that she injured Robert Harris in self-defense…
POLICE OFFICER	[*Sighs.*] Unfortunately, Mr. Uehara, the Okinawan courts have no power to summon an American as a witness. He doesn't have to testify against his will.
UEHARA	Well, then, suppose Robert Harris agrees to testify voluntarily?
POLICE OFFICER	[*Surprised.*] Voluntarily?
UEHARA	We'll convince him—no, no. I mean we'll ask him to testify. Politely.
POLICE OFFICER	It won't work. No, it's impossible. American military personnel, as I've said, have absolute immunity in Okinawan courts.
UEHARA	I have a couple of American acquaintances who might help. If we can prove legitimate self-defense in the Okinawan district court, wouldn't it then be possible to convict this man in the court-martial?
POLICE OFFICER	No, the court-martial is a separate procedure. The military judges won't even consider the outcome of the trial against your daughter. Besides, it may be difficult for her to claim self-defense. You said Harris was injured after they struggled. The best she can do, under the law, is plead mitigating circumstances.
UEHARA	I will arrange it so that the witness appears in court.
POLICE OFFICER	All right. We will file the complaint after you've persuaded him.

Uehara crosses the stage to Miller.

UEHARA	I never realized before how unjust it is to have separate legal systems for Okinawans and Americans.
MILLER	Nevertheless, the Okinawan officer is correct.
UEHARA	And that is why I need you to help me persuade Harris to testify in court!
MILLER	This is so sudden…I don't know what to say…
UEHARA	I apologize for asking, but you're the only person who can help.
MILLER	If I get involved, this case could lead to a very serious confrontation between Americans and Okinawans.

UEHARA	It already has.
MILLER	Not yet…so far, at least. This can still be seen as something that happened between one young man and one young woman. It could have happened anywhere in the world. But if you think of it as an injury done by an American to an Okinawan, it could escalate into something larger.
UEHARA	What do you mean?
MILLER	Think about it. Why ask me to help you prosecute a young American soldier?
UEHARA	Is my request too much trouble for you?
MILLER	No, that's not what I'm saying. But we should talk to each other as individuals. If I knew this Robert Harris, my involvement would make sense. But, like you, I'm a complete stranger to him. We've tried very hard to build friendships in Okinawa that transcend race and nationality. This sort of case could undo our efforts.
UEHARA	Friendships can be mended later. Right now, I desperately need someone—a neutral third party—who is willing to help me speak to Harris.
MILLER	How about Mr. Yang then? He is a lawyer. And, he is neither American nor Okinawan. He would be an ideal mediator.
UEHARA	Is it unpleasant for you, as an American, to confront another American's shameful behavior?
MILLER	I really hate to say this, but quite honestly, I have no evidence that Robert Harris actually did something shameful, and I'm in no position to investigate the case myself. That's why Mr. Yang would be much better. He's not an American and he is a lawyer, which makes him a logical intermediary.
UEHARA	I see. I'm sorry to have taken so much of your time tonight.
MILLER	Wait. Please don't get the wrong idea. I would like you to remember that I've worked hard to build goodwill between America and Okinawa. It's for a good reason I can't help you: we need to avoid unnecessary conflicts if we are to preserve our friendship with Okinawans. Please understand this.
UEHARA	I'll try.
HELEN	[*Entering.*] Are you leaving already? What have you decided to do?
	Uehara stares at Helen as "Stars and Stripes Forever" starts playing. The cyclorama displays these words:

"Civil Administration Ordinance No. 144, The Code of Penal Law and Procedure of the Civil Administration of the Ryūkyū Islands, Chapter 2. Offences Against Safety:

"2.2.3. Any person who rapes, or assaults with intent to rape, any female United States Forces Personnel may be punished by death or such other punishment as the U.S. Civil Administration court may order."

Scene Two

Garden of Mr. Yang's house. Uehara and Ogawa are in the midst of explaining the situation to Yang as he waters his plants.

UEHARA	[*Irritated.*] Well, Mr. Yang, what do you say?
OGAWA	Mr. Yang, I too am asking you to help Mr. Uehara. Please, say something.
YANG	Mr. Ogawa, you are a Japanese citizen, and Mr. Miller is an American. And yet, you don't think *your* intervention can make a difference. Why then do you think that I, a Chinese, can be of help to Mr. Uehara?
OGAWA	Unlike Mr. Miller, I have no status here as a Japanese citizen. You, however, are a lawyer. In addition, I believe you have a strong sense of justice.
YANG	[*Picking a flower.*] In Hawaii, this is called a hibiscus…A beautiful flower.
	The cyclorama displays a crimson hibiscus.
	In Okinawa, it is called the flower of the next world. Did you know it is native to China? Like the seeds of this flower, I've been carried from place to place.
OGAWA	Is that your answer to Mr. Uehara's request?
UEHARA	The seeds may drift, but the flowers are welcome wherever they bloom. I fully understand your position as a foreigner in Okinawa is difficult. I ask only that you help me as a lawyer.
OGAWA	[*Pointing into the audience.*] Look at how beautiful and difficult this place is. That's the East China Sea. Over here to the north and south runs Military Highway No. 1. Along the highway you can see military bases occupying the land. The number of American military personnel is about fifty thousand, and there are over one million Okinawans. But why is there such difference in their rights? Okinawans did not

Higa Yasuo: Maternal Deities

Imploring the Gods (Kami-nigai)
Kume Island, Maja, Umachī
1977

choose this situation. Mr. Yang, you fled from the Communist revolution in China and came here. The residential area where you live is safe and beautiful for foreigners such as you. But can you be happy on those occasions when you are defending the rights of Americans?

YANG   This housing area is pleasant, but don't forget it's surrounded by an American military base.

OGAWA   You're a lawyer, and can stand up for yourself.

YANG   That's not entirely true. I'm a foreigner, so my position is not secure.

OGAWA   But you're aware that Okinawans today do not have the legal right to defend themselves in their own country…in their own homes.

YANG   Mr. Ogawa. You're a Japanese, a compatriot of Okinawans, but you're not defending Okinawans either. For example, Mr. Uehara's daughter—

OGAWA   As a Japanese national from the northern islands, I am considered an alien citizen by the American administration.

UEHARA   Mr. Yang, I've asked Mr. Ogawa to help me in his capacity as a newspaper reporter. I'm simply asking you to help me as a lawyer.

YANG   Let me ask you both a question: what were you doing on August 15, 1945?

OGAWA   The day World War II ended—when the Emperor broadcast Japan's surrender—I was a student in Beijing, a fifth-year student in a junior high school under the prewar education system. It was my last summer vacation, and I was on a trip to Inner Mongolia.

YANG   Did you face any dangerous situations when the news of the Japanese defeat was announced?

OGAWA   The news reached China while I was on my way back to Beijing. I wasn't aware of it until I arrived in the city.

YANG   I imagine it was hard for you, after you arrived in Beijing. But did you sense anything unusual during your trip, any change?

OGAWA   Like what?

YANG   For example, did you sense any slight difference in the way Mongolians looked at you? A warmth or hostility in their gaze?

OGAWA	People were kind to us students, though I don't know how they treated soldiers.
YANG	Do you think their kindness was sincere?
OGAWA	What are you getting at?
YANG	You personally didn't do anything wrong. You were just a student. But didn't you pretend to be indifferent to the Japanese treatment of the Chinese during the war?
OGAWA	And this is the kind of indifference you are pretending to feel now?
YANG	Yes. I'm embarrassed about it. I will have to confess my own sins someday. But, still, I feel critical of you for what the Japanese did in China and for your indifference at the time. [*To Uehara.*] You once told me you were an army officer stationed in Wuhan in Sichuan Province.
UEHARA	Yes. Why are you asking me about this now?
	As Uehara listens to Yang, he remembers what happened in China. The stage goes dark as the crimson hibiscus on the cyclorama is replaced by an image of Second Lieutenant Uehara about to execute Chinese prisoners. He is standing with his sword raised overhead but lacks the courage to kill them. In this flashback, Uehara's voice and the voices of two other soldiers—a commander (CO) and a noncommissioned officer (NCO)—are heard off-stage.
CO'S VOICE	Lieutenant Uehara, what's the matter with you! Why are you hesitating? Kill them! How can you be a platoon commander if you can't execute prisoners! Maybe I should get another platoon leader to replace you. Even a noncom can do it!
NCO'S VOICE	Lieutenant! You are making the commander lose face. Let me do it!
CO'S VOICE	Lieutenant Uehara, you should be ashamed of yourself! These prisoners may have killed Japanese soldiers. Don't you want revenge against your enemy? War begins in hatred. To hate is a mark of honor. To hate the Chinese is the very essence of a Japanese soldier. OK, get someone else to execute these prisoners!
UEHARA'S VOICE	No, Commander, I will do it. *Yaah!*
	Lights rise, and the image of the crimson hibiscus returns to the cyclorama. Uehara's face is pale.

OGAWA	You're being unfair, Mr. Yang. You're diverting us from the matter at hand.
UEHARA	It's all right, Mr. Ogawa. My attitude toward the Chinese during the war deserves Mr. Yang's condemnation. We should leave him alone.
OGAWA	Still…
YANG	Are you giving it up, Mr. Uehara?

Uehara stares at Yang in confusion.

	I am asking if you're giving up your attitude…I merely wished for you to recognize the relationship between your former and present positions—and also to be honest to my own feelings about the war and the behavior of the Japanese in China. America and Okinawa—Japan and China…Such things are beyond our control…
UEHARA	What are you saying?
YANG	I will try to help you, whether we succeed or not. We Chinese have always risked our lives this way. Let's go meet this young man, Robert Harris.
UEHARA	Thank you, Mr. Yang.
YANG	No need to thank me now. We don't yet know what will happen.
UEHARA	I'm deeply grateful.

Blackout.

Scene Three

Light on Robert Harris sitting up in a hospital bed. Uehara, Ogawa, and Yang are beside the bed.

HARRIS	I know why you're here. Are you a Japanese lawyer?
YANG	Chinese.
HARRIS	Oh yeah, I heard Uehara could speak Chinese. So a Chinese lawyer is going to defend his daughter.
YANG	I will not defend anyone.
HARRIS	Then why do you want to talk to me? This room is full of sick and injured people. You've got no right to come in here and upset them. Anyway, I don't need a lecture on what we already know.

YANG	Of course not. We did not come here to impose any legalities on you, nor do we have the right to do so. Therefore, you needn't get upset. We just want to have a calm discussion with you.
HARRIS	Whatever happened was by mutual consent. Afterwards, she attacked me when I wasn't looking, then lied about it.
YANG	Would you testify to that in court?
HARRIS	What?
YANG	I don't want you to misunderstand our intention, Mr. Harris. We are not thinking of accusing you of anything. This man's daughter is under indictment in civil court for a crime against you. Will you testify at her trial?
HARRIS	Testify to what?
YANG	You just said it was by mutual consent, and you were the victim of a betrayal. Will you testify to that? Of course, you are not being indicted in the civil trial, but unless you testify to your side of the story, the girl will not stop accusing you, and suspicions against you will never be dispelled. Okinawans will think you—
HARRIS	What an underhanded trick! You can't fool me. It is an undeniable fact that she injured me. And I know I don't have to testify in any Okinawan court. I know that much about the law.
YANG	Certainly, the law made by Americans favors Americans.
UEHARA	What happened to Michiko, your girlfriend?
HARRIS	That's none of your business.
YANG	You have the right—
HARRIS	I don't understand this. Aren't you Chinese? I've heard—
YANG	Heard what?
HARRIS	I've heard Uehara here was an officer in the Japanese army and fought in China. [*To Uehara.*] Didn't you kill Chinese? Do you think you have the right to judge me?
UEHARA	My past has nothing to do with you.
HARRIS	How about Mr. Lawyer there. You're Chinese. How could you work for a former Japanese officer?
YANG	That is none of your business.
HARRIS	Well, isn't this ironic? Yes, thanks to you people, I now fully

understand the great irony of it all. You should have just let it go.

OGAWA   What?

UEHARA   This is enough, Mr. Ogawa. Let's leave.

Blackout.

Scene Four

"Stars and Stripes Forever" is heard in the darkened theater. Lights come on, and Uehara, Ogawa, and Yang enter. Ambient sounds indicate they are outdoors.

OGAWA   This guy's tough.

YANG   He can't just hide behind his legal rights and obligations. How easy life would be if we could all do that.

UEHARA   I didn't want you to know about my years in China.

YANG   Surely you've thought about our relationship—what it means to have someone like myself as your friend?

UEHARA   I don't know what to say.

YANG   I chose to be a lawyer in order to pursue "legal rights and obligations." I thought it would make life simpler. And I've followed a life of legal "clarity" for the past thirty years.

UEHARA   What the Japanese army did in China was certainly beyond the pale of "legal rights and obligations."

YANG   So, it was in Wuhan that you killed the prisoners?

UEHARA   Yes.

YANG   My younger brother died in the battle in Wuhan. I heard he was first taken prisoner and then died—

OGAWA   Are you suggesting that one of the prisoners killed by Mr. Uehara might have been your brother? You're going too far—no one can know that for a fact. The mere suggestion has hurt Mr. Uehara deeply.

YANG   No, that's not what I'm saying. I'm not accusing him personally. Some things are beyond our control. But I became a lawyer because I wanted to find whatever limits there are to "legal rights and obligations" in such tragedies.

UEHARA   It's too late for me to become a lawyer.

OGAWA   You're not going to drop your case without protest, are you?

UEHARA	[*Weakly.*] I don't know…That's the last thing I want to do, but…
	Ogawa takes Uehara aside, unfolds a sheet of paper, and hands it to him.
OGAWA	Look. I have something to show you.
UEHARA	The members of the American-Ryūkyūan Goodwill Committee?
OGAWA	[*Pointing.*] Here…
UEHARA	Mr. Miller's name…
OGAWA	And his occupation is?
UEHARA	C.I.C.! Army Counter-Intelligence Corps! I had no idea. That's why he never answered my questions about his job.
OGAWA	We were his friends, chatting away on the assumption we had a mutual interest in practicing our Chinese, and we never suspected who he really was.
UEHARA	What do you think he wanted from us?
OGAWA	Your reaction to the unfortunate incident involving your daughter was perhaps an example of what he wanted to find out.
UEHARA	I was a fool to ask him for help.
OGAWA	As they say, nothing is certain in this world.
UEHARA	Okinawans are like Sun Wu-Kung, the Monkey King, who dances in the palm of the Buddha. In this case, America is the Buddha's palm. So who then does this land belong to?
YANG	Beautiful islands. Many things take place here that are not what they seem. Do you see those two men walking over there?
OGAWA	The ones who just got out of that car? Yes. They're headed to the golf course.
YANG	On the surface it looks friendly enough. But they may be talking about a mountain of debts. Today, they may be partners, but tomorrow they may be mortal enemies.
OGAWA	Such a worldview doesn't solve anything.
YANG	But that's where we must start—from life as it is. Speaking from my own limited experiences, there are things that can

be solved by "legal rights and obligations." Others, as if fated, may transcend the boundaries of such legalities. We survive by trying, in our own small ways, to hold on to our humanity while torn between the moral and the legal, the individual and the nation.

UEHARA   [*Finally understanding something.*] Thank you, Mr. Yang. I know what to do now.

YANG   I couldn't help you.

UEHARA   But you taught me something today.

OGAWA   What are you going to do now?

Blackout.

YŌKO'S VOICE   No! You mustn't do that. Accuse him? You are only think-ing of your own pride! What about me?

UEHARA'S VOICE   If I was only thinking of myself, I would swallow everything in silence.

YŌKO'S VOICE   Well, then, just leave me out of it!

Scene Five

A dinner club on the military base. Light jazz plays in the background. Uehara, Yang, Ogawa, and the Millers are eating.

HELEN   Mr. Uehara, now that your daughter has returned to school, I look forward to seeing her again in my English class.

OGAWA   Mr. Miller, I've heard about these clubs on the army base, but this is the first time I have been in one. Thank you for inviting us.

MILLER   You're welcome. I can arrange a dinner like this anytime.

OGAWA   Between the two of us: are you attempting a reconciliation with Mr. Uehara?

MILLER   Well, let's just call it a get-together. Besides, Mr. Uehara has completely recovered himself, and I'm sure there are no hard feelings.

OGAWA   I see.

HELEN   [*Looking at the door.*] Oh, here comes Mr. Lincoln.

LINCOLN   Sorry I'm late.

MILLER   Not at all. We're delighted you made it.

LINCOLN	There's a fine banner over the entrance: "Prosperity to Ryūkyūans, and may Ryūkyūans and Americans always be friends." Beautiful words! Someone told me that's what Commodore Perry said in a toast at a formal reception. He was invited to the Ryūkyūan palace in 1853. We here are a perfect example of what he was talking about. Oh, by the way, I've got news. Did you hear that Mr. Morgan brought charges against his maid?
UEHARA	What?!
	Uehara and Ogawa stand up. Uehara drops his fork on the floor.
	Is that true?
LINCOLN	Yep. A friend of mine who works at the C.I.D. told me. They're still investigating and asking her questions. I just don't know what to make of this all. I wish we could return to the age of "may Ryūkyūans and Americans always be friends…"
MILLER	That was Perry's first visit to Okinawa…when American and Okinawan contact began. But Okinawan relations with China are far older, isn't that so?
UEHARA	[*Impatient.*] Are you really so interested in discussing Okinawan history?
MILLER	[*Puzzled.*] What? Yes, of course. You know I am. I was just trying to begin our regular meeting with the history of cultural exchanges.
UEHARA	I doubt that's really your intention.
MILLER	But—
UEHARA	I can't help but wonder about the real purpose of our meetings.
MILLER	Are you still—
UEHARA	After you refused to help me, Mr. Yang went to the hospital with me to persuade Harris.
MILLER	Yes…?
UEHARA	You said Mr. Yang would be an ideal person. But this is a case that is beyond Mr. Yang's professional powers.
MILLER	I realize the case has been hurtful to you. I truly thought Mr. Yang would be able to handle it.
UEHARA	But it wasn't just a legal matter.

MILLER	What do you mean?
UEHARA	The way Robert Harris treated me, for example. If I told you I was insulted by an American, how would you feel?
MILLER	It depends on the nature of the insult. And the circumstance as well…and your rights and his…
UEHARA	It was the second time I've been insulted by an American. The first was in September 1945, in Shanghai, one month after the war ended. Since I could speak Chinese, I was sent from the POW camp to work in a civilian office. One day, I was walking on a deserted street. I didn't have a weapon, but I was wearing a uniform. A young white man walking in the opposite direction suddenly punched me hard in the stomach. I dropped down on the street in pain. That's when I realized what it means to lose a war.
YANG	The Chinese generally treated Japanese kindly after the war.
UEHARA	Yes, I was surprised. The Chinese soldiers who came from the west were especially kind. That's why Japanese in China didn't suffer as much as we might have—the nationals of a defeated country. So the punch from the young man came as a terrible shock to me.
MILLER	How do you know he was an American?
UEHARA	I'm not certain that he was. People from various countries were in China then, so he may not have been. But at the time, I was convinced that he was American.
MILLER	Pardon me. I'm not unsympathetic to your being struck, but why did you automatically assume that the man who injured you was an American? I suspect you were influenced by the fact that Japan lost the war to the United States. However, it's unlike you, Mr. Uehara, to direct those same emotional accusations at me because of my reluctance to get involved in your daughter's case.
UEHARA	Perhaps I am a bit emotional. But Robert Harris followed his legalistic logic to the end. He said he had no obligation to answer my request, he had his rights, and the Okinawan legal system had no power to summon him to testify at Yōko's trial. I'm not ignorant of this logic of rights and obligations. But in this instance, I find it unacceptable, and it was an act of inhumanity for Harris to use such logic with me.
MILLER	Logic and laws sometimes require sacrifice.

UEHARA	Mr. Yang and I discussed this very point. He said he too was following an inescapable logic. But in reality, in our daily lives, are we rigorously faithful in separating legal obligations from other kinds?
OGAWA	[*Aside to Uehara, speaking in Japanese.*] Uehara-*san*, you shouldn't say the rest.
UEHARA	[*Responding to him in Japanese.*]Arigatō, Ogawa-*san*, but I haven't said yet what I really want to say. [*Then to all, in English.*] Did everyone understand what Mr. Ogawa was trying to do just now? He's worried that I will upset the stable but delicate balance among us. But that does not prevent me from saying what I must—since this balance is based entirely on pretension. Mr. Miller, you said it was regrettable that I took out my resentment on you because I was punched by another American in Shanghai. But how are you different from any other American to me? For example, I heard only recently that you're an intelligence officer, which made me realize that you deliberately misled me when I asked you about your job.
MILLER	I had no ulterior motives. I am forced to conceal the nature of my work. I would call my evasiveness—if that's what you consider it—professional manners.
UEHARA	But now that I know your job, it is only natural for me to believe that you did have ulterior motives. There's a wide gap between you and me.
YANG	Mr. Uehara, you're destroying everything that I've worked so hard to create.
UEHARA	Mr. Yang, you tried, and your efforts are commendable, but you neglected what was really necessary.
MILLER	[*To Yang.*] What were you working so hard to create?
YANG	Toward the end of the war, President Chiang Kai-Shek gave an address to the Chinese army and Chinese people. He said we would win the war, and then he urged us to be good friends to the Japanese after they were defeated. He pointed out that our true enemies were Japan's extreme militarists, not the nation's people.
UEHARA	I too heard that speech. That's why the Chinese were kind to us—and we nevertheless tried to take advantage of their generosity.
OGAWA	Are you sure, though, that the Chinese really forgave the Japanese?

MILLER	Of course not. Whatever the justification, how can people forget the atrocities that happened?
YANG	During the twenty-five years since the end of the war, we haven't forgotten, but we've tried to overcome our resentment—to be friends again. We've done our best. I know there are now twenty-five years of resentment in Okinawa to overcome. But you've destroyed these kinds of efforts.
UEHARA	Not me. Not Mr. Ogawa. Robert Harris destroyed your ideals of friendship and forgiveness. Mr. Miller destroyed them, and Mr. Morgan destroyed them.
MILLER	This is ridiculous. You don't know what it means to be friends across national boundaries. The friendship of the peoples of two countries must be based on friendships between individuals. This is also true of hatreds. Yes, there are national hatreds. But there are many individual friendships. We try to create as many friendships as possible. Between common people. Even though we hold animosities sometimes against each other, we hope that someday we can be friends again.
UEHARA	No, it's only a pretense. You put on a mask to make people believe that the friendship you talk about means something.
MILLER	It's not a pretense. It's the truth. Friendship is the only hope that we can believe in. My strong hope—that friendship is everything—is not a mask.
UEHARA	It works only in theory. You have never been hurt and felt the rupture in your logic. Once you get hurt, you'll understand that it's also logical to hate the hurt. You put on a mask to conceal this aspect of the truth. I've got to expose the deception in your logic.
MILLER	What will you do?
UEHARA	I'll file a complaint against Robert Harris.
OGAWA	But, Mr. Uehara, you decided not to do that.
UEHARA	I've been fooled by Mr. Miller's false logic. I sensed the falseness, but I didn't think deeply enough about it. I tried to accept it. It makes me angry now that I thought it would be possible to simply put aside the insults and betrayals. Now, I will fight this case through to the end.
YANG	You will only make your daughter suffer.
UEHARA	We'll be prepared for anything.
YANG	Are you doing this just to save your own sense of dignity?

UEHARA	It's a matter of Okinawan dignity. No, it's even more than that. It's a matter of basic human dignity.
YANG	I still believe that Mr. Miller's logic of masking our feelings in the hope of forging friendships is correct. Your wound is not as deep as mine. But I endure it, and wear a mask. Otherwise, I could not have lived.
UEHARA	But you removed your mask the other day. You took it off on your own. And you stared at us with your raw gaze. You sounded as if you had been waiting for twenty-five years for the opportunity to make us confront our crimes in China. Now I'm determined to do the same thing.
YANG	You and I are not the same. In your case, you will cause your daughter to suffer unnecessarily.
UEHARA	Mr. Yang, it was you who opened my eyes. Atoning for what I did in your country and seeking justice for my daughter are the same thing; they cannot be separated. What is required most now is to be absolutely unforgiving of our sins. Let me repeat this: what I'm seeking is our mutual understanding of the ethics that are fundamental and unconditional for all humanity. What I want to indict is not just one crime by one young American, but the cocktail parties that would conceal fundamental ethics under the *pretext* of reconciliation.
MILLER	It's unfortunate that we can't see eye to eye.
UEHARA	[*Beat.*] Mr. Miller, are you familiar with Civil Administration Ordinance No. 144, The Code of Penal Law and Procedure of the Civil Administration of the Ryūkyū Islands, Chapter 2. Offences Against Safety, article 2.2.3?
MILLER	Article 2.2.3?

The cyclorama displays these words:

"Any person who rapes, or assaults with intent to rape, any female United States Forces Personnel may be punished by death or such other punishment as the U.S. Civil Administration court may order."

| UEHARA | I hope you will get around to reading it. It spells out the penalty for rape committed against U.S. military personnel by Okinawans. U.S. law establishes one kind of justice for the occupier and another for the occupied. As long as such injustice exists, your hopes will be illusory. Goodbye. [*Exits.*] |

| YŌKO | [*From off-stage.*] Why, Otōsan, why? |
| YANG | [*Looking up at the ceiling.*] Is this really what we wanted? |

Fade to black.

Act Four

Washington, D.C., 1995. Living room of Ben and Yōko's home. A long silence.

BEN	What a story! Was the case actually tried?
	Uehara nods.
	Didn't Yōko resist testifying at the trial?
UEHARA	She didn't resist at all, and that's what worried me.
BEN	I know how Yōko must have felt. Fighting alone, standing by herself in the witness box. I can imagine how the cross-examination went. Did Yōko have to testify in two courts—military and civilian?
UEHARA	I guess Yōko hasn't told you about it.
BEN	No, but she didn't have to. I love the Yōko I met in the United States.
	Yōko enters and stands close to Ben.
UEHARA	I thought many times about dropping the charges—before and during the trial.
BEN	But you couldn't turn back—you had to save face—
UEHARA	I didn't fight to save face. I fought for fundamental human rights. For democracy. For a truthful understanding of ethics and justice. It was very difficult for me to sacrifice Yōko for my beliefs.
BEN	[*To Yōko.*] Did you understand from the beginning why your father did what he did?
YŌKO	I resented it. I thought in theory it might be good to fight for democratic rights, but why me? I struggled to understand why I had to suffer as an individual for something that seemed so abstract. The worst thing was when everyone involved in the trial was taken to the crime scene. The cape was beautiful that day. The Okinawan ocean is the most beautiful sight in the world—more beautiful than the Caribbean, Ben. During the prosecution's questioning at the crime scene, I was forced to describe every detail of that

	day. Starting at a spot about thirty feet from the edge of the cliff, I had to relive each moment…
BEN	I know it must have been terrible for you.
UEHARA	The judge asked Yōko to repeat the details over and over. Listening to her, I also felt terrible anguish.
YŌKO	During the cross-examination at the cape, I gradually realized that I was entirely alone after all. Don't get the wrong idea, Otōsan. I know how much you and Mom love and care for me. But on the cliff, listening to the waves, enduring the questions and accusations altered my view of life. I know it's hard to believe that a seventeen-year-old girl could change so suddenly and so fundamentally. But it's true. I felt that beyond the cliff, all the way to the horizon, there was just myself, standing alone. The sound of the waves gave me the courage to face this reality, and I knew then that I could endure anything and still be my own person.
BEN	I admire your courage, Yōko. [*Beat.*] What was the final decision?
YŌKO	I was a minor and there were extenuating circumstances, and so I received probation. But I didn't care about the decision. After the trial, I was shattered. It took a long time for me to regain my mental balance.
BEN	What happened to Harris?
UEHARA	Not guilty. I was not even allowed to attend the court-martial. I only heard about the decision from your father.
YŌKO	I was alone at the court-martial, too.
UEHARA	It was deeply frustrating. The decision in Harris's case was just as I expected. But I'm not sure if I could have kept calm listening to Yōko's testimony again.
YŌKO	That's why I came to America as soon as I finished high school.
BEN	I can imagine it would be easier to recover from your wounds if you were in a foreign country.
YŌKO	I came to America to see democracy and equal rights in practice.
BEN	It was the right thing to do, Yōko.
UEHARA	I was more concerned about her wounds than I was surprised at her decision to come to America. It dampened

Higa Yasuo: Maternal Deities

Imploring the Gods (Kami-nigai)
Tonaki Island, Shimanōshi
1989

	what should have been happiness at her being accepted by an American university.
BEN	Well, I'm grateful to have met a wonderful woman.
UEHARA	So have you been satisfied with America's justice and equal rights?
YŌKO	I have conflicting feelings.
BEN	[*Teasing.*] I hope I'm on the positive side of your conflicted feelings.
YŌKO	Yes, but it would be easier at the moment if you were not a lawyer.
BEN	[*Serious.*] What's wrong with being a lawyer?
YŌKO	The veterans' association.
BEN	What?! Are you upset that I'm the association's legal advisor?
YŌKO	I like your friends in the association. They are all nice people, and I know that you agreed to advise them because of your friendship with them. And two of them are coming to our party tonight. I really do like them.
BEN	Well, then, what are you unhappy about?
YŌKO	Their protest against the A-bomb exhibition.
BEN	Well, I've told you…They are not protesting the exhibition itself, but the fact that the planners—and the Japanese—seem to have forgotten about Pearl Harbor.
UEHARA	Ben, what if people in other countries tried to have an exhibition commemorating, for example, the end of the Viet Nam War? Would you object if the Vietnamese emphasized the atrocities of using Agent Orange and other defoliants?
BEN	I can't be held personally responsible for what the United States has done.
UEHARA	Ben, you're making exactly the same mistake your father did.
BEN	What do you mean?
UEHARA	Your father told me that what happened to Yōko and Robert Harris was a problem that occurred between two individuals. He then said that we could not translate such a problem into that of two nations.
BEN	I'm not saying that. I'm a lawyer, and I'm grappling with a

particular legal question: to what extent was the use of the A-bomb legally acceptable in international laws. I'm not ready to answer questions beyond that.

YŌKO   In terms of international law, Pearl Harbor may be more forgivable because at least the main targets were warships. The attack wasn't aimed at civilians.

BEN   As I've said before, Pearl Harbor was more a violation of human decency than of international laws. A surprise attack is unethical, a stab in the back. But I don't understand why you're saying this now, Yōko; you've never disagreed with my view of Pearl Harbor.

YŌKO   Seeing my father again, something awakened in me—something that has been sleeping.

UEHARA   If you want to talk about human decency, Americans must pay serious attention to what's going on in Okinawa today.

BEN   [*Despairing.*] Now what is all this? Yōko, you sound like a stranger talking.

YŌKO   Please, don't get the wrong idea. I'm just saying, as Otōsan just said, sometimes it's impossible to separate politics and individual lives.

BEN   [*Holding his head.*] I don't know. Now what will happen to tonight's party? I just wanted your father to meet my close friends.

UEHARA   I'm sorry, but unless we have a clear understanding about the issue, everyone will end up going his separate way, as we did twenty-four years ago in Okinawa. Ben, I don't want you, as Yōko's husband, to make the same mistake your father made. I want you to understand that it's not easy for me to enjoy a party with people who oppose an exhibition that includes American culpability in using atomic bombs. I would like you to know that this is my final position.

BEN   Couldn't you assume that you heard about the exhibition one day later than this?

UEHARA   One day? August 15, 1945—the day that the Japanese surrendered. If that day had come one day earlier for me, I wouldn't have had to commit a horrible sin.

BEN   A horrible sin? Oh, you mean what happened in China. But Mr. Yang tried to forget it.

UEHARA   He forced himself to try to forget. But he never could. That's most natural. By forcing yourself to forget

	something, you end up postponing a real solution. In 1971, I put myself in Mr. Yang's position and decided to press charges against Robert Harris.
BEN	And you made Yōko suffer.
UEHARA	Not just Yōko. Can you imagine how much I suffered? I opposed the wishes of my daughter, my wife—and betrayed the goodwill of my friends.
BEN	Do you think we should forgive both Pearl Harbor and the atomic bombs?
UEHARA	No, I'm thinking of protesting against both. As countries and as individuals we are each victims and victimizers. Only by recognizing this fact, can a new millennium of reconciliation begin. We need to punish ourselves, and we need to be absolutely unforgiving of what we have done. Only by looking first at ourselves do we obtain the right to judge the other side. Choosing this path will cause us to suffer, but this is the only path that is humane.
BEN	In law, we take extenuating circumstances into consideration.
UEHARA	Aren't laws grounded in ethics? It's like original sin in Christianity. We need to be conscious of our own first sin.
BEN	OK, then, I will begin dwelling on it starting tomorrow. Please give me one day; otherwise I don't know how to face my guests from the veterans' association tonight.
UEHARA	You haven't understood my point!
	The doorbell rings.
YŌKO	Are they here already? [*Exits and returns with flowers.*] A messenger from Mr. MacKinley. He has urgent business and cannot make it tonight. [*Handing the flowers.*] For you, Otōsan.
UEHARA	[*Receiving it.*] Thanks. It's very nice of him.
YŌKO	What happened? He was looking forward to seeing you.
BEN	He didn't know how to tell me. He received a medal in Viet Nam, and now he has conflicting feelings about having accepted it.
UEHARA	Could you explain?
	As Ben tries to explain, "Stars and Stripes Forever" is heard from outside the window.

BEN	MacKinley realized today what you realized all those years ago in Okinawa.
YŌKO	[*Looking out the window.*] There are still some people protesting.
BEN	Is MacKinley among them?
YŌKO	I doubt it.
BEN	That's right. He wouldn't be there.
	Beat.
YŌKO	Ben. Can we talk about it tomorrow? Otōsan, could we?
	The doorbell rings.
UEHARA	Yes, I respect Ben's thoughtfulness. We can think about it again tomorrow. And today is not August 15, 1945.
BEN	No, but today is August 14, 1995. If we avoid talking about it today, tomorrow may be too late. My guests will welcome this discussion. Well, they may not welcome it, but we all need to have it. One of the expected guests is a survivor of Pearl Harbor. I'm sure even he'll listen to what you will say.

The swelling sound of "Stars and Stripes Forever." Fade to black.

Translation by Katsunori Yamazato and Frank Stewart

The Paper Plane at the Empire State Building

Pawing the ground, lowering its head, the black bull watches her with its small red eyes. Foam splashes from its nostrils as it drags at the ground with its left foreleg. Between its horns, a tuft of black ringlets glistens, the ears flick, stand erect, and point toward her. It keeps watching her, pawing the ground. Kana turns and runs. The bull leaps forward, goring her from behind. The thick horns hook into her back and toss her high above the beast's head. She is being taken somewhere on those horns, until she is awakened by her own screams.

Kana shuddered. In the places below her shoulder blades where the horns had pierced her in the nightmare, she felt stabbing pain. The bull was gone with the dream, but the pain remained. It was dragging her back into the darkness of the dream. Maybe the pain was real, because she had been cramped in the airplane seat for too long, twisted uncomfortably between the seat and the cold window before finally landing. Whether the dream had intensified the pain or the pain had produced the nightmare, she couldn't tell.

Kana rolled over in bed and closed her eyes. After a while, she sat up and turned on the lamp. She poured herself a glass of water, drank it, placed the empty glass back on the table, and buried her face in the pillow. The bull inside her head had chased away her drowsiness. So she got up and sat on a chair in the corner of the hotel room. Pulling her legs under her to fight the cold, she curled up in her thin robe. What an ominous dream while on a trip, she thought.

Once, long ago, Kana had helped slaughter a bull. It was soon after the Viet Nam War began. The staff in the meat section of her grocery claimed that the price of imported meat was too high, and the customers wanted cheaper, freshly killed meat. At last she had to give in, and they secretly slaughtered a bull in the warehouse. A farmer from the northern part of Okinawa walked one of his poor animals to Kana's place overnight to avoid detection. When they arrived, the bull's legs were white from the dust. Kana felt sorry for the bull. To think it had to walk all night only to be killed here at dawn.

The workers tied the bull's dusty legs together, covered its head with a hemp sack, and then the butcher who delivered meat to Kana's store struck the animal in the middle of its forehead with an axe. It slumped to the floor without a sound. Kana and her employees couldn't bear the horrible sight, and that was the first and the last bull to be killed in the warehouse. The dream reminded Kana of the pitiful black creature, though the incident at the warehouse had happened more than ten years before. Triggered by her fatigue, the faint memory of the slaughter must have returned in the form of the nightmare. The trip had worn her out. Kana was irritated that her tired mind had stirred up such an unwanted memory.

Instead of going back to bed, she dozed while curled up in the chair, awakening to the booming of a metal drum being tossed and rolled. The sound grew louder, and she glimpsed the white light of dawn through the curtains. She looked out to see a garbage truck working its way up the street. Steam rose from the grates in the pavement, and she could see a worker in a white helmet rolling a trash can about. Finally, Kana had a real sense that she was in New York City.

She closed the window and went into the bathroom, pulling off her new pajamas. She drew a hot bath and lay down in the water with her eyes closed. She had arrived at the hotel just past ten the night before. Owned by a Japanese, it was well lighted and comfortable. Her room on the seventh floor was clean and smelled new. Outside the window, the Chrysler Building had glowed pale blue against the night sky. Kana recognized it from postcards and guidebooks. As soon as the bellboy had brought in her luggage, she had impatiently changed her clothes and crawled into bed. Unable to sleep on the airplane, she had been totally exhausted.

After her long, hot bath, Kana felt revived. She dried herself, put on fresh clothes, and applied her makeup. Then she made herself a cup of coffee. The instant coffee tasted awful, like a paper cup. After a sip, she placed it on the side table and fished her date book out of her purse. Putting on her glasses, she found and dialed the telephone number for Sonan Toshi in Washington, D.C. The phone rang for a while before someone answered.

"Hello."

She heard Toshi's familiar voice. "Is that you, Toshi?"

"Yes."

Kana switched from English to Japanese. "It's me, Higa Kana, from the supermarket."

"Oh yes, Auntie. Are you here in America?"

"Yes, I am here."

"Where are you calling from?"

"Hotel Nishino in Manhattan. Park Avenue, I guess. It's near the Grand Central Station."

"You've come a long way." Toshi laughed quietly. Kana heard a male voice in the background, apparently Toshi's husband, say, "Moshi, moshi," followed by the high-pitched laugh of a child. The husband and the boy seemed to be teasing Toshi for speaking in Japanese, which she probably seldom did anymore.

"I might stay here for a week or so. Do you think you can help me out?"

"Of course I can. Henry leaves for California tomorrow. I can come to New York the day after. Is that okay with you?"

"Fine. I'll take care of the travel expenses."

"Oh, you don't have to worry about that," Toshi said cheerfully.

After she hung up, Kana went down to the lobby. Lighting a cigarette, she watched the other guests. Most of them were Japanese, and several appeared to be newlyweds.

At the newsstand in the lobby, Kana bought a map of New York City and a paperback Japanese-language guidebook. She opened the map and located her hotel, approximately halfway up Park Avenue, near Grand Central Station and the Pan American Building. Fifth Avenue and Central Park were close by, and the Empire State Building was less than four blocks away.

Where should I go first? she thought. Many places came to mind. Each brought with it a memory of Mike. In the rush of nostalgia, she felt a desire to visit all of the sights Mike used to tell her about when they were together. She sighed to think of herself as being on a kind of sentimental journey, following Mike's shadow. It could well be the truth. She smiled a little at the thought. At any rate, she felt, she should first go to Central Park, where Toshi told her she had seen Mike. Kana folded the map and pushed the revolving door to go outside.

The sky looked white in the early morning light reflecting off the sides of the tall buildings. It was only November, but the air had the chill of winter. Pulling her autumn coat around her, Kana waited for a taxi. None came by, maybe because it was early morning. Impatient, she walked north along Park Avenue, then down a steep slope. She crossed under an overpass, then reached a broad intersection. A building facing the T-junction was swallowing a great number of pedestrians. Kana stopped and checked the map. She saw that this was the main entrance to Grand Central Station. Near the doorways, she spotted a bum in a red-checkered cap sitting on a newspaper. She gave him a quick glance. Too young. He was ranting and making wild gestures, and Kana thought he must have had a mental disorder. Obviously, it wasn't Mike.

Entering the station hesitantly, she saw to her left another bum sprawled on the floor. The man was Black. For some reason, his ragged jacket was wet and heavy, and his short boots were muddy. A brown liquor bottle and a half-eaten piece of pizza were on the floor beside him. She hurried by, then glanced back. His eyes met hers. They seemed to be blaming her.

The high-ceilinged lobby of Grand Central Station reminded her of Umeda Station on the Hankyū line. The lights were dim, and the place was crowded, mostly with Blacks and dark-skinned people who had probably come from Central and South America. Men and women waited in short lines in front of the ticket windows. In one corner, a gray-haired man in a black suit—probably around sixty-three or -four—was playing a harmonica. Beside him was a small woman who could have been his wife. She crouched behind an old suitcase that lay open on the floor, exposing the cassette tapes inside. She sometimes made feeble smiles, looking around her. Kana joined the little crowd of people listening to the man play. The tune, with its quick tempo, sounded like a march. But she also sensed sadness in the music. She thought the couple might be gypsies. She paused, wondering if she should get on the subway. That would give her more chances to find Mike. Her courage failing, she cut through the crowd and went outside.

She took a taxi to Central Park, getting out at a circular intersection surrounded by trees. A statue stood on a tall column in the middle. The autumn colors were beautiful. She saw a few horse-drawn buggies along the curb under the roadside trees. They were attended by young coachmen in silk hats, white shirts, and blue jeans. The young men turned their smiling eyes to her.

She checked her guidebook and found that she was at Columbus Circle. The statue was of the explorer himself. Scarcely any people were nearby. The fallen leaves on the sidewalk were thick and moist. Squirrels ran under the withered branches, scattering the sparrows and the dead leaves.

Kana soon found herself beside a small coffee-colored pond—called a reservoir on the map—circled by white chairs and benches. She put down her little Boston bag and sat on one of the chairs. About ten other people, mostly old folks with canes, sat facing the pond. They appeared to be pensioners from the nearby apartment buildings. Toshi had told Kana that she had seen Mike near this pond. Kana's other friend, Matsuda Kazuo, had said he'd seen him in Battery Park. Kana thought she would wait here since this was the spot Toshi had mentioned first.

A month ago, Kana's phone rang a little after three in the afternoon as she was on her way from the Awase branch of her supermarket chain to the Sonda branch. A new, oversized refrigerator had just been delivered and was being stocked with produce.

"Hello, Auntie?" It was an overseas phone call. The voice from the receiver echoed and buzzed, and when Kana responded, she heard her own voice come back to her after a slight delay.

"It's me, Toshi. I used to work at your store. Remember me?"

"Uh, Toshi-*chan?*" Kana tried to remember Toshi's face. How many years had passed? The last time Kana had seen her, Toshi was a high school student living in the neighborhood and occasionally helping Kana with her store. The one humble grocery store was all she had owned in those days. Toshi slightly resembled Kana's dead sister, and so Kana adored being around her. Later, Toshi married a young American GI and went to the States with him. The women had continued to exchange letters for some time. And then Toshi's husband retired and found a job with a construction company. Because of his work, the family moved around a lot, and the women's correspondence had ended. What could Toshi possibly want after all these years? The thought made Kana mildly uncomfortable.

"Auntie, actually, I…" Toshi hesitated. Her breathing sounded uneven, as though she were having second thoughts about what to say.

"What's the matter, Toshi-*chan?*" Kana raised her voice, a little irritated by Toshi's silence. Maybe she was calling to ask for a loan. The thought alarmed Kana, but she encouraged Toshi to go on.

"What happened, dear?" Kana asked, trying her best to sound cheerful.

Toshi must have detected Kana's irritation. "I saw Mike-*san*, Auntie," she blurted out awkwardly.

Kana fell silent. She knew she should say something, but her tongue would not move. Her body tensed. She could feel an old wound opening. It had been thirty years since Mike had fled back to the States. He had told Kana that he had been assigned to work in Pusan, then he had simply left Kadena. She hadn't heard from him since then. When she had inquired, the consulate told her that Mike had gone straight back to the States from Pusan without stopping in Okinawa. Once he arrived in the States, he had gotten his discharge. The consulate had traced him to Brooklyn, where he had stayed for about six months, and then he had left to work for a shipping company in Cleveland. After that, they had lost track of him. But Kana couldn't let her search end there. She had borrowed money from all her relatives and hired a high school English teacher as an interpreter to go with her to the States. They searched not only in New York, but in the major cities in Ohio, Pennsylvania, and Michigan. No trace whatsoever. Time passed and brought no further news of him. That was how the story had gone until now.

"Where did you meet him?" Kana's words sounded almost like a cross-examination.

"In New York."

"New York?"

"Yes. In Central Park. He was from New York, wasn't he?"

"Yes, that is so, but…" Kana tried to sound calm, but her voice cracked. "Was it really him?"

"Yes, it was." Toshi's voice was excited and confident.

"Are you sure?"

"I'm sure. I actually spoke with him."

"You talked to him?"

"Yes."

"About what…? Give me more details."

It distressed Kana to think that Toshi would hear in her voice her lingering affection for Mike. But her words undermined her pride the more she spoke. Her heart pounded with vexation.

"I went to New York last week to attend the wedding of Henry's sister. After the ceremony, I went to Central Park, the place I had always dreamed of visiting. I was sitting on a bench at the reservoir, and a man dressed like a bum came close to me and said in Japanese, 'Please have mercy on me and spare me a quarter.'"

Kana waited to hear more.

"I didn't recognize his face at first, but his fluent Japanese made me wonder...Then I looked closely at his face..."

"And it was Mike." Kana finished Toshi's sentence for her.

"It was. His hair was totally white, and his face was partially covered by his beard, but I'm sure it was Mike. I asked him, 'Excuse me, but...is that you, Mike-*san*?' As soon as he heard my words, his face froze and he ran away. No mistake. Anyway, how many Americans can speak Japanese well enough to use a word like *mercy*? Not a regular American guy."

Kana thanked her, wrote down her D.C. telephone number, and hung up. It was hard to believe. At the same time, maybe something that she had been secretly afraid of was finally becoming real.

Toshi's call was the first one; the second came a few days later. It was Kana's classmate from elementary school, Matsuda Kazuo, who now ran a pharmacy in Naha.

"What a shock, Kana-*chan*," Matsuda started abruptly. "I was in Battery Park, you see, where you can get on a ferry to take you to the Statue of Liberty. An American who spoke fairly good Japanese begged money from me. Can you believe it? It was your ex-husband, Mike. Boy, was I flabbergasted."

Matsuda's voice was hot with excitement. When he had asked the beggar if he was Mike, the man had fled in panic. Matsuda's story did not shock Kana the way Toshi's had. Still, for the whole day she couldn't settle down to work. Over the next month, other phone calls followed. The man who delivered lunch boxes to Kana's stores called next. He had been Mike and Kana's neighbor years before. He said he had visited New York with members of the Food Union and had run into Mike on the tour. Then a man who used to work for Kana and who now ran a small security company said he saw Mike while on a group tour to New York. More reports from people who had seen Mike began to surface. Many of them were about encounters in Central Park or Battery Park. Whoever this man was—and it could well have been Mike—he seemed to be approaching Japanese tourists to beg for small change.

What should I do? Kana asked herself in the shock and depression that each phone call brought with it.

Kana had married Mike in 1949, right after World War II. She had lost her parents and sister during the Battle of Okinawa and had been working as a housemaid on Kadena Air Base. Of the few jobs available to Okinawans—even those with high school diplomas—most were on the U.S. military base mowing lawns or washing clothes at a laundry. Only later were Okinawans able to find positions such as typists and clerks at the PX. Luckily, one of Kana's father's friends worked in the base's personnel office, and he helped her find work as a housemaid.

The first job Kana got was with a family named Smedley. The husband, John Smedley, was a lieutenant colonel in the air force and had only recently been stationed at Kadena. His wife, who used to teach at a high school in Oklahoma, volunteered to give English lessons to Okinawan housemaids in her neighborhood. The arrangement was ideal for Kana, whose English conversation skills were only dim memories from her high school classes. Unfortunately, Lieutenant Colonel Smedley soon received a promotion, and the family moved from Okinawa to Korea.

After the Smedleys left, Kana was assigned to the family of an air force sergeant. Mike Bobcock was tall and spindly, a generic American who had no distinct features but was a knowledgeable speaker of Japanese. His wife, Sarah, was slim, blonde, and beautiful and had no desire to do housework. They had a two-year-old daughter. From the day Kana began working for the Bobcocks, she had to deal with huge piles of dirty clothes and dishes. She worked constantly, from eight to five.

Kana saw that as with most American families she'd observed, the Bobcocks lived under the rule of the petticoat government. Sarah had a boyfriend on base, and this caused constant fights between the couple. Less than six months after Kana had been assigned to their home, Sarah started talking about going back to the States. A month later, she left, taking their daughter with her.

Kana recognized the danger of staying in the house without Sarah and began to hope for a transfer to another family or for a change of jobs. It was too awkward to leave the Bobcock residence right away, and if she quit, there might be no place else to work. She was reluctant to ask for a transfer at the personnel office, fearing that her reason—working in a home with a divorced man—might sound trivial or be misunderstood.

After Sarah and the child had left, Mike started to drink heavily and was often absent from duty; but soon the effects of the separation subsided. After about a month, he looked as though the evil spirit that had possessed him had finally gone. Kana lingered on in her job, and slowly she became intimate with Mike. Looking back, she felt that there had always been a secret desire in her, and she had known that sooner or later it would emerge if she stayed.

At first, Mike would hold Kana from behind as she was wiping the floor and ask for a kiss. Kana tried to escape from him. Finally, one day she relented and let him take her to bed. Frightened by his large body, she feared her own might be destroyed. But in the end, she accepted him. She had known no other man before Mike, and their two years together were the only time she ever lived with a man.

Kana couldn't say she loved Mike. She didn't love him, though she didn't dislike him either. Her reserve could have been caused by the hostility she had witnessed between him and Sarah. Furthermore, Kana had just lost her family in the war and was trying to protect her heart from further injury.

Mike had spent two years in Tachikawa before coming to Okinawa, and he had become enthusiastic about all things Japanese. He was terrific at languages. In the mish-mash of Americans and Japanese crowded together on this tiny island, even simple-minded GIs picked up a few common words, such as *ohayō, kon'nichiwa,* and *ikaga desu ka.* In contrast, Mike's Japanese was exceptional. Before long, he and Kana moved off the base and started living together in Koza, where he was known as "Mike-*san,* the excellent speaker of Japanese." Their neighbors all liked him. Mike loved children, and their parents were grateful to him because he would join in community activities and sponsor the kids' baseball team. He was an affectionate man, very different from when he had lived with Sarah. When he came home early, he taught Kana English; and when they were tired of English lessons, he sang in a loud voice, beating time with his hands, and they danced round and round under the tin roof of their little house. At first, Kana didn't know how to dance. In the PE classes at the girl's high school she attended before the end of the war, students were only trained to hold wooden rifles and charge at straw figures.

"Dance, dance, Kana. Follow me!" Mike insisted. She tried little by little to move her body, following Mike. What a surprise when she learned to dance! Kana found out later that the music they danced to was "The Beer Barrel Polka," a song taught in American elementary schools. Kana would be in high spirits, laughing like a child as she danced to the upbeat tempo. Such things had been absent in the closed world of her youth. She wondered if this was what they called getting a taste of America. Maybe this is what democracy is like, she thought, and maybe this was her first genuine encounter with America and the new age.

Mike would do anything for Kana. Gradually, it drew him into the world of the black market. Shortly after they married, Mike helped her open a small grocery store. For the sake of appearances, she displayed cheap household goods and vegetables grown in Okinawa. In reality, though, the store sold black-market liquor, cigarettes, ham, chocolate, and other goods that Mike and his friends bought at the PX. Later, after Mike left her, Kana devoted herself to the grocery store. Located near the corner of the main street, the store couldn't have been situated better. The Korean War, and especially the Viet Nam War, expanded Koza into a big city. Rice paddies and fields were cleared and transformed into bars and cabarets. The girls who had worked in the fields and on the military bases as housemaids soon became bar hostesses, entertaining the soldiers.

When there weren't enough girls in the towns and farm villages of Okinawa island, young women were recruited from Amami Ōshima, Miyako, and Yaeyama. Kana focused her business on those girls, selling cosmetics and women's clothes. Other shops sprang up like mushrooms after the rain,

Higa Yasuo: Maternal Deities

Dancing with the Gods (Kami-ashibi)
Kudaka Island, Hokama-tun, New Year
1976

but only sold liquor and foods; as a result, Kana's store flourished. When business trade with Hong Kong was liberalized, she was quick to import beds, furniture, and tableware, which turned out to be another good business decision. Her store expanded rapidly and she opened several branch stores. After the reversion of Okinawa to Japan in 1972, Kana incorporated, renovated the main store, and turned the branches into supermarkets. She formed an affiliation with Tōyū, a big department store in mainland Japan, and soon she was the owner of one of the top businesses in the city, both in the size of her stores and annual turnover of inventory. This had all started long ago, when she and Mike had been together and he had helped her with the first small store.

Mike was a very kind person. He had never made fun of Kana or gotten angry, no matter how naive her questions, and he had made her laugh with his witty answers. When they started living together, she once asked him where in New York his hometown was. Mike pushed back his chair and stood up. Sliding his hand from shoulder to knee, he said, "This is New York City." Then he unbuttoned his pants, pulled out his penis, which became erect in a flash, and said, "This is Coney Island. I was born here."

Kana had turned her face away and smiled, but not in disgust. His joke was not meant to demean her but to make her laugh.

At that time, all she knew about America were the names of President Lincoln and the Empire State Building. The fact that Kana had heard of the Empire State Building pleased Mike a great deal.

"Good lord! You know about the Empire State Building, Kana." He was as happy as if Kana had complimented his father.

"Any Okinawan knows the Empire State Building," she said. "Is it true, though, that the top of the building is in the clouds and cannot be seen?" Kana asked, standing on her tiptoes and raising her arms.

"Of course! It's the tallest building in the world, you know. It's a hundred and two stories high, and they say that if pigeons fly up to the top, the birds will be too scared to come down."

"Then they'll freeze to death?" Kana imagined a flock of pigeons huddled on a ledge, freezing in the clouds.

"No, they won't. The caretaker will catch them and bring them down in the elevator to the first floor."

"They are too frightened to fly down?"

"That's right. It's the highest in the world, you see."

"What will happen if you fly a paper plane from the top?" Kana asked. She was remembering the time she had made a glider in her high-school handicrafts class and had flown it from the rooftop of the building. Perhaps because it had caught the strongest wind or ridden the right current of air, her glider had flown the farthest. Mr. Hamada, the popular crafts teacher, complimented her greatly on her glider, and she received an A. It was the first and the last time she got an A in handicrafts; Kana was actually very clumsy with tools. She still remembered the joy she had felt when the paper glider had flown so far. She smiled at Mike, knowing he would not think her question was childish. Then she grew rather serious. What would happen if you flew such a plane from the top of the Empire State Building?

"I have no idea. Never tried it myself," Mike said. "But I would think it would fly toward the East River or the Statue of Liberty."

With a serious expression, Mike covered his head with a plate and posed as the Statue of Liberty, raising a make-believe torch in one hand. Her heart warmed at the thought of her own paper plane majestically gliding over New York City.

Kana said, "I wanna try that sometime."

"Yes, we'll do that sometime."

From then on, it had been their dream to fly a paper plane from the top of the Empire State Building. Less than two years later, Mike was gone. But those years had been the most fearless and carefree of Kana's life.

So gentle, a Japanophile. Kana still didn't understand why he suddenly disappeared. Had he been corresponding with Sarah, back in the States, and decided to reunite with her? Or, as much as it pained Kana to think of it, did he just get tired of living with her?

Many American soldiers left Okinawa and never came back. It had been six years since the end of the war, so their leaving was understandable. Not only their Okinawan wives, but the whole town felt it was forgivable. The islanders were tolerant of those young soldiers from the victorious nation and did not reproach them for their conduct.

But Mike had seemed different. A true Japanophile. So popular with the children, he seemed completely at home in the town. Who could imagine that he would do the same thing as those thoughtless GIs, deserting his wife and running away? When he left for Korea, their neighbors expected him to return and even took the trouble to see him off at the terminal on Kadena Air Force Base. Kana remembered the day clearly. The sun was merciless. A fighter jet streaked into the sky with a thundering shock wave, ripping the heavens with its sharp, triangular tail. As Mike went up the gangway of the plane that would take him to Korea, he looked back at Kana and the neighbors only once. And that was the last time Kana ever saw him. The plane tottered along the tarmac and passed by in front of them like an awkward seabird with drooping, uncertain wings. The engine blew the ash-colored dust and gravel toward the townspeople as the plane taxied to the end of the runway and slowly turned its nose into the wind. The monotonous sound of its engine droned for a while, then with a roar that stirred the air, the plane started rolling. The ash-colored dust rose again, then shrouded the observation deck.

In a fluster, many people took out handkerchiefs and covered their noses. Others ran inside the terminal. Kana stood watching. The plane soared over the camouflaged radar dome, shrinking until it was only a metallic glint. She watched until it disappeared into a thunderhead over the tip of Zampa Point in the East China Sea.

A bum carrying a dog under his arm suddenly appeared from nowhere. Kana saw that he was a middle-aged white man with long hair tied at the back like an Indian's. His dark-red, tanned forehead was peeling, leaving pink spots on his skin, and he had a ragged, light-brown beard. His thread-bare shirt hung below his light-blue jacket. He wore wrinkled corduroy pants and torn army boots that were too big for his feet.

The man sat on a park bench, and the dog stood next to him. He took out a big comb, unbound his hair, and began to drag the comb through the tan-gled mat, which Kana thought probably smelled terrible. The dog had its tail between its hind legs, as if scared, and watched the man's face. The dog was not a puppy, but not yet mature either. After the man finished combing, he bound his hair again, stood up, and walked toward the water fountain. Jumping up, the dog followed him. When the man turned on the tap, the dog looked at him expectantly. The man turned the tap farther, and the water spouted in an arc beyond the fountain and onto the ground. The dog bounded on its hind legs, trying to catch the water with its mouth, but it kept missing, and its effort to drink became a game.

The man laughed. So did Kana. He picked up the thin dog and tried to hold it steady so that the dog could drink. The water gushed at the dog's face and splashed everywhere. The dog struggled in the man's arms as he laughed in a loud voice. He kept aiming the dog toward the water, but not much was going into the animal's mouth. Kana grew impatient, then began to feel annoyed. How could he be so clumsy? An old man sitting on the bench across from Kana yelled something like "The poor dog will drown or die of thirst!" The bum put down the dog. It sneezed painfully, then began to lap up the water from the concrete.

What a relief. Kana looked around. The seats around the pond had started to fill up. No one who appeared to be Mike had shown up. No Japanese tourists either.

Kana estimated that about fifty old men and women were now occupy-ing the chairs and benches. She heard the sound of an ocarina coming from behind a nearby hedge. She followed the sound and found an old man sitting in the grass, looking up at the sky, and playing a tune. He couldn't play very well and hit the wrong notes a couple of times before he finished the tune. Nonetheless, he played earnestly, and the effort made his face red. The tune sounded to her like a traditional American folk song, but she couldn't tell for sure. Some people clapped when the man finished playing. The old man smiled happily, his cheeks flushed, and bowed slightly to the people around him.

By Kana's watch, it was shortly after two. The wind rustled the trees and blew the fallen leaves onto the surface of the pond.

She had been sitting on the bench for almost five hours, and there was still no sign of a bum who looked like Mike. She rose and walked slowly through the fallen leaves and across the yellow lawn, following the winding path that led further into the park. According to the guidebook, she would eventually reach the art museum if she headed north, and Bethesda Fountain if she went west.

Kana decided to go west. After walking for a while, she came to a fountain that was somewhat larger than the previous one. In the center stood a statue of a winged angel. She assumed that water should be coming out of the spouts around the angel. She checked the guidebook for the meaning of the word *Bethesda* but found nothing. Four or five boats floated on the nearby pond. A helicopter circled overhead. Kana sat down on a bench beside the fountain.

She waited until the sun burnt the autumn leaves a bright red. Still, no sign of Mike.

The next morning, having finished breakfast, Kana gazed about the hotel lobby. In the center of the room, a group of middle-aged tourists were standing around a young man. Pinned to their lapels were identical imitation flowers attached to tags printed with the name of a travel agency in Kansai. As Kana walked behind them, they glanced at her, then turned back to the young man.

She went outside. It was a refreshing day, with a high, clear sky. Across the street was a line of trees covered in autumn leaves. Dressed in sweat suits, a couple leaned against a low brick wall, embracing each other. A man who looked to Kana like a bum stopped and watched them. A woman pushing a baby carriage went around a flock of pigeons and turned the corner. Following the woman was a boy wearing a red knit cap and crying hard.

Kana again took a taxi to Central Park. She noticed that many people were jogging on the paths. A buggy with tourists passed her by. She sat on the same bench near Bethesda Fountain where she had waited the day before. Sailboats of many colors were drifting on the pond. Old men on the shore manipulated the toy boats using remote-control devices. Sometimes they would lose control, and the boats would crash or even sink, causing the nearby children to laugh, shout, and scream.

Here and there, Kana saw a few tourists who looked Japanese, though not as many as she had expected. Maybe Central Park is not so interesting to them, she thought; they're probably shopping on Fifth Avenue. A squirrel scampered past her feet.

Kana bought a hot dog and juice at the stand near the lake and stayed in the area until evening. It was almost dusk when a flock of birds circled over her head. She noticed the changing colors of twilight. No one who could be Mike showed up. Feeling tired, she went back to her hotel when it got dark.

Early the next day, she went back to Grand Central Station. She strolled around inside for a while, then decided to take the subway to Battery Park. Sightseeing ferries for the Statue of Liberty would be leaving from there.

Instructed by her guidebook, Kana bought a small token, dropped it in the automated ticket gate, and followed a narrow passage marked with green arrows. She soon found herself on the subway platform. It was a little dirty, but not so different from the subways in Tokyo and Osaka.

She got off at Bowling Green Station, went up to the ground level, and walked till she reached a grove of trees surrounded by an iron fence. She could see the lead-gray river through the branches of poplar trees. The wind carried the cold smell of the sea. This must be the mouth of the Hudson River, which flows into the Atlantic, and this is Battery Park, she thought. Through the mist beyond the reflection of the water, she could see the Statue of Liberty. On its right was a slightly larger island. That's probably Ellis Island, Kana thought. She breathed deeply and felt the wind brush back the loose hair on her forehead.

Kana stood by the pier where visitors waited for the ferry that would take them to the Statue of Liberty. Office workers were forming a crowd, waiting to board ferries headed for Staten Island. It was still early in the morning, and tourists had not arrived yet. Kana crossed into the park and sat on one of the benches closest to the wharf. She would wait for Mike there since it was where Matsuda Kazuo had reported seeing him.

From the direction of the pier, an elderly white woman in a baggy sweater strolled along the path. She took out a piece of bread from the basket she carried and began to throw pieces to the pigeons. More pigeons came, flocking together, along with some sparrows. When the woman threw the bread, the sparrows were quicker and got the pieces first. But the pigeons flapped their large wings, got in the way, and were able to eat their share.

Just before nine, people started gathering for the Statue of Liberty ferry. They arrived in tour buses that pulled in by twos and threes.

In moments, the pier was lively with tourists. Many of them were Asian, possibly Japanese or Korean. Meanwhile, the ferry was docking at the pier, kicking up white waves and gunning its engines. It slowed as it neared the wharf, turned its bow, and came to a stop. The gangway was lowered, and the lines of tourists hurried cheerfully aboard.

After the ferry left, the wharf was quiet. Again the water looked lead colored to Kana. She took out a small pair of glasses and put them on to follow the white wake of the ferry for as long as possible.

Soon, a tour bus arrived and Kana saw many Japanese tourists. A large group of elderly people was gathering around a young man holding up a purple flag. It was almost eleven. If Mike was going to appear at all, this would be the time. Kana looked around her. Without her noticing, quite a few people had come into the park to sit on the benches and watch the ferries. Some were standing in the shade of the trees or leaning on the rail, looking out at the ocean. Many old people were among them. Another ferry arrived. After it docked, sixty or seventy passengers got off and the party of Japanese tourists went on board.

Around noon, Kana rose from her bench and walked around the park. She came across a dark-red stone building and saw a crowd gathering at its entrance. It looked like an old museum fort. On the map, it was labelled CASTLE CLINTON. Farther along the path, she saw a food stand with a beach umbrella perched on top of it. A short white man wearing a baseball cap was cooking dull-colored sausages on a smoke-stained iron plate. Beside the plate was a heap of sliced onions. They glistened like slimy creatures and had an unbearable stench. When Kana frowned, disgusted with the smell, the man looked hard at her. She bowed slightly as though apologizing and bought a cola and a pretzel that resembled a Japanese rice cracker. She went back to the bench, tore off a piece of the pretzel, and put it in her mouth. It was too salty to eat. She wrapped it in tissues, put it in her purse, and drank the cola. There was another spot that Japanese tourists visited called the World Trade Center, but she didn't feel like going there.

After two, the clouds over the bay began to turn gray. The shadows were deeper on the pier and in the trees. As the light dimmed, the temperature dropped, and the breeze that slipped through Kana's blouse felt cold. The chilly air began to drive away the people who had come to the park to stroll, leaving only a few. The colder it became, the more Kana sensed the futility of her journey. Her hopes seemed as fragile as the wind whirling among the fallen leaves and dust. She looked around the park. Why am I here? she wondered. For a moment, the sense of perplexity and restlessness she had felt the day Toshi had called came back to her, together with the memory of Mike's departure and her feelings of loss. For her to be shivering in the wind in the park of an unknown land seemed like a dream.

Kana suddenly missed her warm office back home. She missed the cup of hot tea on her little writing desk that a cleaning lady prepared for her every morning. She thought of giving up her search. Would I be throwing everything away? she wondered. She resented Toshi and Kazuo for telephoning her, burdening her life with this huge, unexpected complexity. Everything had been going well enough. No major complaints. Maybe I shouldn't have come, she thought. Something like regret flashed across her mind, but did not linger. More than anything, she now wanted Mike to show up and bring her uncertainty to a conclusion.

Kana remained sitting on the cold bench by the pier until four, waiting for the last ferry to leave. People who looked like office workers were again gathering at the pier for Staten Island. The wind grew colder. Still, a man who could be Mike did not appear. Kana's body was now chilled to the bone, and she longed for a cup of hot coffee. She was terribly tired. She watched the last ferry of the day depart, then stood, turned up the collar of her coat, and took a taxi back to the hotel, where Toshi might be waiting.

Entering the hotel, Kana saw a petite woman about forty-five years old sitting in the lobby, reading a Japanese newspaper. When she saw Kana, she stood up and walked toward her with a smile. With her grayish hair curling up on her narrow forehead and with her thin legs, she reminded Kana of a poor laborer's wife. They could have passed each other without recognizing one another if they hadn't made an appointment by phone.

"You grew old...," they said at the same time.

"How is your husband?" Kana asked.

"Fine. He's running around as usual."

"And your children?"

"The oldest, our daughter, got married last year. The younger ones are now a senior and a junior in high school."

"Both boys?"

"Yes, two of them."

Kana led Toshi to the hotel restaurant.

"So, how is your search? Have you been able to look around?"

After they had ordered tea and Japanese meals, Toshi began questioning Kana in a manner that seemed more probing than Kana was prepared for.

"Yesterday and the day before yesterday, I went to Central Park," Kana replied. "And Battery Park today. I didn't see anyone who looked like him. You don't think he knew I was coming and has been hiding somewhere, do you?" Kana laughed as she took a cigarette out of her purse. She felt her face suddenly redden.

Toshi ignored Kana's joke. "New York is a big city, you know. A search for someone here is like trying to catch a little fish who jumped back into the ocean. And maybe we have to go to the Bronx to look for someone like Mike-*san*, but it's a little dangerous out there. It's possible that we should ask the police for help, but they are probably too busy to help search for a runaway person."

"We don't know if Mike is a runaway, do we? He might have a family like everybody else." She remembered Sarah's face and wondered for a moment if Mike was with his first wife again. If so, there would certainly be no room for Kana in his life. But Mike's living with Sarah was unimaginable. She was convinced of it.

"It's not the kind of search you can go to the police for," Kana added.

"I guess we just have to wait for him where Japanese tourists gather."

"I guess so—for now anyway."

Kana lit her cigarette, took off her glasses, and pressed her eyes with her hand. She put on her glasses again and looked up at Toshi's quizzical face through a thin haze of cigarette smoke. Kana pushed the ashtray to the side.

Toshi blinked. "I wonder...though...may I ask you one thing, Auntie? I guess it's not really my place to ask this because I'm the one who called and started all this. But, Auntie, why are you here? If I were you, I would be content to have learned that he's alive."

Toshi's expression conveyed something Kana could not read. She fell silent, unable to answer. Toshi's words had touched the heart of the matter, the very thing Kana herself couldn't fathom.

"Why? I don't know. I don't understand it myself."

Kana extinguished her cigarette in the ashtray and smiled weakly. What is it really? She had come all the way to New York to look for a man she had lived with three decades ago, and for only two years. What drove her to do this? She didn't know.

"For one thing…I still appreciate the help Mike gave me when I first opened the store."

"Well, that's for sure…"

Kana nodded and took a deep breath, then slowly exhaled. "But, I guess that's not the only reason." Kana paused after each word as though she were fishing for it through layers of years. "I was deserted by him; but when I look back, those years weren't all that bad. Good things happened. When I heard that the man is begging for his bread in his home country—how could someone not care?"

Kana's voice was almost trembling. She moved her eyes to the TV screen in the corner of the lobby to control her emotions. Both women were silent as they watched the waitress pour tea into their cups, then leave.

"Is this what those *uyanma* used to do?" Toshi asked. A mischievous smile crossed her face as she squeezed some lemon into her tea.

"Uh, *uyanma*…am I like them?"

Kana tried to imagine the lives of the women called *uyanma* in the Yaeyama Islands. When the Ryūkyūs were under Japanese rule and categorized as one of the clans, or *han,* political prisoners of the samurai class from Shuri, the capital, were sent to the Yaeyama Islands. There was a custom in Yaeyama that a local woman attended the samurai officer as a wife while he was exiled there. Such women were called *uyanma.* After completing their sentences, these officers separated from their local wives and went back to the capital. Quite a few, they say, could not forget their wives in Yaeyama and returned, abandoning their positions in Shuri. At the same time, there were *uyanma* who went to Shuri to help their husbands in times of financial difficulties. Those women, Kana thought, devoted themselves to their husbands. Compared to them, how much had she devoted to Mike? She felt sad. Touched by Toshi's words, Kana identified herself with the *uyanma* in the capital, but only for a moment, until the difference in her position and theirs turned her smile bitter. Unlike the former samurai officers in Shuri, the ex-GIs wouldn't welcome the Okinawan women coming out of their past from the occupied land in the East and showing up on their doorsteps. In fact, Toshi had said that the man she called out to ran away in a panic. Kana felt empty. She was beginning to see that she was playing the role of the unwelcomed *uyanma,* and she regretted it. But she knew she should have expected these emotions when she left Okinawa.

Higa Yasuo: Maternal Deities

Dancing with the Gods (Kami-ashibi)
Okinawa Island, Ada, Shinugu
1975

"I think…I know how you feel. If Henry did the same, I might search for him like you," Toshi said.

"We are women of passion."

The two women from Okinawa looked at each other and laughed out loud.

"But, Auntie…" Toshi had a serious look again. "What are you going to do if you actually find him? I'm rather concerned about that. The bums here, you know, they are ninety-nine percent junkies—either alcoholics or drug addicts. I think you know that."

Kana stared at Toshi's face without a word.

"Toshi-*chan*," she said finally, "I think I'm going to take him home with me if he's not with Sarah. Is that too rash of me?"

Those words from her own mouth startled Kana. Her mouth, it seemed, had started speaking for her heart. Kana was amazed to think that she had been unconsciously preparing these feelings to surface ever since Toshi had called about a month ago.

"How many more years does he have?" Kana asked. "If he has been on the road without Sarah, his health must be ruined. I don't think he has much time. If it's okay with him, I'd like to take him back to the island and have him spend his last days there. Do you think that would be possible?"

As she spoke to Toshi, Kana began to understand her feelings for the first time and felt them leading her to a conclusion. Let me be one of those *uyanma*, she thought—the *uyanma* with unrequited love. That's fine.

"We might have new kinds of troubles if I take him back to Okinawa. But let it be. There are many retired military personnel spending their remaining years in Koza."

"I couldn't do it, Auntie, but you could. If I were in your place, I would give him a hundred dollars and go home," Toshi said.

"You are still young. That's why you can be so decisive. I envy you."

"Shall we put a halter on him and drag him to Okinawa?" Toshi said half-seriously.

The trays arrived. The women took up their chopsticks in silence.

Unfortunately, it rained the next day. Toshi and Kana bought raincoats at the newsstand and walked to Times Square. They stood in the entryway of a movie theater for shelter until the rain stopped, and then made their way along Broadway to Columbus Circle. Walking through the theater district just after the rain, Kana felt empty and weak. As Toshi said, it was like looking for a tiny fish lost in the ocean. They might be trapped in an endless search, thought Kana sadly. As she watched the carefree people strolling on Broadway, she felt ashamed of herself, the oddball who didn't belong, who had a completely different purpose for being there. They entered Central Park and spent that afternoon in the museum. In the evening, they parted. Toshi went to Carnegie Hall to hear the singer Atō Tokiko, and Kana went back to her hotel alone. She placed a telephone call to Okinawa to check on her store and on other matters.

The next day was clear and calm. There was little trace of the rain that had fallen overnight. This was Kana's sixth day in New York. She and Toshi decided to walk along Fifth Avenue, from the New York City Library toward Rockefeller Center. When they arrived, the RCA Building was filled with people and light. The huge ginkgo trees were scattering their golden leaves on the sidewalk, and glints of sunlight were dancing on the statue of Prometheus in the Lower Plaza. The flags behind the sculpture swayed gently when the water from the fountain spouted from time to time. In the center of the plaza, the wind lifted the Stars and Stripes. On one side of the American flag was the national flag of Switzerland, and on the other that of Brazil. Kana looked for the Japanese flag, but couldn't find it among more than fifty flags there. She occasionally saw some Japanese people, though fewer than she expected. You can't trust what people tell you, she thought.

From the Lower Plaza, they walked slowly north. The street was flooded with people. On the right was St. Patrick's Cathedral. The women walked until they reached the square in front of the Museum of Modern Art. Kana's eyes had been scanning the figures of bums the entire time. When she focused her attention, she could find them under trees, in the shade of porches, in the shadows under stairways—they were everywhere. Most were young men, but the females and the old were also there. Whenever Kana saw a white bum about the same age as Mike, she slowed down and observed him out of the corners of her eyes.

Past the Plaza Hotel, they found themselves at the south entrance to Central Park. They walked on the paths of leaves, which were now familiar to Kana. Birds sang in the trees. The women passed by the children's zoo. The sound of Stephen Foster's music drew them toward an old, green building, where they saw a merry-go-round with about twenty gorgeously decorated wooden horses going round and round. Only three of the horses had riders. It was a weekday morning, thought Kana, and that must be the reason it was so empty. Each of the riders was a little child being steadied by a father. The children were in high spirits, but the fathers had serious looks. When their eyes met Kana's, they smiled shyly.

The faces of the riderless horses looked sad.

Near Bethesda Fountain, Kana again saw the bum with the dog. The dog came to Kana and sniffed at her shoes, wagging its tail. Being a dog lover, Kana crouched down and petted it on the head.

All of a sudden, Kana heard Toshi's high-pitched voice and looked up. "There he is. Look. That's him!" Toshi exclaimed. She turned to Kana, appearing tense and pale.

As Kana moved her eyes in the direction where Toshi pointed, she saw a tall, old white man. He was surrounded by five or six Japanese tourists. He was pointing and telling them something about the statue of the angel high on top of the fountain. He was quite a distance away, but Kana thought she recognized something familiar in the way he looked. Her legs trembled. She could feel her face turning pale.

Kana hesitantly approached the group of tourists, all the while concentrating on the old man. When she was about five meters away from him, she stopped. The light-green worn-out coat. The wrinkled pants with stains of coal tar. The dusty lace-ups. Under his dirty, cream-colored hunting cap, Kana saw the man's tiny ears, dark-red from too much exposure to the sun, and his long, wild beard. She could smell solitude in his body odor.

Kana braced herself. "Mike," she called out.

The man turned toward Kana. She gazed into his face. He stared back.

For a while, they just looked at one another.

It's not him, she thought. All the strength left Kana's body. The man's age and face could have been Mike's, but it wasn't him.

"What can I do for you?" the old man asked in fluent Japanese. But the voice wasn't Mike's either. Kana felt nervous and bowed to him.

"Excuse me. I mistook you for someone else."

The old man stared at Kana's face for a while, then suddenly jabbered something in English, shook his yellowish beard, and walked backwards through the crowd. Then he turned around and started walking quickly. Occasionally, he glanced over his shoulder, which made him trip. His back appeared both pitiful and humorous to Kana. Toshi and Kana watched his figure disappear into a grove of trees.

"I thought for sure that was Mike-*san*," Toshi said. She sounded disappointed and aplogetic. "Sorry…"

Kana, however, was partly relieved. She had mixed feelings.

"He did look like Mike, though," Kana said, trying to comfort Toshi. Then a question entered her mind: what sort of past does that man have? She somehow felt she knew what he had been going through. Like Mike, he may have deserted a wife and children somewhere in Japan. Her heart ached. She couldn't breathe, imagining the misfortune that had caused him to lose so much while being so fluent in Japanese. Mike, like this man, would also be suffering from the memory of having deserted his wife, if he were still alive. The choking in her chest eased as she thought about it. She felt a little better. She understood that what she had seen could be the greatest gift of her trip. If so, it was worth it, she thought.

Kana was skimming through her guidebook as she sat on the subway. The car moved in fits and starts. When it reached her station, she watched a white man with silver hair and a ruddy face put his arm around his wife's waist. Kana fell in behind them as they exited. Behind her was an African couple with a toddler, speaking in an unknown language. Kana was seeing Toshi off at La Guardia Airport. On the way, Toshi apologized, saying that she would have shown Kana around New York if she had known the city

Higa Yasuo: Maternal Deities

Dancing with the Gods (Kami-ashibi)
Ishigaki Island, Shiraho, Harvest Festival
1977

better. Trying to comfort Toshi, Kana told her that it was okay and she no longer had any regrets.

As she said goodbye, she pushed an envelope that contained a large sum of money into Toshi's purse. Toshi looked upset, but Kana said to her, "I was going to give it to Mike anyway, if I had found him," and she laughed.

Kana hurried back to Manhattan after saying goodbye to Toshi. Her own plane would leave JFK for Narita at 1:30 P.M. She still had some time left before her flight. She caught a taxi to the Empire State Building. It was close to ten, but the shadow of the building fell on the entryway. She looked up. She couldn't see the distinct steeple. She barely saw the Star and Stripes over the entrance. The guidebook had said:

> The Empire State Building: 102 stories above ground level and two beneath, 381 meters high, 450 meters in height including the broadcast tower. Construction started in May 1929. Construction was completed in May 1931. The total cost of construction was $42 million.

Kana pushed open the heavy door. The floor was cold, and a draft was coming from somewhere even though she was already inside the building. The ticket booth for the observatory was in the basement. When she got there, about ten people were waiting in line. She paid three dollars and fifty cents, went back to the first floor, and waited in line again in front of the elevator.

With about twenty other tourists, she rode up to the eightieth floor in a rush of speed—just like flying in an unpressurized plane. Her eardrums were ringing. Everyone got off on the eightieth floor, showed a ticket, and got on another elevator to ride to the eighty-sixth floor.

Inside the observatory on the eighty-sixth floor was a carpeted hall with a store at the end. The air was stuffy and overheated. Kana pushed open a thick plastic door to the outside deck. The strong wind hit her immediately. It was colder than she had expected. A thin layer of clouds moved overhead, blocking the sunlight and dimming everything. The coldness and strange light were things Kana had not imagined when she dreamed of the building back in Okinawa.

She looked up. The cold air and white light enveloped her. It felt like the coldest winter. She gazed toward the ocean and saw the Statue of Liberty far away through the white fog. To her left, the mouth of the East River was a gleaming gray. On her right, the Hudson River separated Manhattan from New Jersey. The clouds were rushing in from that direction. The next moment, everything was swallowed in the white fog. Kana couldn't see anything. The cold, moist air shrouded her body and slipped into her clothes, chilling her neck, breast, and back.

From this place, Mike and I had planned to fly a paper airplane, Kana thought.

Higa Yasuo: Maternal Deities

Seeing the Gods Off (Kami-ukui)
Kōri Island, Ungami
1976

She looked around. The observatory was surrounded by a concrete barrier about one meter high, topped with a transparent plastic panel another two meters high. Above the panel, a steel fence curved sharply inward. It wouldn't be impossible to fly a paper plane over the fence.

When she went back inside, she saw people waiting in line to go up to the observatory on the hundred and second floor. She followed them. The top floor was an airtight chamber about thirty-three square meters. The view from there was not any better than from the eighty-sixth floor. She stayed about ten minutes and went back down to the lower observatory, then bought a container of hot tea and sat down on a vinyl bench to drink it. The tea was good. She was overcome by a sense of partial fulfillment just for being in the observatory of the Empire State Building. Reaching for her handkerchief, she opened her purse and saw the pretzel she had bought in Battery Park. As she put a small piece of it in her mouth, she remembered the story Mike had told her about the pigeons that were too scared to fly down. She had the urge to fly the paper plane. Indeed! Flying a paper plane when she was almost sixty years old, she thought, slightly embarrassed. Yet that had been her longtime dream. If not now, then when? She could not imagine that she would ever be standing there again.

Kana found a sheet of paper in her purse and folded it into an airplane. Then she went outside to the lookout deck. About ten people were peering into telescopes or taking photographs. She walked behind the visitors, hiding the little plane in her pocket. Too many people to try. She gave up on the east side and went around to the west, facing the Hudson River. She looked around to be sure there was no one watching.

Kana threw the plane steeply upward.

It flew over the fence with ease and immediately was caught in the cold, foggy wind. In a flash, the plane was headed toward the East River.

Kana looked around again to see if there had been any witnesses. There was no one, only the moist wind humming gently to itself, dampening her face. From over the far Jersey shoreline, the clouds were sweeping in again.

Translation by Shinjō Tomoko and Frank Stewart

Higa Yasuo: Maternal Deities

Seeing the Gods Off (Kami-ukui)
Aguni Island, Mushinkuchi
1990

About the Contributors

Christopher Drake has translated and written about *haiku* as well as Ryūkyūan *omoro* and shaman songs. His translated books include *Copying Bird Calls: A Hundred Linked Haikai* by Nishiyama Sōin (1605–1682) and *Haikai on Love: A Hundred-Verse Linked Sequence* by Matsuki Tantan (1674–1761). He is also co-translator of *Early Modern Japanese Literature: An Anthology, 1600–1900*, edited by Haruo Shirane.

David Fahy teaches in the Department of East Asian Languages and Cultures of the University of California–Davis. Among his published translations is another story by Matayoshi Eiki, *Kaho wa umi kara* (Fortunes by the Sea), in *Southern Exposure* (2000), edited by Michael Molasky and Steve Rabson.

Kathy Foley is a professor of theatre arts at the University of California–Santa Cruz and editor of *Asian Theatre Journal.* Her exhibitions of Asian performing arts have been displayed at National Geographic, the Center for Puppetry Arts, and the East-West Center Gallery.

Hamagawa Hitoshi received a master's degree in English from Southern Illinois University and is an associate professor in the Department of English Communication at Okinawa Christian University. He has published numerous essays and articles on the modern literature of Okinawa.

Kyle Ikeda received his doctorate in Japanese from the University of Hawai'i–Mānoa in 2007 and is now assistant professor of Japanese language and literature at the University of Vermont. His translation of Medoruma's "Mabuigumi" first appeared in a different version in *Fiction International* 40 (fall 2007).

Kawamitsu Shinichi was born on Miyako Island. His work includes three books of essays and two books of poetry. "The Hawks" was published in *Poems of Kawamitsu Shinichi* (1977).

Makiminato Tokuzō was born in 1912 in Naha, Okinawa. A survivor of the Battle of Okinawa, he published four books of essays and two books of poetry. "The Well" is from *Okinawan Elegies* (1982), a book of poetry with woodcuts by Gima Hiroshi.

Matayoshi Eiki was born in Urasoe, Okinawa, and graduated from the University of the Ryukyus. He has received the *Ryūkyū Shimpo* Short Story Prize, the Kyūshū Arts Festival Literary Prize, and the 1995 Akutagawa Prize, for his novel *Buta no mukui* (The Pig's Retribution). "The Wild Boar That George Gunned Down" was published in 1978 and was inspired by a true incident.

Medoruma Shun was born in Nakijin, Okinawa. A graduate of the University of the Ryukyus, he was awarded the Akutagawa Prize in 1997 for his short story *"Suiteki"* (Droplets). "Mabuigumi" received the Kawabata Yasunari and Kiyama Shōhei Literary Prizes in 2000. He also wrote the screenplay for the film *Fūon: The Crying Wind* (2004), which received the Innovation Award at the Montreal World Film Festival.

Nagadō Eikichi was born in Naha, Okinawa, and began writing novels at age thirty. In 1987, he won the Northern Literary Award for his Nahaibai songs "Scattered Pieces," and in 1988, the *Okinawa Times* Art Award. He has been awarded the Okinawa Art Award and the fiftieth annual Art Encouragement Prize. His fiction has appeared in *Complete Okinawan Literature* and the *Kyūshū Art Festival Literary Awards Anthology.*

Nagadō Madoka received her bachelor's and master's degrees in English from Kobe City University of Foreign Studies and a second master's in English from University of Hull, in the United Kingdom. She is a doctoral candidate in English at the University of Hawai'i–Mānoa.

Nakawaka Naoko has had her fiction published in the *Anthology of Okinawan Short Stories, New Okinawan Literature, Complete Okinawan Literature,* and the *Kyūshū Art Festival Literary Awards Anthology.*

Nobuko Miyama Ochner is associate professor of Japanese in the Department of East Asian Languages and Literatures at the University of Hawai'i–Mānoa. She earned a bachelor's in English from Tokyo Kyōiku Daigaku (Tokyo University of Education). She received her master's degrees in English and Japanese literature and her doctorate in Asian languages and Japanese literature from the University of Hawai'i–Mānoa. She has published numerous articles on twentieth-century Japanese writers and co-edited two collections of essays on Japanese literature.

Ōshiro Sadatoshi is an award-wining writer and associate professor of Japanese at the University of the Ryukyus. He has won several literary awards, including the 1994 Okinawa City Theatre Prize.

Ōshiro Tatsuhiro was born in 1925 in Nakagusuku, Okinawa. After middle school, he attended an academy in Shanghai. He returned to Okinawa at the end of World War II and began to publish books and articles on Okinawan culture and history, as well as works of fiction and drama. The novella *Kakuteru pātī* (The Cocktail Party) first appeared in the magazine *Shin Okinawa bungaku* (New literature of Okinawa) in 1967 and was awarded the Akutagawa Prize the same year.

Sakiyama Tami was born on Iriomote, an outlying Okinawan island, and lived there until the age of fourteen. She later graduated from the University of the Ryukyus, where she studied Japanese literature. In 1989, "Round-trip over the Ocean" won the Kyūshū Arts Festival Literary Prize and was nominated for the Akutagawa Prize. In 1991, "Island Confinement" was also nominated for the Akutagawa Prize. In her recent fiction, she experiments with mixing Japanese and the Okinawan language.

Shinjō Tomoko was born in Okinawa in 1958 and studied at the University of the Ryukyus and the University of Vermont. After completing the MAT program (Master of Arts in Teaching with concentration in British and American Literature) at the University of Vermont, she returned to Okinawa to teach English.

Sminkey Takuma (né Paul Sminkey) has been living in Japan for over twenty years and acquired Japanese citizenship in 2010. He received a master's degree in English literature from Temple University and a master's in advanced Japanese studies from Sheffield University. He teaches at Okinawa International University in the Department of British and American Language and Culture. His translations include *A Rabbit's Eyes* by Haitani Kenjirō (2005) and *Ichigensan—The Newcomer* by David Zoppetti (2011).

Taira Buntarō was a pioneer in translating Okinawan poetry into English, and for many years was a professor of literature at the University of the Ryukyus. His book *My Fifty Favorite Okinawan Poems* was published in 1955. The book was later expanded to include seventy-seven poems and was reprinted in 1969 as *My Favorite Okinawan Poems*.

Takara Ben was born in 1949 in Tamagusuku, Okinawa. He received a bachelor's degree in chemistry from Shizuoka University and attended graduate school in the Philippines. His first poetry collection was published in 1979. Since then, he has published several books of criticism and poetry, including *Misaki* (1984), and is the recipient of numerous Okinawan literary awards.

Wesley Iwao Ueunten is an Okinawan *sansei* who was born on Kauaʻi. He received his doctorate in comparative ethnic studies from the University of California–Berkeley and is an assistant professor of Asian American studies at San Francisco State University. He has published articles on Okinawan identity and is the co-founder of Genyukai Berkeley, a group that performs Okinawan music.

Yamanoguchi Baku (1903–1963) was born in Naha, Okinawa, and in 1922 moved to Tokyo, where he lived most of his life. He began publishing poetry while still a teenager. A prize named in his honor is awarded annually to a promising poet.

Katsunori Yamazato received his doctorate from the University of California at Davis and is a professor of American literature and culture at the University of the Ryukyus. His books include *Poetics of Place: Reading Gary Snyder* (2006) and *A Narrative History of Ryudai, 1947–1972* (2010). Among his translations from English to Japanese are Gary Snyder's *Place in Space* (2000) and *Rivers and Mountains without End* (2002). He co-edited *Voices from Okinawa*, the summer 2009 volume in the *Mānoa* series. At present, he is the director of the Pacific North/South American Research Project "Human Migration and the Twenty-First Century Global Society."

Yonaha Mikio was born in Hirara City, on Miyako Island, Okinawa, in 1939. He has published two books of poems, *The Love of Red Soil* and *What the Wind Says*.